James Junius Marks

The Peninsula Campaign in Virginia

Or, incidents and scenes on the battlefields and in Richmond

James Junius Marks

The Peninsula Campaign in Virginia
Or, incidents and scenes on the battlefields and in Richmond

ISBN/EAN: 9783337426200

Printed in Europe, USA, Canada, Australia, Japan

Cover: Foto ©ninafisch / pixelio.de

More available books at **www.hansebooks.com**

THE

PENINSULA

CAMPAIGN IN VIRGINIA,

OR

INCIDENTS AND SCENES

ON

THE BATTLE-FIELDS AND IN RICHMOND.

BY

REV. J. J. MARKS, D.D.

PHILADELPHIA:
J. B. LIPPINCOTT & CO.
1864.

TO

Samuel Small, Esq.,

OF YORK, PENNSYLVANIA,

THIS WORK IS MOST RESPECTFULLY DEDICATED,

AS A MARK OF ESTEEM AND AFFECTION FOR ONE WHO DESERVES THE
HIGHEST PLACE IN THE REGARDS OF THE AUTHOR FOR MANY
ACTS OF FRIENDSHIP AND HOSPITALITY SHOWN HIM WHEN
A STRANGER; BUT MORE ESPECIALLY TO GIVE VOICE
TO THE GRATITUDE OF THOUSANDS FOR A CHARITY
MOST MUNIFICENT AND UNCEASING, WHICH
HAS SOLACED AND COMFORTED MULTI-
TUDES OF OUR SOLDIERS, DISABLED
AND WOUNDED IN THE SER-
VICE OF THEIR COUNTRY.

JAMES J. MARKS.

PREFACE.

THIS work is given to the public with many misgivings, for it has been prepared by camp-fires, in the midst of hospital labors and marches on the Rappahannock, in the mountains of Virginia, and under the pressure of exhausting duties. The author has had no time for retirement, for consultation of authorities, or trimming away excrescences and redundancies. He is, therefore, painfully conscious of a thousand defects and blemishes, which are the consequences of hasty preparation.

He might never have obtruded himself upon the notice of more than a few too partial friends, had not disease, induced by exposure, compelled his leaving the army in the field; and urged to the effort by many companions in tribulation, he could not resist the temptation to gather from his portfolio the fragmentary memorials of a never-to-be-forgotten campaign. Encouraged by the approbation of many friends, he has given to the world the memories of those days.

He has been prompted to this, in part, from the desire to show to the country the gratitude due to the noble Army of the Potomac, by the record of its labors and sufferings. He likewise hoped to contribute one or more leaves to the history yet to be written,—for, in this early twilight, no man is able to

1*   (v)

write a history of the Peninsular campaign worthy of the name. Time is a great teacher; and every year, for the next quarter of a century, will break the seals of mystery, and disclose the hidden causes of movements which for a long time mocked our curiosity, and eluded our research. He has not, therefore, had the presumption to attempt to write the history of that celebrated campaign, but has aimed rather to give personal impressions, and to record the scenes and events of which he was the witness.

In the haste of such compilation he may have made criticisms too sweeping, and seemingly too severe, as is intimated by my excellent friend, Dr. Swinburne; but let it be remembered that no man's vices in the army are pushed into such an odious and unendurable prominence as those of a self-indulgent, intemperate, and heartless surgeon. No one endures more, and perils more, than the faithful surgeon. The author cannot but hope that all who read his work will do him the justice to believe that, if he has spoken too severely, it has been because cases of shameless neglect of duty have forced themselves upon his notice; but for no class of men does he entertain profounder respect, and sincerer friendship, than for those surgeons who made it their constant effort to relieve the miseries of sickness, and to heal by all the resources of their art, and humane attentions, the wounds received in battle.

THE AUTHOR.

CONTENTS.

CHAPTER VI.

CHAPTER VII.

CHAPTER VIII.

CHAPTER IX.

CHAPTER X.

CHAPTER XI.

CHAPTER XII.

CHAPTER XIII.

CHAPTER XIV.

CHAPTER XV.

CHAPTER XVI.

SUNDAY, June 29th.

CHAPTER XVII.

MONDAY MORNING, June 30th.

CHAPTER XVIII.

MONDAY, June 30th.

CHAPTER XIX.

MALVERN HILL.

INTRODUCTION.

"WRITE," says my friend, the author, "an introduction to my book." This request, coming to me, as it did, from a gentleman whose good qualities of head and heart I learned, during *my campaign* on the Peninsula, to love, and whose self-sacrificing patriotism was admired by all who came within the influence of his presence, addresses me with the most potent influences urging me to compliance. And yet what shall I write? Can I improve upon *the work* itself? Can aught that I may say render more valuable, or even aid to call attention to, the truthful descriptions, interesting incidents, and really valuable contents of the book? These questions have naturally suggested themselves to my mind; and at all times negative answers have been forced upon me. And yet, *perhaps* I may say something to add to the interest which a perusal of "The Peninsular Campaign; or, Incidents and Scenes on the Battle-fields and in Richmond," must everywhere incite in the glorious cause of the battle of freedom against rebellion, anarchy, and tyranny, which is now shaking our whole country, North and South, as with the throes of an earthquake; and upon the hopes of this, *perhaps* induced mostly by love for my friend, and anxiety for the cause of our country, I was led to attempt to comply with the request of Dr. Marks.

The rebellion of the so-called "Confederate States" against the United States Government has brought with it an era in the progress of our country upon which historians, for ages to come, will write, and yet fail to exhaust the subject. But in no instance will any history be so valued as those coming from men who were participants in the scenes their willing pens depict. And it may be remarked, too, that the truth-fulness and value of any history of this rebellion will depend upon the near or remote degree in which the writer was re-lated to, or participated in, the scenes, views, and incidents he assumes to describe. In this view, this book will go down to posterity as a most valued and truthful, as it is now the most interesting, history of an important period in this con-test, which has found no lukewarm spectators within the sec-tions of country now claimed by, or allied to, either of the contending parties. This history of the Peninsular campaign will be sought for by the inhabitants especially of the Eastern, Middle, and Western States, with greater avidity than that of any other portion of the history of this rebellion, for the reasons that its brilliant commencement sent electric thrills of highest hope through the heart of every truly loyal man of the North and West; its progress so tedious, for causes now known to but few outside the pale of the chiefs of the military departments of our Government (but which will, of course, be developed by the future historian), for months kept the hearts of the people of those districts in an agony of anxious suspense, impelling them frequently to heap upon the Govern-ment, and the officers in command of our forces, scathing criticisms and bitter imprecations; and its whole history was marked by the loss of the lives of thousands upon thousands of men, whose memories " will be green" in the hearts of their relatives, friends, and descendants in the North and West for ages to come.

These losses, occurring as they did not alone by the rav-ages of "grim-visaged war," in their usual phases, but in numerous instances by want of care, disease, pestilence, and almost famine, in the camp and hospital, upon the roads and in the field, struck home to the hearts of the friends of the victims with more awful and grief-bearing effect than would have been the case had the news been brought to them that their relatives had died on the field, while nobly fighting against the enemies of the "good old flag," which has, for over eighty years past,

over all the world, been recognized as the emblem of freedom, and is even now the ensign of the noblest nation of the
earth; enshrouded, it is true, in the darkening, damning palls
of civil war, yet looked upon, revered, and respected by the
people of all other countries as the brightest star in the con-
stellation of the universe of nations.

This awful destruction of life outside the usual course of
war has been attributed, by friends and supporters of the different parties of the country, and by the followers of different
officers of the Government, to as many different causes as there
have been parties and officers interested or implicated in the
matter. Many of the alleged causes are truthful, to a certain
extent, but all of them are overdrawn; and very many more
are entirely unfounded, disgraceful to those charging them,
and only arising out of the evident desire of their supporters
to heap unwarranted contumely upon the Government, or the
officers by them arraigned; and that, too, with a design thereby
to further the still more evident and grossly treasonable intent *to hinder the Government in the speedy and successful
prosecution of the war*, and thus give aid and comfort to the
enemy in such a covert manner as to shield the authors from
the penalties of *open treason*.

Foremost among these assigned causes (and the only cause
which the profession of the writer will justify him in discussing to any extent) has been the alleged inefficiency in the conduct of the medical department of the service during this
campaign. It will be recollected that the celebrated Dr. Tripler, an old army surgeon, whose most valuable works upon
military surgery have justly attained a fame as world-wide as
the subject itself, was Medical Director of the Army of the
Potomac at that time. It has been charged that, by reason
of his neglect, the Army of the Peninsula was left without
many things which were absolutely requisite for the proper
administration of the medical department of that army; and
that thus the soldiers, worn out by the fatigues of the march,

2

weakened by exposure to severe storms, and the dangerous miasmas of the swamps, and brought down to the hospital by disease, were literally allowed to die from want of these necessaries, when they could have been promptly obtained at any time, as it is said, upon proper call. This charge, it has occurred to me, is grossly unjust to one whose highest aim in life has been to serve his country faithfully, and make himself a useful and a shining ornament to the glorious profession he has adopted, and a lasting benefit to the human race. The office and duties of a faithful surgeon, even in civil life, is no sinecure; and when a surgeon of noblest mind and purest purpose, impelled by love of country, has chosen to abandon even the emoluments to be derived from the practice of his profession as a civilian, and is willing, for the paltry pittance allowed by Government, to assume the responsibilities and devote his utmost energies to the duties of Medical Director of an army so large as that over which Dr. Tripler had charge, it seems to me that even the pardonable anxiety of the friends of those dying under his charge is not excusable for a violation toward him of the ordinary rules of charity which are, in the "Book of Books," laid down for our conduct toward *all* men. It has been made apparent to me, as well by the declarations of men who were in position to know the facts, as by my own experience in the matter, that the lack of proper materials in the medical service of the army, at that time, was caused, not by the neglect of Dr. Tripler to call for them at the proper places under Government, but by the failure or inability of the Government to supply the articles he ordered.

In my own experience in the Peninsular campaign, many incidents of which are referred to in this work, by the author, in terms of praise which have afforded me the most ample and gratifying reward for all I there endured, I found it at all times difficult to obtain a sufficient supply of many materials which were absolutely necessary for the proper care and cure of the sick and wounded, and, in fact, I was many times utterly unable to obtain articles most needed; and yet I have had the most convincing proof that the Medical Director cannot be justly held responsible for this.   The fault, I am convinced, laid nearer to the Government at Washington.   To my mind the Surgeon-general (superior officer to the Medical Director) having the means at hand at Washington for ascertaining, if he did not know, the proportions of war the campaign was assuming, — and knowing, as he must have known, the size of the army, the dangers by which that army were beset from the effects of the climate, the character of the country, and the probabilities of battle, — was in duty bound to see that all necessary material was provided for the medical department of the service; and it would be but a sickly compliment (as it is an illy-consoling excuse) for that officer to say that, perhaps, he did not realize all the necessities of the case.   And yet the fact is patent, that there was, during the whole of this campaign, a lack of supplies for the medical and hospital departments, which, without doubt, was the cause of more deaths than occurred by the other and more direct casualties of war.

It may be remarked here, in defence of Dr. Tripler, that although he has not, for a long time past, filled the office of Medical Director, yet at every battle since the removal of the army from Harrison's Landing (as I have been informed by a number of returned surgeons whose capacity and credibility cannot be questioned), the same lamentable defects in the medical service of the army have existed to a greater or less extent; as, for instance, in the location of, and supplies for, the hospital at Windmill Point, where days are said to have elapsed before necessary food and medical supplies were obtained, and a great number of our men actually died from lack of them; the medical history of the battle of Antietam, at which it is charged, by Dr. Agnew, that at least five hundred men died from the want of medical supplies; the late battle of Chancellorsville, where thousands were, it seems to me, needlessly left in the hands of the enemy, when they might and should have been transferred to the other side of the river, and there received proper surgical attendance. It is said that, after this battle, our brave wounded soldiers, in many instances, laid for days without proper (and in some cases without any) food, and with no medical relief, many of them left to the mercies of the enemy, a large number dying from sheer neglect, and many more were buried alive in fires occasioned by the contending armies in shelling the woods, and in burning the Chancellor House.

Where now rests the responsibility for all these incidents of lack of proper care and exertion in providing for the medical department of the service? Not on Dr. Tripler, certainly. If there were any faults in that gentleman's administration of the medical department of the Army of the Potomac, it seems apparent at a glance that those above him at the time, and yet in office, have not profited, or at any rate have not, for the advantage of the soldiers (who are, after all, most interested), availed themselves of and acted upon the instruction which should have been derived from the development of such faults.

The writer of this was one of a number of surgeons (all more or less known for their attainments in surgery, and many of them occupying the foremost ranks in their profession) who obeyed with alacrity the call for help which came forth, almost as with the wail of despair, from the Government and the officers and soldiers of our army, in anticipation of the heavy engagements which were to take place on the Peninsula. These men, without reward, all left lucrative employment at home, and afforded most substantial assistance to the sick and wounded throughout the campaign; and I am convinced not one of them can be found who will not coincide with me in my views as to the origin of the defects in the medical service of that campaign. Those men, knowing these defects, have called attention to them and their causes at home; and the result has been, that although many, if not all of them have been at all times since willing to extend the same assistance they at that time afforded to our sick and wounded, yet, by the *fiat* of those in power, they have been interdicted from so doing.   The reason for this *may* be found in an aversion, in high places, to the assistance of volunteer surgeons, who, seeing defects in the conduct of the department of the service pertaining to their profession, *may* deem it their duty to expose them.   But enough of this.   It is my intention to examine this subject more fully at another place; and at that time I shall deem it my duty, and it shall be my agreeable privilege, to discuss the matter, and expose the source of evil to its full extent.

There have been many defects connected with the Peninsular campaign (originating, no doubt, from the fact that the war of the rebellion had suddenly assumed proportions which no man, either North or South, had anticipated) which have since been successfully remedied by the Government.   Many of these have been ably set forth by the author of this work. And indeed we may say with truth, the wonder now is that a Government so unaccustomed to war as ours had been has, in the space of two years and more of the most hotly contested struggle that ever convulsed a nation, exhibited so few failings, and committed so few mistakes.   What man is there among us who, two years ago to-day, would not have laughed to scorn the person who would have dared predict that this rebellion could have lasted to this day?   Who at that time dreamed that, before this hell-conceived uprising of a portion of our people against God's favored Government should cease, the armies upon either side would extend to millions?   And yet here, after two years of war, we find in the field, with either of the contestants, an army larger than has been supported by any Government for ages past.   While, therefore, we all should claim the right to discuss freely (yet with charity) manifest errors or omissions of duty on the part of the Government, or its representatives in the field, in the conduct of the war, we must not fail to render thanks to the "God of battles" that he has enabled us, during the terrible contest

2 *

hitherto, to travel in the right path so far as we have. It must be conceded at all times, however, that *errors winked at always grow upon us ;* and it is, therefore, the duty of every citizen who loves his country at all times fearlessly to call attention to manifest imperfection and mismanagement, or wilful misconduct in the administration of any branch of the Government, without regard to the question as to whose interests or feelings may be affected by the exposure. Let the idea once obtain, that citizens must wink at or pass silently over demonstrated derelictions, or even indiscretions, in the Government or its officials (whether in times of war or peace), simply because they are the derelictions or indiscretions of the Government or its officers, and we surrender at once the right of the master (the people) to hold the servant (their representative in office) to accountability for his stewardship. An honestly intended administration of the Government never can be weakened (but will always profit) by a frank exhibition of its defects; and that public officer who is unwilling to have his attention, or that of his sovereigns (the people), called to errors in his administration as an officer, is a dishonest man, and will always be an unsafe and unreliable servant of the people. I have deemed proper thus to remark upon this subject, because of the dangerous extent to which the expression, *" hold on until the war is over,"* is now being used, whenever any one has the frankness to point out errors or indiscretions in the conduct of *any department* in reference to the war. My idea is, call attention to and cure these errors and indiscretions, if you would hasten the speedy and successful termination of this unhappy contest.

For these reasons I have full confidence that, hereafter, the good sense of the people will, with one accord, render heartfelt thanks to Dr. Marks for the fearless manner in which, at times during the progress of his narrative, he has pointed out what he conceived to be errors of omission or commission in the conduct of the Peninsular campaign; and whether the reader agree or disagree with the conclusions of the author, all will be compelled to acknowledge that the tone of the work affords ample proof of his sincerity in the matter. Thus, I myself am compelled to differ, to some extent, with him in his conclusions as to the standard and character of the surgeons of the army as a body; and yet I must admit that there are, and have been, numbers in that branch of the service to whom his strictures (and even more severe), are justly applicable. In my experience with the Army of the Potomac I found the majority of the surgeons to be competent, faithful, and efficient men, always attentive to the interests of the sick and wounded, and never avoiding, but always courting "the post of danger as the post of duty." As a body, a more reliable set of officers could not be found in the service. If the proportion of better surgeons in the army has since decreased, it is highly probable that this decrease has been caused by the manifest defects in the management of the medical department, for which they were in no wise responsible, and which have been referred to in this work by Dr. Marks, and in this introduction by myself. Men of the highest attainments, and purest motives, will not always consent to stand silently by and see faults, for the effects of which they themselves may be blamed, even though they may be convinced that, by remaining and suffering, they may yet do some good: and it is not yet clear to a demonstration that *many* valuable men have not *been driven* from the corps of surgeons of the army by their aversion to undergo the military necessity of remaining silent as to defects and abuses in the medical department, which are detrimental more to their patients than themselves, and yet for which they are not in any way accountable. But the poorer class, caring nothing for these things, would naturally remain; and hence, perhaps, the strictures often now indulged in against the surgeons as a class.

And now a few words as to the author of this work. I met him, a stranger, at the White House. With a natural disposition, on my part, to exercise the utmost caution in the selection of my friends and confidents, I found in him a man who, from the commencement of our acquaintance, enweaved himself in my affections; and even before we had encountered half the harrowing scenes through which a Divine Providence guided each of us in safety, I learned to look up to and love him for himself. A more useful man was not connected with the army at that time. No man came within the sphere of *his* duties, who was not most favorably impressed by his presence; and the thousands of soldiers now living, who from time to time, during those *"days of blood,"* were the recipients of his goodly counsels, and most kind attentions, will, in after years, whenever the name of Dr. Marks is mentioned, "rise up and call him blessed." A true Christian, who had learned the importance of at times addressing men's souls through their physical necessities, and the (to the pastor) still more important duty of adapting himself to the vicissitudes of life, that he might the more effectually carry out his Christian mission, he everywhere and on all occasions, by all his acts, demonstrated to those around him the dignity and usefulness of the pastorate, and the excellency and divinity of Gospel Christianity. The influence of such a man in the army must have been seen to be appreciated. With such men for teachers, comforters, and counsellors, no army can be conquered, no nation subdued. His usefulness as a chaplain did not, however, to the least extent, transcend his capacities in the hospital; and all who are acquainted with the facts will willingly concede that the advance hospital station left in his charge was at all times maintained and managed by him in a more cleanly, efficient, and orderly manner than any others connected with the Army of the Peninsula.

That Dr. Marks may, by his book, and by all his works in life, accomplish all the good the Almighty designed for him, and he so much desires; and that he, with all true patriots, may now be permitted to rejoice in the rebellion crushed, and the good old Union restored, is the most earnest wish of his friend,

JOHN SWINBURNE, M. D.

July 23d, 1863.

INCIDENTS AND SCENES

OF THE

PENINSULAR CAMPAIGN.

~~~~~~~~~~~~~~~~~~~~~~~~

CHAPTER I.

Early Camp-life — Dr. John Crawford — Memorials of many
Virginia Families — Fairfax Seminary — Bishop Meade.

WE reached Washington City in August, 1861,
— the companies composing the 63d Pennsylvania
arriving at intervals of several days. Colonel (now
General) A. Hays joined the regiment on the
16th of September; and on Saturday, the 27th of
September, we crossed the Potomac, going in boats
to Alexandria.

On the morning of the following day we disem-
barked, and marched to a new encampment on the
Leesburg road. Our tents were pitched on the
property of Mrs. Dr. Powell, under the shadow of
the fruit-trees in her orchard, around her mansion.
We were now 1070 strong; the men were large,
robust, and full of life; the regiment excited the

(21)

interest of all the troops of the various States near us.

We were at first included in the division commanded by General Franklin, but were in a few days transferred to that of General Heintzleman.

During our stay at Camp Hays, near Washington, Dr. John Crawford came from Kittanning, Pa., and immediately commenced amongst us the duties of regimental surgeon. He was then in firm health, full of life, and enjoyed with the zest of a boy the strange scenes and novel adventures of camp-life. His presence was a constant charm to the men; his face, always radiant and kindly, invited to trust in his sympathy. He was, moreover, a man of gentle and loving nature, highly gifted, not so much with the treasures of scholarship as with a memory that never failed him. Ardent in his nature, enthusiastic for all that was good and noble, he imparted his sympathies and emotions, like magnetic fire, to every one around him. He had the keenest relish for all that he esteemed beautiful and grand : every striking scene, picture, or event unsealed the fountain, and there flowed forth the stream of song. Every hour spent in his company gave us some of the most precious gems of classical and English poetry. His nature was most affectionate, leaning, probably, too much for happiness on his friends. Few men had a keener relish for society, and fewer still could impart so much genuine enjoyment. Noble man! how sincerely we all mourned his loss, — passing away from us as he did in the very zenith of his power, and when there was opened for him the prospect so bright for usefulness to his country!

But if our loss was great, who can conceive the
irreparable one to his family? He imparted, in the
few days that he was with us, the sunshine of hope;
and how much of the light of life must have fled
from those who looked up to him as.the solace and
the strength of the future!

Opposite to our encampment was the yellow oc-
tagonal house of Mrs. Lee. The houses of the inhabitants of the country were nearly all deserted. The
families that resided in this section were the most
aristocratic in the State—the Lees, the Masons,
Washingtons, Hunters, Spotswoods, Fairfaxes, were
represented, and some of them still retained broad
ancestral lands. In the South, the most wealthy
and polished people are not the dwellers in cities
and towns; but the planters and country gentlemen
are the representatives of the old families; and
everything rich in ancestral memorials is found in
their homes. Many of these families lived in the
greatest opulence and ease. The summer, with the
exception of an occasional excursion to Hampton
Roads and Cape May, was spent on their estates.
The winter was given to Washington; and hence
the influence that Virginia for a long time exerted
on the National Government was owing to the social
power of many highly polished families, who, every
season, gave themselves to the plottings and pleas-
ures of the capital. The sons of these old aristocratic families were thus aided to obtain all the
situations which they desired in the army, navy, and
foreign embassies; and the marriage of the daughters of these wealthy and noble houses to members
of Congress, officers in the army, and other distin-

guished citizens, spread the network of Virginia's
influence over the entire land.

Of these families, residing in the neighborhood
of Alexandria, not one remained, except where extreme sickness or age prevented a removal.   It was
a strange spectacle, — those sumptuous and elegant
mansions, with their rich furniture and paintings
abandoned, and a few aged, helpless negroes and
sick soldiers the only occupants.   In a short time,
all that was valuable in these houses disappeared;
the walls were blackened, the mirrors shattered, and
everything interesting and beautiful destroyed.   The
fences were soon gone; the orchards and gardens
became encampments; and the once green fields
were trodden into dustiness, the forests cut down,
and everything we looked upon bore the blight
of war.

In many of these houses were found interesting
family memorials, such as letters written in the last
century, and were from fathers, sisters, and brothers,
descriptive of travel, adventures, and marriages, and
sometimes of narratives of conversations with distinguished men: these letters were well written in
the style of the old English authors in the days of
Addison, Johnson, and Pope.   I will be pardoned
for alluding to these; for they were found lying in
open drawers and, in many instances, scattered upon
the floor.   One of them was an elegantly written
epistle of a father to his son, then in a Northern
medical school, recalling the experiences of his own
youth; and, in words full of philosophy and piety,
counsels him to "beware of the snares and tempta-
tions which are the ruin of so many, and from which

they hope that repentance and reform can deliver them; but the consequences are sure to come in sorrow, in confirmed habits of evil, in a thousand pains and ills, and, worst of all, in fear of an avenging Providence, which neither infidelity nor occupation can drive away from the mind." This letter is written in the bold round hand of the olden time.

Another is the letter of a father to a young Dr. Powell, in answer to one requesting the hand of his daughter in marriage. The letter is written in a style so manly and noble that I felt acquainted with the writer, and regretted that one so calculated to adorn and bless had to die. Others of these letters conduct to the interior history of the family, depicting the anxieties, sorrows, and hopes of parents, — the unhappy events and conflicts of some years, and the bereavements and death-scenes of others. These letters are interesting and instructive as family records, and teaching us the lesson that those who have gone before us had our trials, buffeted with the same troubles, loved and feared and joyed and hoped as we do now. One of these writers was a highly gifted woman, full of wit, and so keenly cutting the outline of the characters she met with, that you know them all, laugh with her at their follies, and enjoy their oddities. The women and the men that she describes stand out so living-like in her tableau, that we know them as though they had been our companions from childhood. In one of these letters she describes in a most amusing and felicitous manner the triumphal journey of an aunt through certain towns of the Old Dominion, where she was

3

everywhere wined, feted, and toasted because the mother of sixteen children.

Amongst the papers found in various places in this house, were many manuscript sermons of the Rev. Mr. Lee, breathing an ardent Christian spirit. Mr. Lee, as I learned, had been dead many years. His wife, a daughter of Mrs. Powell, soon followed her husband; and thus, two of the good of the land were taken away from the evil to come. Mr. Lee had been during his life a professor in Fairfax Theological Seminary. This institution, belonging to the Episcopal Church, had for its patrons and founders such men as Bishops Moore, Meade, and Johns, — men whose praise for piety, wisdom, and eloquence is in the mouths of thousands, North and South. In this Seminary were educated men ardently devoted to the cause of religion, who were broad and catholic in their views. Bishop Meade especially was unfriendly to slavery, and favored the great movement of 1825–30, looking to emancipation, when many distinguished men in Virginia committed themselves so earnestly to the cause of human freedom. At this time, Bishop Meade was behind no one in urging on the people of his State the duty and expediency of emancipation; and he farther depicted in glowing and prophetic language the dangers of the future, if, from motives of avarice, interest, and ease, they deferred action. And yet, this conscientious and far-sighted man defended on his dying bed the secession of the Southern States, though he well knew that the root principle of the rebellion was the determination to uphold and perpetuate human slavery. Such is the glory and the shame of man! To-day a prophet with a speech which none can answer or resist, with an eye that reads the truth under any veil, and with a heart that welcomes all its self-denial and reproach; but, to-morrow, a wretched trembler in the presence of enemies whom his wisdom and eloquence have collected, and with a darkened face and the heart of a child, fleeing from dangers which he had once welcomed!

CHAPTER II.

Encampment on the Farm of George Mason, Esq. — Character
of this Man — Appearance of the Country — General Desolation — The Discipline of the Camp — General Jameson —
Mrs. Jameson — The Daily Life of the Army — Personal Influence of Officers.

AFTER remaining in Camp Shields about three
weeks, we were transferred to the command of
Major-General Heintzleman, and removed with
several regiments to the extreme left of the Army
of the Potomac. The new encampment was on the
farm of George Mason, Esq. This gentleman had
for a long time held a prominent position in Virginia, both as a lawyer and politician. His boast
and glory was that the blood of the Stuarts flowed
in his veins, being a descendant of Charles II.; and
certainly the general contour of his face strikingly
reminded one of many of the portraits of that
family; and in the expression of cold, savage brutality, he fell short of none of his illustrious ancestors. This man is one of the few of whom I have
yet to learn of a single good act to shine like a gem
in the general waste of a barren life. As a son, by
his unnatural cruelty he brought upon himself the
curse of his mother; as a magistrate, he was as
remorseless as James II.; as a master, there are no

words in the English language to paint him. In his front grounds, near his house, now stand two large posts, with rings and chains in each. One he called by the suggestive name of Tiger; the other by the equally expressive name of Lion. To these posts he had poor whites and free negroes whom, as a magistrate, he condemned to be whipped for petty larcenies and trading with slaves, chained and whipped, —at the first execution giving them a taste of Lion, and dismissing the bleeding, cowering wretches with gleeful satisfaction, "hoping that they might be brought before him again, and the next time Tiger should tickle them with his soft and furry claw!" This man, as a prominent lawyer and wealthy planter, had much to do in embittering the citizens of Virginia towards their countrymen of the North. He drew up in the Convention the celebrated bill for the expulsion of all Northern men from the State. He was known as an ardent advocate of all the doctrines of Secession.

When Ellsworth first broke into Alexandria, the tidings of the coming and near presence of the Yankees were soon borne along every highway; and to none brought more consternation than to the Hon. George Mason. He packed up in all haste his plate and valuables, gathered his slaves, ordered out his carriages, and, in the wildest haste, urged immediate flight to Richmond. His family, followed by a long retinue of servants, had already reached the avenue gate, when the procession was arrested by the appearance of our cavalry. The panic and scene that followed can be imagined. Mr. Mason most passionately complained of this indignity

3 *

heaped upon a citizen of Virginia. The ladies begged him to be quiet and submit, and wept and sobbed as though plunged into the very depths of misery. The negroes grinned with delight, enjoying the dilemma and mortification of "Massa," but more "de comin' ob de wah."

Mr. Mason was marched back, provided with comfortable quarters in his own house, and protected by guard from all unreasonable intrusion. He was closely watched, and never permitted to leave his premises. No clients came to his door; his functions as magistrate were suspended; his negroes were going and returning, riding his horses and selling his grain, without restraint. His fields were encampments; his fences were consumed for fuel; his forest lands were soon treeless; and Mr. Mason could look over his wide farm and see everywhere desolation. This was the winter of his discontent. The very presence of our soldiers filled him with frenzy, and his rage was beyond disguise. But after a time his avarice mastered every other passion. In order to obtain damages for the ruin of his property, he took the oath of allegiance, brought in a bill of eighty thousand dollars against the Government, — charging twenty thousand dollars for the cord-wood we cut, and eighty dollars an acre for the injury done the land on which we encamped, and ten thousand dollars for his fences. A commission audited his bills, but with what result I never heard. Such is one of the aristocrats who plunged the whole country into war, and brought ruin on Virginia.

We now began to assume all the peculiarities of

camp-life; and military discipline gradually cur-
tailed personal liberty, but with a wisdom which I
shall always admire. Colonel Hays (now General
Hays) did not suddenly place on the necks of the
soldiers the iron yoke of military law. He gradually accustomed the men to submission; went
through the ranks and instructed them, — being
more patient than one could have anticipated, from
his fiery nature, with their slowness and errors. At
first, he made the lash of discipline fall most heavily
on the officers; and little by little accustomed the
men to the stern *régime* essential for the success of
an army. He knew well that rigid military rule
would be at first intolerably oppressive to those who
had possessed liberty to the utmost license. He
made no effort to whip and scourge the men into
order, but left this to time and training. To this
immediate extinguishment of the liberty of the citizen may be traced much of the insubordination and
sickness of the army in the autumn of 1861. Many,
stung to madness by the tyranny of those no way
their superiors, and smarting under a discipline ca-
pricious and unmerciful, became eager to throw
themselves away in dissipation, and in acts of fool-
hardiness; others, contrasting their "grievous bondage" with the enjoyment and quiet liberty of their
homes, sunk into a state bitter and gloomy, caring
little for their lives, became indifferent to their persons and duties, and welcomed wounds or death as
an escape from a despotism they could not endure.
These nameless injuries and insults suffered under
the name of discipline, excited my pity for the
soldier more than even his sickness and wounds.

In the ordinary adjustments of society there are many restraints upon men of selfish, resentful, and cruel natures; but such a man in the army as an officer can gratify to the full the malignity of his heart. There is no man who more fully deserves the gratitude of his country than the volunteer soldier in our armies. He has left his home, sacrificed his interests, thrown himself out of employment, relinquished for years all his plans for the future, given up his personal liberty, and, at the call of his country, laid on her altar all that man holds most dear. All honor to our noble volunteer! May the country they have helped to redeem for freedom, never forget them, and their children honor with the deepest love their memory!

It is due to General Hays to say that, while he was always active, — no effort fatiguing him, nor length of march wearying him, — he was patient with the men, and never permitted any one to be wronged, if he knew it. He was restless, impulsive, and fiery in temper, therefore sometimes erring in haste of judgment, but underneath all there was really a warm, generous nature. He had the singular power of infusing his own spirit into his men, — making the weakest strong, and controlling the most turbulent by a glance of his eye, or wave of his hand; a man whom nature designed for the position he occupied. Very soon after our removal to Camp Johnson our brigade was placed under the command of General C. Jameson. I have met no one in the army with soldierlike qualities superior to this man. With a tall, noble person, as commanding in look as Julius Cæsar, in a group of a thousand officers the eye would have selected him as the finest model of manhood.

At the commencement of the rebellion, he occupied a distinguished position at the bar in his native State—Maine. He was one of the first to offer his life to his country. He came out as commander of the 3d Maine, and was in the thickest of the fight at Bull's Run. By his coolness and bravery on that fatal field, he won for himself the thanks of the army and the nation. As the commander of our brigade, he was impartial,—easily approached by officers and soldiers in the ranks. He had none of that hauteur and silent sternness assumed by many officers, who, dressed in a little brief authority, listen to complaints with impatience, and reply with insults. To him every soldier was still a man and a brother. As an officer, training and disciplining his brigade, few in the army were his superiors. He mastered with ease the most difficult and complicated movements, and showed himself equal to every emergency. If it had pleased Providence to spare him, there was no doubt a brilliant and successful future before him. From his earnest enthusiasm, generous kindness, and ardent devotion to the cause of his country, one portion of the army derived much of that moral force which bore it so successfully through the Peninsular campaign. Mrs. Jameson accompanied her husband to his tent when he first came amongst us, and remained during the winter. Of this lady, as of one who will never emerge from the shadow of her widowhood, it may not be improper nor indelicate to speak. Not more than thirty years of age, her countenance had lost none of the radiancy of her girlhood. With a person uncommonly graceful, she had a face that shone on us like the star of the morning,—always hopeful and benignant. With refined and polished manners, delighting in good books, and in conversation naturally diffusing the precious odors collected in those gardens of spices,—lowly in her estimate of herself, humble before God, meek and gentle in spirit, —she appeared to us as one clothed in the purity of the Madonna. She was all one could desire in a companion and friend of the heart. The presence of this excellent lady in our portion of the army was of a value never to be estimated. As she passed through the camp and hospitals in familiar visitations, as she attended our meetings for prayer and public worship, the officers and soldiers were reminded of their mothers, wives, sisters, and daughters; and home affections were revived. The very sight of a woman of spotless purity in the camp, is like the visit of an angel.

We had at this time in our brigade the 99th Pennsylvania, commanded by Colonel Lujeane; the 105th Pennsylvania, commanded by Colonel McKnight; the 61st Pennsylvania, commanded by Colonel Rippey; the 57th Pennsylvania, commanded by Colonel C. Campbell; the 87th New York, commanded by Colonel Dodge; the 63d Pennsylvania, commanded by Colonel Hays. The usual camp duties were: the reveille beat at six o'clock in the morning, and in five minutes after, the roll was called in the street of each company, and every soldier was obliged to report himself dressed and ready for duty. At seven o'clock breakfast was served by the company cooks to each mess. The breakfast was generally camp crackers, called "Hard Tack," coffee without milk, and a piece of pork or beef. If we were so fortunate as to have a sutler in camp, we added to our luxuries a little butter or molasses. Then commenced the daily cleaning and scouring of guns, which lasted until half-past eight o'clock, when the guard-mounting began. From forty to eighty men were daily in requisition for guarding camp, head-quarters, and commissary stores. The men required from each regiment were marched to brigade head-quarters, and then assigned their several posts of duty, and at nine o'clock returned, and resumed their appointed beat or watch. At nine o'clock, except when the weather was very bad, the various companies were marched to some neighboring field for drill and manœuvre. They were sometimes commanded by a captain, but more frequently by a lieutenant, or orderly sergeant. This continued until twelve o'clock, when they returned to camp for dinner. At that meal we had crackers, bean-soup, boiled meat, and coffee, but rarely potatoes. At half-past one, the camp was again all bustle, — the men strapping on their overcoats and knapsacks, cleaning, washing, and blacking, for regimental or brigade drill. At two o'clock they marched into the field, and continued to practise all those movements and evolutions which enable men to act in concert, and facilitate the use of the weapons of war. At four o'clock, in the winter, the men returned to camp, rested a few moments, and then again fell into line for dress parade. This always struck me as the most imposing of all our military ceremonials. The men were expected to wear their best clothing; the companies, without the delay of a moment, fell into the line from their own camp-street; and, when the men took their places, a perfect silence succeeded the noise of a thousand feet, and all assumed a solemn, statue-like rigidity.

The band-corps standing on the extreme right of the regiment now strike up some military air; and the drum-major stands in front of the band, looking for all the world like the buckram soldier in a musical box. The impressiveness of this officer's appearance is heightened by the great staff which he bears in his hand, with an enormous gilt head. Of what this staff and its big head are emblematic, I never could learn, — possibly designed to be an impressive symbol of the fact that all bands are likely to be afflicted with that fantastic disease, the "big head." As the Persian kings had their coffins borne before them when they entered the royal palace to be crowned,—reminding them that all earthly power and splendor ended in the grave, — so this huge-headed staff may be borne before the band, and, in the hand, be made to perform a part so fantastic and ridiculous, to remind them that they might become empty-headed, foolish, vain, and worthless. With a most solemn step, the major now advances, elevates his staff, shakes it at some power in the air, then lowers it, as before some imaginary divinity, and, with many elevations, quivers, and shakes of the staff, wheels on the left and commences his majestic march. It is always essential that this officer should look fierce, and bring down his heel on the ground with indignant force, as if calling upon the earth to pulsate to his tread. The band slowly marches along the entire line, and, when it reaches the extreme of the left wing, wheels, and with a much more rapid strain and quicker step returns to the head of the regiment.

In front of the line, and about a hundred feet in advance of the centre, stands the colonel. The officers, at a given command from the adjutant, advance in front of their companies; then comes from out of each company the orderly sergeant, and all advance to the centre of the line, and give their evening report of officers or men absent without leave. After the return of the orderlies to their position at the head of their companies, the adjutant reads any orders which may have been received from the War Department, from the general-in-chief of the division, or brigadier-general, or from the colonel, inflicting punishment for offences, or granting promotions. After this, the officers advance in line and greet the colonel with a military salute. If the commander has any instructions to give to the officers, they listen with the deepest respect; and in a few moments, with a mutual wave of the hand, the officers separate, the companies deploy into their camp-street, break ranks, the military work of the day is over; and the deep silence of the last hour is succeeded by the shouts, the songs, and laughter of those who have thrown off the yoke and burden of another day. Poor fellows! they little know what may be in wait for them.

Very soon after we entered our new encampment, the men commenced building little cabins, large

4

enough to contain four, eight, or twelve persons.
In these they built chimneys, and in a little while
were quite comfortable. Many of the enjoyments
of civilization were borne into these cabins. Nearly
every soldier had his Bible, almost all a hymn-book;
many of them possessed libraries of several valuable
volumes, and spent much of the night in reading.
Others spent their nights around the camp-fire, and
many were the stories told,—the wild legends of Indian, Celtic, and German life,—fierce were the con-
troversies in regard to politics, religious faith, and
the virtues and vices of various races; and there
was always some one the butt of all, and mercilessly
the subject of caricature.

In the first organization of a regiment, the officers
who have the severest labor are the captains, adju-
tants, and orderlies. All the others may escape
from constant watchfulness and exertion, but with
these it is impossible; for daily reports have to be
made to the colonel and to brigade head-quarters,
and censure and severe discipline follow any neglect of duty. These daily reports descend to the
most minute details: the number of men in camp;
the number sick; the number sick in quarters;
the sick in the hospitals; the number in the company present for duty; the number detailed for
special service; and where those absent from camp,
whether on passes or furlough; the rations drawn,
etc. etc. Every few weeks these reports are rendered more voluminous, and incredibly difficult of
preparation, by the clothing account, in which is
charged to each soldier all the articles of dress he
draws,—he being allowed clothing to the amount of

forty-two dollars a year; and if he draws less will receive pay to that amount, and if more it will be deducted from his monthly pay. These reports must in all things conform to strict military rule,—which, like the law of the Medes and Persians, changeth not. There must be no mistakes, nothing to be corrected, or left to be understood.

In a little time after the organization of a regiment, the isolation of the men composing it from the world becomes almost complete. His regiment constitutes the whole world to the man. It is but rarely he can obtain a pass to go without the lines; and when he could visit some old friend or neighbor in another regiment, camp duties, repairing his cabin, washing his clothes, or mending his garments, occupy his spare moments. Thus, the soldier in the army, like the man digging a well, gradually sinks out of the sight of men; and his own vision of the world becomes every hour more narrow. Regiments lying alongside of each other will not have the slightest intercourse, and in months will scarcely know each other's name or numbers; and this is more especially the case if they are from different States.

This is one of the results of service in the army most deeply to be deplored,—that the officers and soldiers lose all American feeling, and have no ambition beyond their own regiment or, at most, corps. Against this, every wise commander of divisions and corps will watch, and take every measure in his power to induce intercourse and friendly sympathy between the officers representing different sections of the country. The ten-

dency of military life is to generate an intense self-
ishness. Away from home and all those blessed
influences which soften and expand the heart in
sympathy, encompassed with masculine grossness,
all the nature hardens, and "is set on fire." The
emotions of tenderness and pity are suppressed, and
the mind fully occupied with the plans of ambition,
stung by insults, or inflamed by rivalry and hate.
There is no spot in the wild chaos of the soul where
the dove of charity can rest. I have wept bitter
tears on the fields of battle, where "the gory,
ghastly spectacle" was too terrible to be endured;
I have felt sincere pity for those who for long
months suffered the pains of wounds and sickness
on the hospital-beds; but nothing has occasioned
me the same profound grief as witnessing the degradation of human nature in the army. What com-
miseration can be deep enough for that soldier who
knows well that he is only valuable in the eyes of
his officers as a creature of muscle, with powers of
endurance beyond those of the camel of the desert,
as he is able to dig trenches, stand guard twenty-
four hours without sleep or rest, — as he can bear
without complaint storm and sunshine, winter's
cold and summer's heat; and, when no longer capable of performing exhausting duties and marches,
he is consigned to the living tomb of some hospital,
with little thought and less pity, left far in the rear,
carried from one hospital to another, forgotten as
the dead, and dropped out of the memory of his
companions.

Many officers, as they ascend in rank in the service, divest themselves of all human feeling.. With them, power hardens the heart and dries up all the springs of generous sympathy; their faces become cold and stern, and their commands have in them a sting which degrades all who have to obey. Under such an officer, the soldier invariably becomes a worse man, often losing all interest in the cause of his country.

As an escape from a despotism which goads them to madness, some desert, others feign sickness, others sink into indifference, and endure with feigned apathy the extra duty of the camp to-day, the guard-house to-morrow, and the handcuffs the next day; and all this because they have become hopeless. They have been treated like brutes, and to brutality they sink.

I know that this stern iron rule — into which not a single element of humanity is permitted to enter — is excused on the principle of necessity. "War has no time for charity," "nor moments which she can give to anointings with the oil of kindness."

To this, the reply is easy. No man is fit to command in the camp or field who does not constantly recognize the great principles of humanity. Men may be drilled into perfect, living machines; but this is not courage. All true bravery springs from confidence in the right of that cause for which all home ties are sacrificed; and in such an hour, every soldier is heroic in proportion to the trust and love which he bears towards his commander.

4 *

In battle, the voice of the man whom the soldier loves, nerves his heart; and, rather than forfeit his esteem by flight, he will remain at his post and die. Much of the devotion of the army to General McClellan was owing to the fact that, as he rode through the ranks, he always looked upon the men kindly; and when he had to press a soldier out of his way, it was never with rudeness or insult. And this was the secret of Kearney's popularity in his division; and among the thousand camp traditions of that singular and gifted man, there is not one of needless insult or cruelty to soldiers in the ranks. For them he had always the looks and language of cheer; while for his officers he had often such words of biting, bitter scorn as only General Kearney could utter, — falling on them like angry flashes of lightning from a storm-cloud. And in all the army I know of no such devotion to a general as was exhibited by the men of Kearney's division.

The soldiers who perform prodigies of valor are those who have formed strong personal attachments for some officer; and they cannot waver under his eye, nor desert his person.

My firm conviction, after nearly two years of observation, is that every officer ought to be dismissed from the service, as worthless for such a position of power, who fails to secure the trust and love of his men. For it will be found in the day of battle that such an officer will be left alone to perish; and, regardless of his fate, every man will consult his own safety.

I have known companies in regiments which, in the earlier Peninsular engagements, never stood firm; but subsequently, by change of officers, became the best and most unfaltering of heroes.

Nothing is lost by honoring in every man the great principles of his manhood.

CHAPTER III.

The Chaplain and his Duties—Distribution of Books—Religious Services — The Obstacles to Success — No Protection nor assigned Duties — Treatment of the Chaplains by many Officers — The Tendencies of Military Law.

I HAD been the chaplain of the 12th regiment Pennsylvania Volunteers in the three months' service; and, while in the service of that regiment, had extended my labors along the line of the Northern Central Railroad from York to Baltimore, — as the regiment was on guard-duty all its term of enlistment on that line.

I re-entered the army as chaplain of the 68d Pennsylvania, and my services commenced about the 1st of September, 1862.

We were then encamped near Washington. Many of the men were young, and fresh from their homes, and entered with a most hearty enthusiasm into everything that promised to interest them and give relief; for they were yearning for something to fill up the place in their hearts left vacant by being separated from all they had loved from childhood.

My first care was to distribute Testaments and hymn-books among them. With these, some had been supplied before leaving home. The first week I appeared in camp I distributed to those who came to my tent four hundred copies of the New Testament, in four different languages, — English, German, French, and Italian, — and during the same week, six hundred small hymn-books, called the "Soldier's Hymn-book,"—drawing my supplies from the American Tract Societies of New York and Boston. From more than one hundred tents the evening hymn ascended to heaven, and those sacred songs were sung with an emotion hitherto unknown; for they reminded them of home, and dear friends, and brought back afresh the most solemn and impressive scenes in their lives.

My custom was to have two public services on the Sabbath. These were held in the open ground of the camp, and were well attended by men and officers. The attendance from the first was voluntary. But I am now convinced, after the experience of nearly two years, that every soldier ought to be compelled to attend the worship of God once on the Sabbath, whatever may be the religious faith of the chaplain. If a man of sense, he will preach on those religious truths and duties which find a response in all minds; and, as much of the power of divine worship, after we reach the years of maturity, is in reviving the sacred impressions of the past, all may be benefited. But according to the present arrangement, the attendance being voluntary, those who most need instruction and rebuke never come under the sound of the chaplain's voice. And if in any way he provokes the hostility of a number of officers, he will find his occupation gone: a mere corporal's guard will attend his Sabbath ministrations, and in a thousand ways will he be snubbed, and made to feel that his presence is a restraint, his life a sinecure, and, as an officer, a useless appendage to the army.

This opposition is easily provoked. Rebukes for drunkenness, gambling, profanity, or undue severity, will be certain to bring down on the offending chaplain a storm of rage. "He has been teaching the men to despise their officers. He has been meddling with things which he has no business to mention or to see. He does not preach the gospel. He is a small-minded busybody. If they had a chaplain who was a gentleman, they would always attend his services and encourage him; but, under this man, there is danger of their becoming heathens and infidels." Thus, the Christian minister in the army, just in proportion as he is a man of true piety and worth, will provoke hostility, and his resignation be compelled. In many cases, some of the best of men have, under unprincipled and infidel officers, suffered months of martyrdom; and nowhere can the chaplain look in hope for help, — the Government giving him, indeed, his commission, but not assigning his duties, nor compelling the other officers of his regiment to help and sustain him in his work. Their duties are prescribed, definite, and minute; but for him, all is uncertainty. The surgeons must have their hour for sick-calls, and be aided by all the officers in finding the disabled of the regiment: their decision with regard to the sick must be respected. The men whom they order to the hospital,. must be sent: those whom they command to remain in their quarters, cannot be called out on duty. But the chaplain is powerless. He has no hour that is his, but can be crowded out of all the Sabbaths of the year by parades, military necessities, etc. etc. There are many complaints in regard to the inefficiency of chaplains in the army. There may be much truth in this; for many of the chaplains are men who have passed the prime of their lives, and have been worn out in the work of the ministry before they entered the army. Beyond other men their habits of thought and action become fixed and permanent. They cannot conform with ease to the new circumstances in which they find themselves; and, in some cases, their teachings are not appropriate to the moral necessities of the men whom they address. But there are many most valuable chaplains in the army,—men of the highest intellectual culture and purest worth, who in talent would stand in the front rank of any profession, and fill the best pulpits in the country. It is most important for the moral welfare of the army, that such men should not be driven from their places. But they deeply feel the indignity inflicted on them by degradation of rank and absence of protection.

So far as the appointment of chaplains is concerned, it was evidently a concession made to the religious sentiment of the country,—one of those formless, shapeless things thrown in to fill up a vacuum. If there was any intention to secure to the army the highest benefit from religious and moral teaching, why leave the whole plan imperfect and, like a roofless dwelling, valueless as a shelter, worthless as a home? Since the chaplain's service is such an immense expense to the Government, why not make it efficient,—prescribing what

the man shall do, compelling its performance, and
the attendance of every man in the regiment on his
teaching? Talk of the man effecting but little when
he and his services can be tossed as an idle ball
from hour to hour! Complain of his want of power
when he is left out shivering in the cold, when for
every other man in the army there are rights and
the protection of law!

Every man who, as an officer or soldier, has been
in the service of the Government, knows that the
purpose of the entire military system is to beget
reverence for law. Law, law, is written on the pu-
pil of the soldier's eye, graved on every bone of his
body, and burned into every muscle. By law, the
light of his tent is extinguished, and he sleeps; by
law, every step of his nightly beat is determined,
and if he slumbers at his post, he dies. By law, he
is awakened in the morning before the dawn, and
brought forth from his tent; it regulates every mor-
sel of his food, the very hour it should be served
to him, and during the entire day he hears no voice
but its commands. Law, like an august monarch,
reigns in the camp, and every instinctive desire of
the soul, love, and friendship have to bow at its feet.
Law prescribes every movement, invests him as a
coat of mail, speaks to him lying down and talks to
him rising up. Law winds the cord around his hat,
ties his shoe-latchet, brushes the dust from his coat,
and rubs the rust from his gun. Law lays its giant
mailed hand on all his natural instincts. At one
time it converts the living, moving man into a rigid
statue of iron, and again hastens him, with the
steady step of one to whom fear is unknown, into

the jaws of death. At one moment, by a wave of its hand, prostrating him in the dust, another moment hurrying him with frantic fury into the face of his enemies. Law scowls at conscience, has contempt for remorse, hate for charity, and freezes the tear of pity on the cheek of him who sheds it. Well may we adopt of military law the expressive language of prophecy: "It is strong and terrible exceedingly." Nothing on earth is so effective in changing the entire nature of man. And when this is the intention, the actual influence of military discipline, is it wise to have a class of officers in the army without its protection and aid? Are they not thrown into a position necessarily isolated and defenceless? Unhesitatingly I say, rather abolish the entire chaplain service than continue it as it is now. If the man has no rights, no assigned sphere, no prescribed duties, no protection from law,—but is occasionally permitted by a colonel, whom unreasoning Mars has placed at the head of his regiment, to hold a religious service, — then his life is a degradation, and his ministry a failure.

For the very reason I have alluded to, because the chaplain has duties without rights, not one officer in twenty will attend any religious service. They soon catch the spirit of many of their superior officers, which is, — tolerate the chaplains, for we cannot without them secure enlistments; but never forget they are a great expense and annoyance, therefore gently but surely get clear of them by never attending their ministrations; by giving them nothing to do; by hindering anything they attempt to accomplish; by never showing them any attention; by leaving them

5

tentless, at the mercy of the other officers; by making all the profanity, the drunkenness, the thieving, and gambling of the regiment the proof of the chaplain's being "a dumb dog;" by giving him no transportation for anything he may have gathered for the good of the men,—such as books,—or a tent for worship; spring on him as many reviews and parades as possible; keep the men a long time standing at Sunday morning inspection,—make this very important. If the chaplain should come around, show undisguisedly your contempt before the men. Jeer and laugh when his back is turned; and when you have prolonged inspection until the heat of the day, go straight to your tent, and advise your men to do the same. Be certain that Sunday shall be the only day of the week when you will consult the ease and comfort of the soldier. Advise sleep and rest. Adjourn the chaplain's service over until night, and then, by having a great deal going on, defer the services as late as possible, and then have tattoo beat during the first hymn or just after the announcement of the text. If after all this he still hangs on, degrade him by making him postmaster and mailboy. If he has no horse on which to carry the mailbag, put him as a nurse into a hospital. If postmaster, take the pound of flesh; make him turn out with the mail in thunder-storms, in winter tempests; make him swim rivers, struggle through sloughs deep enough to engulf armies. If he demurs at conveying the mail on Sundays, let him know most distinctly that no officer has any business with a conscience in the United States service; but if he still refuses to go, take as a matter of compromise the most drunken, furious soldier in the camp, borrow for him the ferocious spurs of the quartermaster, mount him on the chaplain's horse, send him with the mail-bag; and if the animal returns windbroken and blind of an eye, pity the horse, curse the chaplain, and reward the soldier.

Let no man think that such wrongs as these were never perpetrated in the army. I could bring the most reliable witnesses to prove that this only faintly hints at the indignities that many chaplains have had to endure; and though this has never been my experience, shall I be so unmanly as to be less indignant because it was the bitter experience of many of my brethren? I have myself in other portions of the army been grossly insulted by men who afterwards apologized, because they thought the chaplains men of little spirit and less value.

I know not that any good can be done by the publication of the infidelity and atheism of many of the officers of the army. But it gives me satisfaction to be now at liberty to say, that the men who were so rigid in exacting the performance of every military duty, habitually neglect the greatest of moral obligations.

With all these discouragements and hindrances, my firm conviction is that the religious teacher who is firm, faithful, and constantly thoughtful of the great interests of which he is the representative, will find friends in every regiment, and his very enemies will make peace with him.

At the same time I am more certain that there are great and radical defects in the present organization of the chaplain service, which loudly demand amendment and change. I fully believe that the chaplains are now performing a service for the country and army of inestimable value; and most sorry should I be to see them driven from their posts. I fear this is inevitable, unless they have a protection and authority not now given.

CHAPTER IV.

The Revival — Gloom and Discontent from Inaction — Tent for Public Worship — Dedication Scene — The Soldier alone with his Mother — The Formation of a Camp Church — Progress of the Revival — Letter of Mansfield Brown, Esq.

FOR the encouragement of those various benevolent societies which send books and papers to the army, I must record my testimony to their signal usefulness.

While we were in the neighborhood of Washington and Alexandria, I obtained weekly supplies of these, and aimed, every Saturday evening and Sabbath morning, to visit all the tents in the regiment, and give to each soldier something for Sabbath reading.

These were uniformly received thankfully, and read.

I collected a library of three or four hundred volumes of historical, scientific, and biographical works. With these I had three hundred numbers of magazines and reviews, such as Harpers', Littell's Living Age, the Eclectic. These found their way into every tent, and were read with manifest benefit. The men, as there were given to them this mental

5 *

nutriment and amusement, felt less temptation to waste time in card-playing, or to seek excitement in intoxication. They were more contented and peaceful, and many made astonishing progress in general knowledge. During the days that were stormy and wet, they spent the entire time, except those on guard, in their tents; and, having books within their reach, the hours were neither dark nor misspent. Many assured me that they had gained more knowledge in the camp, during the winter of 1862, than in all the years of their previous lives.

One hundred and twenty volumes of very valuable books, entirely new, were contributed by W. M. Shinn, Esq., of Pittsburg. Others were received from the Soldiers' Aid Association, in Pittsburg; others were from the United States Sanitary Commission; others from the American Tract Societies of Boston and New York. These contributions secured a benefit never to be estimated in time.

Very soon I found it essential to secure a tent for public worship. One was obtained from the Rev. M. Brown, of Georgetown. It was a tent which had been used for several years for camp-meeting purposes. This the strong winds of October blew to pieces. We were then for several weeks without any covering or shelter. Until the 1st of December we held our meetings in a large guard-house which had been reared; but this we found very unsuitable and smoky.

Most dark and gloomy at this hour was our prospect for doing good. There had set in a long season of storm: the mud was fabulously deep. The tents were frequently flooded. The men were becoming

restless and desponding. A great change had occurred at home. All manufacturing interests had
started anew, and wages were higher than ever before,
while the families of the soldiers were suffering with
sickness, poverty, and cold. Now they began to
feel the corroding of the fetter. Their friends and
neighbors who had remained at home were reaping
a golden harvest.

All these things angered the soldiers. Their
faces became gloomy and their hearts sad. Their
wives and children came to them at night in their
dreams, weeping and haggard; and by day they
were haunted with a sorrow they could not shake
off. Some sunk into languor and home-sickness, —
which mocked all the usual remedies for disease,
and sent them to the hospital, and in the end to the
grave.

It now became a matter of the highest moment
to amuse the men, and bear their thoughts to those
truths which have ever stilled the tumult of human
passion. We made arrangements to start in the
camp various classes for mutual instruction. Two
in the Latin language, one in the study of German,
one in arithmetic, and, most important of all, a de-
bating society. In order to carry successfully into
execution all these plans for improvement, I wrote to
my friends, Mansfield Brown and Joseph McKnight,
of Pittsburg, for the means to purchase a tent for
public worship, and such assemblies as would con-
duce to the benefit of the regiment. Most generously, and without the delay of an hour, they responded, authorizing the purchase of a tent. The
very day their letter was received, a large tent was

offered for sale in a neighboring camp. This I immediately purchased; and before night had it pitched, a floor laid down, and a stove placed in it.

Thus, everything was arranged for Sabbath worship. This was about the 1st of January, 1862. We met in the tent on Sabbath morning, a large congregation, some seated on camp-stools, some on rude benches, some on the floor, many standing at the entrance of the tent. The interest of the occasion was greatly increased by the presence of Mrs. General Hays, who was then on a visit to her husband, Mrs. General Jameson, Mrs. Maria Hayes, the excellent matron of our hospital, whom all loved as a mother, and Miss Gilliam, and Miss Herr, who, with a self-denial ever to be commended, had become nurses in our hospital. The season was one of the greatest interest and pleasure. It was the bursting of sunshine through the darkness that had hung over us like a pall. It gave hope of future benefit and enjoyment; it reminded us of home; it was almost a church. Many eyes swam in tears, and many voices choked with emotion as we sang,

"Jesus, lover of my soul,"

And again,

"The Lord's my Shepherd,
I'll not want."

The tent gave me the theme of that morning. I told them the history of its purchase, of the generous proffer of further aid, of books, etc. etc.; and that these were but slight tokens of the deep interest felt in their welfare at home. I reminded them of the scenes attending their departure from home; of the

prayers, tears, and vows of the last Sabbath they
spent amongst their kindred; of the irrepressible
anguish of their mothers, wives, children, and sisters when they parted with them; of the promises
they had made. They had never known before how
large a place they had filled in the hearts of those
who loved them. I reminded them that at this very
hour, as their parents and kindred were assembled
in the houses of worship, they were in the hearts of
all, and the holy song was broken by sobs, and
faces of prayer were wet with tears, because they
were not there; how essential they were to the happiness and life of many. I alluded to the hundreds
of letters we were every week receiving, all breathing the same sentiment, exhorting and entreating
them by all that was dear and sacred to follow the
teachings of their ministers, and to revere the memories of home; and there was committed to them
the most sacred of all trusts,—the earthly happiness
of those to whom God had bound them. I asked
them if they could be so cruel as to blast the hopes
and embitter the life of one that loved them, and
bend down their venerable parents with a weight
that would crush them to the grave; and if they
thought there was any sacrifice too great for them
to make for those in whose hearts they were daily
borne. I reminded them of the incurable anguish
they would endure if they heard of their sins; that
they had fallen before temptation, had gone to dens
of shame, had indulged in drunkenness, had become
profane: to themselves these sins would bring only
evil now, and in the end remorse. Yet they might find
some relief from conscious degradation in the ex-

citements of the camp, in the occupations and activities of a soldier; but what balm could be found to heal the hearts they had broken, and who could comfort those who mourned over their sons as fallen from virtue and piety? I exhorted them, for the sake of all whose interests they represented, not to fall into sin, but to shun those evil ways which set on fire of hell the whole course of nature. And if they were determined to have nothing to do with religion, and to dismiss from their hearts all fear of God, yet every sentiment of manliness and every principle of honor demanded they should not disgrace the name they bore. They were here the representatives of their fathers' houses; and if they were churlish, quarrelsome, drunken, and profane, they not only degraded themselves, but dishonored their parents, — for the tree was judged by its fruits. I mentioned the case of a young soldier of a neighboring camp, who had fallen since he left home into many of the sins of the army, who, while playing cards, had become angered, and broken out into such blasphemy as confounded even his companions. While still angry and disputing, some one handed him a letter just brought into camp. It was from his mother, and she a widow. After he had read the first few words the letter fell from his hands, and he burst into tears, exclaiming, "My mother! my mother! If she knew of my sins, she would die of a broken heart!" Then, lifting the letter again, he read a few more lines and sobbed out, "Yes, mother, I will, I will, I will read the Bible you gave me. I will try to pray: I will break off my sins. Oh, my mother, I thank God you do not know how low I have sunk!'" And with many passionate exclamations and tears he continued to read the words of warning and love. One by one his companions went out and left him alone with his mother.

I entreated them to remember that the habits of sin, once contracted, were not easily thrown off. Some thought that sin was as easily cast out of the soul as a snow-flake was shaken from the hand. But this was against all human experience; "for sooner shall the Ethiopian change his skin, and the leopard his spots, than those who have learned to do evil shall learn to do well," etc. And with many other like words I reasoned with them.

The effect of this address was most manifest. All listened with increasing interest; many with tears.

At night, I again preached on Luke xii. I urged to the confession of Christ, and spoke of the danger and temptation to which they would be exposed, — the perils of sickness and battle; and they needed above everything to be made hopeful and strong by faith in an almighty, merciful, ever-present Friend. The impression of the morning was increased at night, and many retired to weep and pray. And on this day commenced one of the most remarkable seasons of religious solemnity I have ever seen. This interest continued unabated in power until we were broken by sickness and battle in the Peninsula.

During these months, hundreds in the camp found the highest joy in religious meetings, and with ever new pleasure they came together to hear the gospel. It was a season never to be forgotten. Nearly all the murmuring and discontent of the camp passed

away. The men were sober, quiet, and cheerful.
Some who had been for years dissipated, abandoned
the cup, and never, within my knowledge, afterwards
fell. Others, who had ever been a burden to their
families, now confessed their guilt, and sent home
the humble acknowledgment and promise of amendment. Others laid open long-concealed sins, and
sought instruction in regard to what they should do
to make atonement for the wrong they had committed. It was a time of great searchings of heart,
and for many weeks my tent was crowded at all
hours, when the men were off duty, by those wishing
to know the way of life.

For the mutual protection and encouragement of
those who desired to begin a new life, I resolved,
after consultation with many officers and friends, to
form a church in the regiment. We had nearly one
hundred men, officers and soldiers, who were members of various churches. For harmony, it was essential to form the church on principles common to
all. I therefore drew up a form of doctrine and
covenant to which all could assent, and which would
bind us in unity, and bear with it all the sanctity of
a sacred agreement.

Before the communion I devoted every hour when
the men were in camp in visiting from tent to tent,
and talked with each one separately, or in the tent
circle, in regard to their religious hopes and views.
I endeavored as far as possible to ascertain their
home history, that I might more perfectly identify
myself with them in sympathy, and adapt my instructions to their moral and spiritual state; for I
found invariably that there were some events, scenes,

and instructions which permanently impressed the
character for good or evil, as if the human mind was
only now and then, and at long intervals, capable
of being moved and changed. I endeavored to find
what circumstance, what lesson, what deed had left
behind an influence which survived all changes. I
found in some cases the mind was embittered and
permanently warped by some act of thoughtless or
designed cruelty, long forgotten by the offender, but
in the heart of him who had suffered, remaining like
a viper's tooth, poisoning the very fountains of life.
In others, some act of duplicity, some deed of hy-
pocrisy, created distrust of all who bore the Christian
name; and too blind and too unjust to see that a
cause may be glorious, while he who represents it is
base, they laid the crime of one at the door of all.
In other cases, some lewd companion or vile book
had debased in sensualism; and the imagination had
hung in all the chambers of the soul the pictures
of evil. Again, there had been indulgence in
childhood, and the suspension of parental authority
at the season when it was most important, producing
a restless aversion to all law. In fact, there were
but few in whom the controlling elements were
reason and conscience; but the many were biased
and led by their appetites, passions, and prejudices,
by pride, vanity, and ambition; and these emotions and vices impelled them in the path they had
chosen, and rendered a change of character almost
impossible. I made it my aim to gain the confidence of all, that I might successfully combat their
errors, enlighten their understandings, and appeal
to their consciences and better natures. This course

6

of visitation made me acquainted with the peculiarities and past history of each one, and enabled me, as I hope, to be more valuable at this time; and my own constant study in regard to the things which most influenced the conduct of men, added to the plainness of my teachings at this period.

Before the day of the communion we had a succession of storms. The mud was beyond fable. The men were confined to their tents. This enabled me to more successfully visit them,—to sit down by their side without the fear of interruption.

On Sabbath, February 9th, 1862, we organized the church, and received into its communion one hundred and seventy members, about sixty of whom for the first time confessed Christ. At the commencement of the services I baptized six young soldiers. They kneeled before me, and I consecrated them to God for life and for death; the majority of them baptized, as it proved, for the dead. I then read the form of covenant and system of faith; to which all gave their assent.

I then read the names of those who wished to enter this fold in the wilderness, enumerating them by companies; those who had made a profession of religion at home, and came to us as members of Christian churches; and those who now came out as the disciples of the Redeemer.

Then followed the communion service. This was one of the most affecting and impressive seasons of my life. The powers of the world to come rested on all minds. The shadow of the great events so soon to follow was creeping over us, giving earnestness and an impressive solemnity to all hearts. It was a day never to be forgotten, as a commencement of a new era in the life of many. It was a scene on which angels might look down with unmingled pleasure; for here the weary found rest; the burdened, the peace of forgiveness; the broken in heart, beauty for ashes. Our position increased in a high degree the interest of the occasion. We were far from our churches and homes, yet we found here the sacred emblems of our religion; and, looking into a future which we knew was full of danger, sickness, and death to many, we here girded ourselves for the conflict. It much resembled the solemn communions of Christians in the time of persecution. Our friends who were present from a distance, of whom there were several, rejoiced greatly that there was such a scene in the army. General Jameson was deeply moved, and afterwards said it was the most solemn and interesting scene of his life.

Again on Sabbath, March 9th, the religious interest continuing, we held another communion. At this time twenty-eight were received into the church. Seven young men were baptized. The interest was even greater than at the former communion; and it gives me now the greatest satisfaction to know that this season, which gave to many the highest enjoyment ever known on earth, where the cup of thanksgiving was mingled with the tears of gratitude, prepared for the sacrifice that was to follow. Many who were there never again partook of the wine of promise until they drank it new in the kingdom of God, and sat down at the marriage-supper of the Lamb. My friend Dr. Crawford was never again at the Lord's table; but was then prepared, by the peace like a river, for entering upon the blessed rest. And many others found their beds softened in sickness by the remembrance of the consecration and joy of those sacred seasons. Others were made tranquil and even triumphant in death, by the vision of the Saviour whom they had first met in the breaking of bread in the camp.

Mansfield Brown, Esq., of Pittsburg, was present at the last communion. His impression and report of the scene deserves a place in the record of mercy, and will be read, by every one into whose hands this book falls, with pleasure and profit:

"DR. McKINNEY:—*Dear Sir:*—I know it will give you pleasure to hear how I spent the Sabbath, March 9th, in the 63d regiment, Colonel Alexander Hays, near Fort Lyon.

"As you are well aware, there has been for some time quite a revival of religion going on. A most interesting, soul-stirring state of things exists among *them.* God is certainly largely blessing them. Never did I see men so deeply in earnest.

"In the morning, at eleven o'clock, Dr. Marks preached in the tent-church to as many as filled the two tents. At the close he said that as it was likely the regiment would move soon, he would hold a communion that night, and invited any persons wishing to join, to meet him.

"At two P. M. we held a most solemn and touching prayer-meeting. The prayers of the soldiers were very ardent and to the purpose. I conversed with many dear young men in their tents and alone, who readily acknowledged their need of salvation.

"At night, the tents were crowded to excess; and, as the evening was pleasant, the ends of the tents were opened and an eager crowd pressed around. A small, rude table was used; common bread, wine made of grape-jelly and water, and two glasses, were placed in the centre. Our tents were lighted by three candles, swung from the centre. Familiar words were well sung. A few introductory remarks and a prayer, then eight stalwart soldiers kneeled around the table and were baptized; the bread and wine were then passed to communicants; even outside the tents all eager to obey the command, 'This do in remembrance of me.' Everybody was weeping. Twenty-nine joined on profession,—the whole membership now being one hundred and eighty-eight. We had sweet singing while Elder Danks (captain) and myself distributed the sacramental elements. Surely, God was there. And it was well calculated to remind us of that dark night in which it was instituted. It was a most solemn, impressive scene, and one never to be forgotten. We closed it by all audibly uniting in saying the Lord's Prayer, and parted,—never all to meet until we meet at the marriage-feast in heaven.

"The soldiers are obliged to put out lights and retire at tap of the drum; but a few of us spent an hour yet in devotion, singing, and conversation in Captain Danks's tent. It was a good meeting. To witness the men's deep emotion at any reference to their families in prayer, and then to hear them say, 'We can die without fear and leave the loved ones with God, content, so our glorious flag is sustained,' gave confidence in the success of our country's cause.

6 *

"I stepped into a tent in which were five young men, Sabbath morning. Three were reading their Testaments; had a pointed conversation with them; found they had all been well *trained at home;* all knew what was their duty; three of them joined the glorious army to-night. Another fine, well-trained young stranger had been halting and hesitating, though greatly exercised for some time; four of his mess had joined, the fifth having died suddenly. He said every letter from his *good father and mother* urged and entreated him to seek religion, but he doubted his fitness. He was that night baptized and communed, and afterwards told Dr. Marks how happy and thankful he felt. His load was all gone. He intends to be a preacher.

"On Monday morning, among the first persons I saw was a stalwart man coming out of the Doctor's cabin, weeping. He grasped my hand and said he was so happy. The Doctor has written to me since that the good work is still increasing. May it go on until every dear soldier in our army shall become a good soldier of the cross!"

CHAPTER V.

Scenes in the Neighborhood of Mount Vernon — The Quakers — Their Loyalty — The Washington Family, and Traditions of General Washington—The Lewis Estate—Our Pickets in that Neighborhood — The Old Church of Washington at Pohick — The various Great Estates in that Neighborhood—A Woman's Revenge.

In this neighborhood the most of the farms were in a poor state of cultivation. The land was exhausted, and the appearance of the fields anything but pleasant to an agriculturist. There were many beautiful modern houses, but these evidently did not represent the generosity of nature, but were the fruits of wealth, gained from some other source than the soil. But at this time these beautiful houses were green spots in a desert. All around there was desolation. The fences had been burnt for camp-fires, the outhouses torn down for tents, the horses and mules of the army roamed without limit over all their lands, the encampments were in the orchards, meadows, and gardens. But few families remained to be witnesses of their ruin. At the approach of our troops they had fled.

The country back of Alexandria for many miles has all the aspects of a blighted land. The original

forests have been cut down, and on the old exhausted fields have sprung up pines, thickets of
dwarf oaks, thorn trees, and briars; and thus the
very forests add to the unsightliness of the scene.
There is enough diversity in the landscape to make
a most beautiful country; but in a land that is
weary of man, and where all the furrows of the field
complain of him, every traveller is compelled to
sympathize with nature.

Mount Vernon is about nine miles from Alexandria, down the Potomac. The main road, that has
been used for two hundred years, winds over the
hills near Fort Lyon, passes the estate of George
Mason, Esq., and again descends from the height
into the valley of the Accotink. The first four
miles of this way carries the pilgrim for Mount
Vernon over desolated fields, through low and
shaggy woods; but at length the road reaches the
summit of the hills embosoming the Mount Vernon
estate, and a vision of rare beauty bursts on the eye.
We looked down on green fields and meadows,
white farm-houses nestling in orchards and vines,
barns and outhouses which betokened abundance
and wealth, good roads, and long lines of evergreens
overshadowing them, like faithful sentinels guarding the ways. By patient industry these lands have
been redeemed, and Mount Vernon made again attractive, — as if when those who bore the venerated
name of Washington were no longer influenced by
his example and virtues, others were sent to secure
from abandonment and restore to primitive fertility
an estate sacred from the name and ashes of the
Father of his Country. Of the Washington family

no descendants now remain on the Mount Vernon estate, or in the neighborhood.

The estate of John A. Washington is a part of the original Mount Vernon property.   To my surprise, I found this man quite popular with his Quaker neighbors.   To them he was the kind and generous friend, and to his negroes an easy and gentle master. But he was improvident and intemperate, and every year found him in deeper indebtedness and nearer to bankruptcy.

At length the sale of a portion of the estate became a necessity.   Then opened that degrading spectacle of one who bore the most honored of names, appearing before his country as willing to prostitute to infamy the spot sacred to mankind, as containing the house and tomb of Washington.

The country was saved from this last degradation by the timely intervention of certain patriotic ladies, who came forward and purchased the estate, when John A. Washington was negotiating its sale to blacklegs and gamblers, who proposed to fit up the grounds as a watering-place, for the amusement of parties of pleasure. These enterprising gentlemen had extensive plans for public entertainment, and proposed to inaugurate every form of dissipation possible within the limits of decency; and soon the whole country would have been shocked by hearing that there were masquerade balls in the room where Washington died, and the orgies of drunkenness around his tomb.   To prevent this the ladies interposed, and paid Mr. Washington one thousand dollars per acre for two hundred and fifty acres.   This included the fields around the house, — the orchards planted and the gardens laid out by Washington. Certain persons now hold the estate in trust for those ladies. Some of them reside on the premises; and, under their eye, the house is being reconstructed, the walks renewed, the walls rebuilt, and the fences repaired. They design to restore the grounds to the state in which Washington left them; and with the most commendable self-denial they remain in the old mansion, and, almost in the solitude of nuns, live to accomplish their promises to the public.

Not much remains to remind one of the great and good man who spent the last years of his life here, and from this dwelling passed from the shadows of earth to the visions of another world. There are only one or two portraits, a few venerable chairs, some pictures of hunting-scenes, one of the battle of Bunker's Hill, but not one of any of the scenes in which Washington was the principal actor. In this, as in everything else, he displayed his good taste and the modesty of true greatness. On the walls in the great hall of the dwelling hangs the key of the Bastile, sent from France to Washington, as one of the emblems of European despotism laid at the feet of the great Liberator of the New World.

One or two autograph letters of Washington remain, written in the full round hand, without blot or erasure, which distinguishes all the productions of his pen. One of these was a letter of sympathy sent to the Rev. Mr. Fairfax, then in Alexandria, on his way to England in pursuit of health; and is full of kindly reminiscences, and assures the sufferer that nothing but the inclemency of the weather prevented Mrs. Washington and himself paying him their respects before his departure. This letter was written but a few months before his death.

The thousand traditions of the neighborhood only confirmed the impression I had before received, that the life of Washington at Mount Vernon was most simple and unostentatious. His house was open to all his neighbors, and he was the friend and counsellor of the poorest.

His love of order was one of his most marked characteristics. Every appointment must be fulfilled at the moment. Settlements must be made on the very day the account or note fell due. On one part of his estate, four miles from Mount Vernon, are now found the ruins of the old mill to which Washington rode on Thursday, the 12th of December, 1799, to settle with the miller, and to receive his accounts for the year. He remained until in the afternoon, and rode home in a violent snowstorm, and never recovered from cold taken on that day. On the following Saturday night, he died of croup or diptheria.

His end was characterized by the remarkable self-possession which so signally distinguished his entire career. After the fatal symptoms were manifest on Saturday, he found great difficulty in speaking; but, as well as he could, he gave instructions to his secretary to "record his letters and papers, to arrange his accounts, and settle his books." To his physician he said: "I feel myself going. You had better not take any more trouble about me, but let me go off quietly. I cannot last long." And again: "Doctor, I die hard; but I am not afraid to go. I believed from the first I should not survive it. My breath

cannot last long." And again: "I should have
been glad, had it pleased God, to die a little easier;
but I doubt not it is for my good." And just before
he died he closed his eyes with his own hands, folded
his arms on his breast, breathing out, "Father of
mercies, take me to thyself." And the last words
he ever uttered were, "'T is well!" Thus died one
of those noble men for whose lives and virtues we
feel thankful to heaven; for they belong, not to one
country, but to the human race. Showing us the
attainments of which man is capable, they shine in
our heavens like the star of the morning, heralds of
that better day when justice and truth, piety and
temperance, shall ennoble and beautify all the great
of every clime.

All the walks and paths about Mount Vernon
were trodden as holy ground; for along the same
paths had been impressed the footsteps of Washington. These trees had been planted by his hands;
on these flagstones under the portico had he often
walked, and looked down on the Potomac; and
there, under our eye, reared the obelisk which
marks the spot where he lies until we shall all
awake from the dust of the earth. Until then, his
grave shall be a shrine to which his countrymen,
and the good of all lands, will come, and learn to be
patient in hope, and self-sacrificing for the future.

During my walks about Mount Vernon, I met
with an old slave of the Washington family, — Joe
Carter. He now lives about five miles from the
Mansion-house, in a cabin of his own. Old Joe is a
negro of character, and bears a greater dignity because a member of the most illustrious family. This

man told me that he was three months old when General Washington died; and that the general, some time before his death, emancipated all his negroes, three hundred and sixty in number, but that nearly all of them remained and worked on the estate; that the general was always good to his slaves, and would not permit them to be beaten or ill used.

He also said that Mrs. Washington had three hundred slaves, and the general had proposed to purchase these from his wife and set them free. She hesitated for some time what to do, but at length decided not to accept the offer; for the paying for them would too seriously embarrass the estate, and she had too many poor kinsmen to permit her to emancipate all her colored people.

Joe bears a high reputation as a man of truth and piety. He is industrious, and lives in a cabin on his own ten acres.

"What are you doing, Joe," said I, "for another life? Are you a Christian?"

"Oh yes, massa. Dis nigger 'bleve in de Lord Jesus. Religion de mostest beautiful ting in dis world. Ole Joe he do drink, cuss, and swear awful. De Lord he make Joe a temp'rance man, and bress de Good Massa, he radder die dan cuss. Yes, massa, religion is de hopenhand to dis ole nigger."

There lives in the Quaker neighborhood a number of families the descendants of the Washington slaves; and from these may no doubt be gathered many most interesting traditions of the distinguished families and persons who have lived in this region.

The Mount Vernon estate, as left by General

7

Washington, was six thousand acres. This was, by
his last testament, left to members of the Washington family, and to Major Lewis, who married Miss
Custis. The house and property of the Lewis family
were sold twenty years ago to John Mason, Esq., who
now resides in the house reared by Major Lewis in
1804. The house was designed by General Washington, and the grounds laid out as directed by him.
This vast baronial dwelling stands on an elevation
of three hundred feet above the Potomac, and commands a magnificent view of the hills of Maryland,
the isles of the river, the house of Mount Vernon,
and the hills around the valley of the Accotink. On
this spectacle the eye never wearies of gazing. This
portion of the estate has suffered, like the rest of it,
from the extravagance and luxury of the proprie-
tors, but more from their absence for a considerable
portion of the year from their homes. Nearly all
these old Virginia families were pensioners on the
Government, and lived during the winter in Washington; hence, their estates near the capital were
neglected, the great houses of their fathers sunk into
ruinous heaps, and their fields became barren. .

Mr. Mason came from New Hampshire. After a
most adventurous life as a sailor, merchant, and
captain of a trading vessel, he at length settled in
Virginia as the owner of the Lewis estate. He was
undoubtedly one of the most remarkable men whom
I have met. Many of the great rooms in the Lewis
House are now unoccupied, and one wing is in ruins.
The rooms occupied by the family are great chambers; and as in ancient halls the sound of your
footsteps awakened echoes which die away in the

distance, and arouse the imagination as in a haunted scene, so here you are so far removed from all the living that you commune with the dead.

There is in this neighborhood one of the most interesting communities in Virginia. Some thirty Quaker families from Pennsylvania and New Jersey came to this State many years since, and purchased a large portion of the Mount Vernon estate; and now form a society of very intelligent, loyal, Christian people. In their hands, the poor, worn-out fields have become again fertile, and every year adds to the prosperity of this peaceful neighboroood. While in every direction around war has ravaged the land, and three-fourths of the farms are deserted and waste, here everything is as quiet, and the families as unmolested, as in time of peace.

These men of peace are known to be hostile to the institution of slavery; but by their uniform honesty and kindness they won the esteem of their disloyal neighbors; and when they fled before our troops, they left in the care of the Friends many things of value. When the Rebel pickets came through their neighborhood, and occasional cavalry scouting parties, they had instructions not to molest the Quaker families; and when our lines extended beyond them, our soldiers and officers experienced the greatest kindness from this entire people, and we formed friendships which will last as long as life.

It is very evident that this is destined to be one of the greenest spots in Virginia; for the economy, industry, and honesty of this people will secure to them wealth. Possessed of fields most amiable and generous, there can be no limit to their prosperity; and another generation will be distinguished by all those arts and refinements which adorn the highly educated and virtuous.

I have spoken of our picket-lines. These are the guards placed from three to ten miles in advance of our camp. The encampments of the enemy on our left wing were beyond the Occoquan, — a river that flows into the Potomac about three miles below Mount Vernon. About six miles from its mouth the Richmond road from Alexandria crossed it at the village of Occoquan. The enemy's lines extended to this river, and Wigfall, with a force of thirty thousand, held the ferries, fords, and heights. Accotink Creek flows into the Potomac a short distance above Occoquan Bay; and the distance from one stream to the other in front of us was about three miles. Our lines extended to the Accotink, and between these streams was the debatable ground run over by the scouts of both armies; and occasionally parties of reconnoissance would from both sides collect forage, and surround houses supposed to harbor spies and enemies.

These parties would sometimes meet, and then there was one of those skirmishes which gave the men a greater taste for battle. The enemy, from their perfect acquaintance with the country and knowledge of the inhabitants, had the advantage. They could almost always in some way receive warning of our advance, and would have time to flee, or lay an ambuscade. In many of these struggles we lost men, who were killed or taken prisoners; but the loss of the enemy was fully equal to ours. The

wretched families living in this field of contest were
in the most pitiable condition; for they were under
the protection of neither army, and were robbed and
insulted by both. Their fields were stripped, their
corn and wheat seized, their cattle and horses stolen,
and, not permitted to cross within the lines of either
army, they were reduced to circumstances of the
deepest distress and want. From many of the houses
thus occupied the men were gone, generally in the
Confederate army; and when our men came to look
into these dwellings, they were uniformly touched
with pity. The entire family were suffering from
cold, sickness, and nakedness: the women in tears,
and the children wan with hunger.

The regiments composing a brigade were sent out
on this picket-service about once in three weeks.
They remained on the outposts about three days,
and then were relieved, and returned to camp. On
this line our picket-posts were about one hundred
yards apart. At one of these posts were placed five
or six men. At the posts they constructed a booth
of boughs and trunks of trees. Within this they retired in stormy weather, and slept when off guard.
The men were placed in line generally along a road
or path, and stood about twenty paces apart. There
was a signal and countersign, and any one advancing
to a picket was halted and asked to give the signal;
when this was given, he was ordered to advance to
the point of the bayonet and give the countersign.
If neither of these could be given, he was placed
under arrest, and sent under guard to the head-
quarters of the brigade general, and he, if not satis-

7 *

fied, sent the prisoner to the head-quarters of the major-general.

The approach to a picket-line is attended with great danger; for the men are looking for an enemy, and. more disposed to shoot than wait. If any one approached the picket at night, he was very liable to be shot; for the picket may halt the man approaching, or not, as he pleases.

It requires the utmost circumspection on the part of the officers, especially if fresh troops are on line, in approaching the pickets. I was once passing down the picket-line near Pohick Church, and, not having received the signal, I approached one picket-post. I heard the command, "Halt!" but I supposed this was not for me. The next moment, as I advanced, I heard the picket ask his officer, "Shall I fire?" The presence of the officer saved my life. I had passed a great number of pickets, but was halted nowhere before. We lost one of our men in this way. There was a night alarm, — several guns, — and young Gardiner, hurrying up the line to inform his officer of strange appearances at his post, was challenged by a picket, and in his haste threw up his gun, as if about to rush on his challenger. The picket fired, and poor Gardiner lived but half an hour. He was from one of the German counties of Pennsylvania. The moment's hesitation in using the English language probably caused his death.

The danger of the picket-line suggested the following beautiful gem, of the authorship of which I am uncertain:

THE PICKET-GUARD.

"'All quiet along the Potomac,' they say,
  'Except now and then a stray picket
Is shot as he walks on his beat to and fro
  By a rifleman hid in the thicket.
'Tis nothing — a private or two now and then
  Will not count in the news of the battle;
Not an officer lost — only one of the men
  Moaning out, all alone, the death-rattle.'

"All quiet along the Potomac to-night,
  Where the soldiers lie peacefully dreaming;
Their tents in the rays of the clear autumn moon,
  Or the light of the watch-fire gleaming.
A tremulous sigh, as the gentle night-wind
  Through the forest-leaves softly is creeping,
While stars up above, with their glittering eyes,
  Keep guard — for the army is sleeping.

"There's only the sound of the lone sentry's tread
  As he tramps from the rock to the fountain;
And thinks of the two in the low trundle-bed,
  Far away in the cot on the mountain.
His musket falls slack — his face, dark and grim,
  Grows gentle with memories tender,
As he mutters a prayer for the children asleep —
  For their mother — may Heaven defend her!

"The moon seems to shine just as brightly as then,
  That night when the love yet unspoken
Leaped up to his lips, when love-murmured vows
  Were pledged to be ever unbroken.
Then drawing his sleeve roughly over his eyes,
  He dashes off tears that are welling,
And gathers his gun closer up to its place,
  As if to keep down the heart-swelling.

"He passes the fountain, the blasted pine-tree,
  The footstep is lagging and weary;
Yet onward he goes, through the broad belt of light,
  Toward the shade of the forest so dreary.
Hark! was it the night-wind that rustled the leaves,
  Was it moonlight so wondrously flashing?
It looked like a rifle—'Ha! Mary, good-bye!'
  And the life-blood is ebbing and plashing.

"All quiet along the Potomac to-night,
  No sound save the rush of the river;
While soft falls the dew on the face of the dead—
  The picket's off duty forever!"

In this section of Virginia there were but few families of true loyalty; but there were memorable exceptions. One was John Underwood, a prominent citizen, born and reared a slaveholder; but having visited the Free States, he returned to Virginia convinced that the great curse of his native State was slavery. In conversation he stated in full his convictions to his fellow-townsmen, and uttered sentiments which sounded in their ears as insurrectionary and fanatical. He was at this time one of the judges of the county court. They resolved to hurl him from the bench, and the judges came to the court-room armed, with the intention of shooting him if he advanced to his usual seat. But Mr. Underwood was there before them, took his seat, and laid his loaded and cocked revolver on the table before him. As the other judges advanced, he commanded them not to put one foot on the platform where he sat, or they should die. They yielded, sat at his feet, and he administered the court; and when the business was over, left the room, where a hundred faces were black with anger and murder, without the quiver of a muscle.

He farther braved the fury of the slaveholders and mob who followed them by erecting a Lincoln pole in the public square of Occoquan. He was now hunted as an incendiary and enemy to his State, fined by the court, and threatened with imprisonment and death.

At the commencement of the rebellion, he, with all those who had co-operated with him, was compelled to seek safety with our army. After filling for months some post about Washington, when our troops took possession of all the country this side of the Rappahannock, Mr. Underwood went down to see his widowed mother; and, in a Rebel raid, was seized and hurried away to Richmond, where, if alive, he now lies in one of their prisons.

There was another man, named Williamson, who was valuable to us as a scout and guide. He was a shrewd, cunning man, who had been injured by some of the wealthy whites; and revenge was, I feared, a stronger motive with him than a desire to benefit his country. We had heard through Williamson that there was a large party of Rebels who crossed the Occoquan nearly every morning, and took position on a ridge of hills in front of us. Here they remained during the day in observation. A plan was laid for their capture. To effect this, Colonel Hays selected about fifty men from different companies, who were commanded by Lieutenant-colonel Morgan. The men left our picket-line about three o'clock in the morning, and passed through dark pine forests, beyond a farm-house, on the way.

When they had gone about half a mile from this house, they came to the road which the enemy usually took from Occoquan. But they, for some unexplained reason, came up that morning by another way, and passed by our men almost within the touch of their hands; but coming along a new path, there was felt some uncertainty in regard to who this strange company were. The impression of some of our officers was, that it was a body of our own men out on scouting duty.

The enemy marched to the house, learned of our passing, and returned and laid an ambuscade for us. After remaining here nearly an hour, the colonel commanded the men to rise and march back to camp. They started to return, and had advanced more than one-fourth of a mile when the click of guns in the heavy forest arrested the four or five in advance. They drew their pistols and peered into the darkness. Instantly the enemy fired, and Captain Chapman, Lieutenant Lisle, and Moore, private in Company G, fell. Captain Chapman and Lieutenant Lisle died in a few moments, and Moore in less than an hour.

Our men returned the fire and rushed into the forest, and drove the foe before them. The enemy lost by our fire three men, and in this number, it was said, their celebrated leader, Burke, who had distinguished himself as a picket murderer.

It was all over in five minutes, the enemy beyond pursuit, and our men in mute horror around the dead bodies of their officers. Captain Chapman was one of the most promising officers in the army. Of a courage that rendered him incapable of fear, of great clearness and penetration of mind, and rapidity of decision, of most commanding personal appearance, with the eye of an eagle, he was the man to lead in daring exploits, and to become in the highest degree the idol of the soldiery. He was descended from a family in the north of Ireland, and his ancestors had been from time immemorial engaged in the military service of Great Britain; and, if I am not mistaken, he had at the time of his death two uncles high in rank in the East Indian Army. His fall — when there was opening before him so illustrious a career, and in circumstances where no brave man would desire to die — gave to all his friends the deepest sorrow. Lieutenant Lisle was our quartermaster, and therefore a volunteer in this skirmish. He was a valuable officer, and deeply regretted by many in the army and at home.

The regiment returned from picket-duty on the day that the officers were killed. The bodies were brought in, however, before the regiment reached camp. It was a spectacle that caused all hearts to cease beating. The wagon containing the dead drove to the tent of Captain Ryan; then there was the pause of several moments in silent awe, as if each one dreaded the terrible disclosure. At length, one more adventurous than the others threw open to our gaze the marblelike faces of the dead. There had passed before each that great mystery which gives a solemn grandeur to every human brow.

Most tenderly, as if sensitive to every touch, were they borne from the wagon to the tent, and laid in fitting positions.

It was hard to convince ourselves that this was

not a frightful dream. Was it possible that those
who an hour before were the most active, whose
voices were heard in command, who walked by our
side full of plans for years to come, were now motionless and silent forever, and that there had fallen
between them and us a veil which no mortal can lift
and live?

This sad event threw a gloom over the regiment
for months; and at every dress parade we looked in
vain for the commanding figure of Captain Chapman, and we were never called to a severe engagement without regretting that he was not there. Yet
he is only one of the many thousands of the noble
and the brave whom ruthless war has taken from
our side.

I have spoken of Pohick Church as one of the
most remarkable relics of the days of Washington.
This church stands to the left of the Richmond
road, and twelve miles west of Alexandria. The
situation is beautiful, on the green hill above Pohick
creek. It was built by various distinguished families who formerly lived in this neighborhood, such
as the Lees, the Masons, McCartys, Washingtons,
Fairfaxes, and Lewises. Of these families but few
survive; and these feeble remnants, like the fragments of a noble vessel broken on the rocks, have
in them little to remind us of the greatness of the
past. Our troops took possession of this church,
and the walls were blackened with a thousand
names. The seats were cut to pieces, and borne
away as memorials of the church of Washington.
The old square pews remained at this time, and
the pew of Washington, nearly untouched, because

probably not known as such by the soldiers. I append here an extract from Bishop Meade:

"My next visit was to Pohick Church, in the vicinity of Mount Vernon, the seat of General Washington. I designed to perform service there on Saturday as well as Sunday; but, through some mistake, no notice was given for the former day. The weather, indeed, was such as to prevent the assemblage of any but those who prize such occasions so much as to be deterred only by very strong considerations. It was still raining when I approached the house, and found no one there. The wide-opened doors invited me to enter, as they do invite, day and night, through the year, not only the passing traveller, but every beast of the field and fowl of the air. These latter, however, seemed to have reverenced the house of God, since few marks of their pollution are to be seen throughout it. The interior of the house, having been well built, is still good. The chancel, communion-table, tables of the law, etc., are still there, and in good order. The roof only is decayed; and, at the time I was there, the rain was dropping on these sacred places, and on other parts of the house. On the doors of the pews, in gilt letters, are still to be seen the names of the principal families which once occupied them. How could I, while for an hour traversing these long aisles, — entering the sacred chancel, ascending the lofty pulpit, — forbear to ask: And is this the house of God which was built by the Washingtons, the Masons, the McCartys, the Grahams, the Lewises, the Fairfaxes,—the house in which they used to worship the God of our fathers,

8

according to the venerable forms of the Episcopal Church, and some of whose names are yet to be found on those deserted pews? Is this also destined to moulder piecemeal away, or, when some signal is given, to become the prey of spoilers, and to be carried hither and thither, and applied to every purpose under heaven?"

Has not this language all the impressiveness of prophecy? Was there not to many minds in Virginia a foreshadowing of the doom near at hand? Did not many see dimly the hand moving on the wall? This struck me as more remarkable, for similar expressions fell from the lips of Jefferson and Madison.

In this same neighborhood, about three miles from Mount Vernon, on the heights over the Potomac, are found the broken walls of the house of Lord Fairfax. It is now a heap of rubbish, and large trees are growing out of the ruins. One can still trace the outline of the garden walls, and here and there a rose-bush and lily live and bloom amid the crumbling timbers and fallen bricks.

The tombstone of one of the Lady Fairfaxes now lies broken in the forest overlooking the Potomac. On this she is described as "very beautiful and too pure for the world."

Lower down on the Potomac is the celebrated Gunston Farm. This was the Mason estate, and for nearly a century the home of that renowned family. Here George Mason, who was distinguished amongst the early founders of our Government, lived and died. He was one of the signers of the

Declaration of Independence, and a member of Congress for many years.

His son, George Mason, was reared to his father's profession, — a lawyer, — and was described to me as a man of most splendid gifts and varied accomplishments, but of the most dissolute manners and basest passions. He had travelled extensively over Europe, mingled with the best society, and enriched his mind by converse with the greatest men of his times. All conceded that he was one of the most captivating of men.

At the age of thirty he was known as the most abandoned of *roués*. He met in society a very charming young lady of the name of Powell. Her beauty, vivacity, and cultivation, though his heart was dead to love, induced Mr. Mason to propose marriage. This, after some hesitation, she accepted, not that she loved him, but her family were in moderate circumstances, and she married for position.

It is to be hoped that there is to be found nowhere in the history of man an instance of one who approaches the brutal excesses, the shameless vileness of Mason. His aim from the first was to subject his wife to all those moral and social indignities which would degrade her and bring her down to his own level; and by exposures the most revolting and vicious, to make her the pity and scorn of her slaves. For twenty years she bore his brutality, exiled herself from society, only finding enjoyment in the company of her child, and some peace in the days' and weeks' absence of her husband. And to her honor be it recorded, that she rose above that slough of odious putridity, like the western lily, that blooms and exhales its sweetness in the midst of death.

But there is an end to wickedness on the one hand, and suffering on the other. Mason died in his prime. Around his bed in his last hours stood many relatives and friends of the family, and the injured wife. When the curtain had fallen between the dead and the living, she closed Mr. Mason's eyes, and said aloud to all "that this was the first act that she had performed for her husband in twenty years with pleasure." It was the voice of nature and virtue, expressing the sense of a great deliverance. The body of death was thrown off forever. But Mrs. Mason's womanly revenge was not yet fully gratified. She erected a tombstone over his dust, recorded his name, age, year and day of his death; and below is found the following lines:

"Brandy, Brandy, bane of life,
  Source of evil, cause of strife,
  If men could half thy vices tell,
  They would wish thee safe in hell."

Such is the epitaph of one of the most gifted and talented men in Virginia, and who might have left a name of honor to his country and his family. Mrs. Mason lived on the estate some years, until her only son died in his youth. She then left the place, and now, if alive, resides with her relatives in another portion of the State.

CHAPTER VI.

The Slaves — Their Condition — Story of Hanson Yerly.

THE old family servants in Virginia are certainly the most interesting characters. They have most retentive memories, and take the greatest pleasure in relating the stories and histories of the past. Their dramatic power and vivacity increases the interest with which one listens to their legends and tales. Certainly to the traveller there is no class of people in Virginia from whom so much that is valuable in tradition can be gleaned.

The negroes of distinguished and wealthy families always felt exalted by being the property of such, and took upon themselves the airs of a slave aristocracy; and in their churches and social gatherings the respect they commanded, and position assigned them, were not decided by their own character or appearance, but by the position of the master. Hence, the slaves of poor farmers or planters were treated with the greatest contempt by those of a wealthy and powerful family.

No man has a greater admiration for rank, and no one is so exacting in claiming all its privileges, as the negro, and none feels so keenly the degradation of poverty. The negro is the most gentle and

8 *

kindly hearted of the human race; and it is the greatest joy of his life to love and honor some one whom he thinks worthy of such worship: consequently, he will be found always reflecting the manners, conversation, and opinions of his master. Hence, one middle-aged negro will assume the grave, pompous manner of the old planter; while his son will wear the smiling, courtly air of young master. The slave of a minister is always known by the solemn reflections he introduces, and his throwing into every sentence, "Speaking after the manner of men." Thus, the slaves exhibit the manners, characteristics, and life of the families to whom they belong; and in all those qualities which awaken interest and sympathy, the negroes of Virginia are superior to the poor whites of the same State. The negro is much the most active, hopeful, and earnest: the white man is ignorant to a proverb, listless and indifferent to all present interests, and unconcerned about his future.

But the negro has a much more lively, cheerful nature, and a shrewd aptitude for acquiring useful arts which throws the whites into the shade. And certainly, to all that is beautiful in song, sweet in music, and rich in eloquence, there is no man more alive than the negro. I have never known a people to whose better nature an appeal could be made with more certainty of response than to this race. And less than all men is his nature vindictive, but cheerful, contented, and patient. They speak of the wrongs they have suffered with a calmness and spirit of forgiveness which, if borne by white men, would place on their heads the crown of martyrdom. From all

I could learn, the old families of Virginia were kinder to their slaves, and more thoughtful for all their interests, than the class of masters who had recently risen to power. On large plantations there were, beyond doubt, many cases of aggravated wrong and cruelty; for the overseers, as a class, were the most brutal and tyrannical of men, selected because they could wring the most labor from human sinews and bones.

The master who owned more than fifty slaves could not have much personal knowledge of each of these; and when the number reached hundreds, he could not have any such acquaintance with their characters and wants as would give them any security against wrong. It was in the power of the overseer to inflict on each of these the deepest injuries, and to drive the slaves to madness and murder, and yet the master be ignorant of all that was going on. In many cases even a humane master shut his eyes to the cruelties of his overseer; for, in order to make anything from slave labor, the authority of the overseer must be sustained. The uniform testimony of the slaves was, that the sorrows of their state were increasing every year. The trade in negroes broke up their family relations, and rendered the servants unhappy and distrustful. The faces of their masters were against them, and one act of cruelty made necessary many more. Something of that universal impulse felt by the human mind in all lands, found its way into every slave cabin, and produced indignation where there was once patience; restlessness where there was formerly contentment; anger and the purpose of revenge in the place of humble submission. If the war had not broken out, the status of slavery in Virginia could not have long continued. There were many signs that the volcanic fires were heaving, and the earth was trembling beneath their feet.

I think one of the most interesting chapters in the history of man might be written from the narratives of slaves now in our army.

While our camp was in the neighborhood of Alexandria, I often heard of the wisdom and piety of a colored man living near, who was called Hanson. I invited my friend, and almost companion, Dr. Crawford, to go on a visit to Hanson. I was more anxious to see him, as I had learned from various conversations with different persons, white and black, that Hanson sometimes preached to his people, and had the highest reputation for sobriety, truthfulness, and industry. We soon reached his house, less than a mile from our camp. We introduced ourselves to his wife, whom we found a bright, pleasant-faced mulatto woman of about forty. The house was neat, well whitewashed, covered with vines without, and carpeted within. We saw about the place three children, much superior to their class in Virginia in manner and dress. They were able to read, and we saw several excellent books arranged on the stand.

One of the children was sent to call Hanson from the field. While the child was absent, we learned from the woman that her husband had purchased some years before the ten acres of land upon which they were living; and, after clearing it, planted some trees, and made the garden. Before the war

they succeeded very well in sustaining themselves
by raising vegetables for the market; but now the
soldiers stole at night their tomatoes, cabbages,
potatoes, and fruit, and reduced them to the necessity of selling pies and cakes in camps, and washing
for officers. There was no bitterness in her manner: their injuries were borne with the unmurmur-
ing patience of the race.

In a few moments Hanson came in. He was a
man of powerful frame, fully six feet high, with a
face much more Anglo-Saxon than African; of remarkable dignity and gravity of manner, reminding
one of many of the Virginia gentlemen of the olden
school, whose style of speech, looks, and demeanor
were much more English than American. While
apparently not broken with age, his head was as
white as snow; but there still remained much of the
force and vivacity of manhood. He thanked us for
coming to see him. After we had conversed with him
a few moments, some allusion was made to his long
and possibly eventful life; and we expressed a desire to hear from him some of the most noteworthy
incidents of his history. He very willingly com-
plied.

In the following story, as we received it from his
lips, I do not profess to give, in all instances, the
precise words he used; neither do I give any Afri-
canisms, for these were not noticeable.

HANSON'S STORY.

"My mother, I was told, was a fair octoroon
woman: she was the slave of my young master's
father. My father was a white man, a Scotch or

English gentleman, one of those who, in old times, came from the old country to visit their relatives in Virginia. I never saw him. He went back, soon after I was born, to the land beyond the sea. My mother died when I was a little child, — my only recollections of her are those of a pale, sickly-looking woman, but to me very beautiful, who often hugged me in her arms and sung me to sleep; and would you believe me, old as I am, I often dream of my mother, and always as pressing me to her bosom, and singing her lullaby. I was a poor child when she died, for I had no one to love me; but I can well remember of crying and sobbing in bitter grief, and asking old master 'when they would bring back mamma from the ground?'

"When I was about seven years of age, I began to hold master's horse, and to run errands. I soon began to wait at table, and became the favorite of young master. He was two years my senior, and acted constantly as my protector, and never allowed me to be maltreated or wronged. He made me his confidant, and poured into my ear all his plans for the future. As I could not read, he often read to me striking stories, and histories of travel; and related, when he returned home, the news of the neighborhood. My young master was an only son. He had sisters; but he needed a boy to open his heart to, and who would always look up to him as better than any one else, and even as the wisest boy in the world. At all events, I was a favorite with my young master, and better treated than the other slave children; and as I was his companion, rather than his slave, in those times, I felt but little of the

weight of those chains that were afterwards so heavy.
My young master was gay, and fond of company;
and as he had many relatives in other counties, he
was nearly half his time from home, and visited
some of the most reputable and wealthy people of
the State.   This gave me, as I always attended him,
an opportunity to see much of the country.

"At that time, master, there was no trade in
slaves. We were happier, less oppressed, and treated
more like human beings, than afterwards.   After
we had passed three or four years in this way, my
master met a young lady of Prince William county,
by the name of Taylor, the daughter of Colonel Taylor, and became attached to her, and proposed marriage.   I was with him when he went to bring
home his bride, and I never can forget the gayety
and splendor of that time.   It was in the month
of May, and everything was in the finest bloom.
We went down in carriages, several of master's
friends going with him.   We drove to Colonel Taylor's in the morning, and looked on a scene such
as is only once beheld in our lives.   There was, as
in front of most of the Virginia houses in those days,
a long avenue of evergreens, poplars, and chestnuts.
Along this avenue were all the slaves of this family,
dressed in their best, some in white, with great tur-
bans on the heads of the women, as was the custom
in those days.   All were dancing, and in a thousand ways showing how much they were interested
in the occasion.   Coming nearer to the house, the
carriages and wagons of the neighbors and friends
of the family lined both sides of the avenue.   As we
approached nearer, the sight was beautiful, master;

such a multitude of ladies, so beautifully dressed, so gay and happy : to look upon their smiling faces, you would think there was no sorrow in the world. Indeed, I have never forgotten it; and often now the scene comes up before me, and I find myself saying, 'Where are they?'

"I remember one of the great figures in the scene was the old minister, with his light silk stockings,' silver shoe and knee-buckles, white gloves, and powdered hair. We never see such sights now, such beautiful ladies, nor such noble-looking men.

"But in the joy of that time commenced my first sorrow. Our young mistress was severe, and never satisfied with the slaves; and from being the happiest and most contented of people, we became morose and unmanageable.

"Even my young master gradually changed, and became severe and exacting. He had often promised that, when I reached the age of thirty, he would give me my liberty. I had been foolish enough to look forward in hope to that time, and to fill my soul with the dream of freedom.

"I had already married a young woman, a slave of master's. She was a good woman, as light in color as myself; and I had arranged in my own mind that I would purchase my wife after I became free.

"When I was thirty, master appeared to have forgotten his promise; and I could see that he thought a promise made to one of his own negroes was not binding. But he was still kind to me, and treated me with some of the old familiarity. I sought an opportunity of speaking to him on the subject. He told me he could not then give me freedom; he had too much work to do; and if he gave me liberty, all the other slaves would become discontented, and demand the same thing; and that his wife was opposed to it. But he promised that he would permit me to make as much by carpenter work during the year as I found possible; and if I gave him one hundred dollars a year, he would be satisfied.

"I was greatly disappointed. I cannot tell you how, for a time, my soul was full of anger towards God and man. But soon I remembered that I had not fulfilled my own vows to God, and my sin had found me out; and I hope that my trial was a blessing to me in the end.

"Just about this time the slave-trade commenced in Virginia. In my early remembrances there was no trade in slaves. If there were any bought and sold, it was in the settlement of estates; and it was made a point of family honor to purchase all the slaves within the circle of the relatives, and not permit families to be separated. In those days people did not speak of negroes as cattle, and as without affection for their children.

"The most of the old planters were kind to their people, not oppressing them with severe work, nor driving them in the fields with cruel overseers. There were not much gambling, drinking, and horse-racing in those days. Indeed, I remember the old Virginia planters, such as Washington, Dr. Powell, Mr. Carter, Judge Washington, and old Mr. Mason; they were temperate, kind, and just; but before I became an old man, all these good and wise men

9

were gone. Their sons were bad men, fought duels, drank, gambled, and were cruel to their slaves.

"When I had been married four or five years, a trader came from North Carolina to Alexandria in a little schooner, loaded with bacon. For this there happened to be a great demand that year. This man had no intention of commencing a trade in slaves; but some of the planters offered him a young boy or girl for bacon, and in this way he began to buy, and collected, I suppose, ten or twelve.

"The next year he returned, and brought with him two vessels loaded with salt pork. At that time, master, we raised very little, in this part of Virginia, but tobacco; and if the crop failed, the planters having to buy much of their meat, were hardly pressed; and there appeared to be some excuse for selling one slave for the benefit of many.

"But the trader came back, and began to be called the 'bacon man.' This time he proposed to take slaves in exchange for his meat; he had opened a profitable trade. This year he bought a large number of slaves; poor planters, dissipated men in debt, widows with estates they could not manage, — all now began to talk of selling slaves.

"From this commenced a great trouble amongst us — our hearts trembled with fear. To be carried away, and sold in those distant new States, was to us the occasion of far greater misery than our fathers endured in being stolen from Africa. Every autumn the 'bacon man' returned, and others came with him, and there was opened a great trade in negroes.

"I never can forget the wretchedness of those years. We all felt as if a sword was hanging over our heads, and as bad as if we had heard the death-angel strike three times on our doors.

"Oh, what dreadful sorrows there were, master, in those years! You have heard it said that slaves feel but little, that we do not grieve as the whites; but in this we are greatly wronged. We love more deeply, because we have but little to love. Our masters and mistresses have their carriages, farms, friends, offices, their slaves, their business; but we have none of these: therefore to a negro man all his life and happiness are in his cabin, and when you have taken away from him his wife and children, he has nothing left. Many have I known to die of a broken heart; others never had any joy again after a child or husband was sold away from them; others I have known to commit suicide.

"When we saw the sails of the 'bacon man' unfurled, and his ships on the way down the Potomac, the panic of that year was over. And thoughtless and careless about the future as the slaves are, the fear of being torn from our friends, and sent away into dreadful hardships, settled like a heavy cloud on all our people. When we came together, it was to hear of some wrong or sorrow that set all our hearts on fire.

"Then commenced that alienation which has gone on ever since, becoming a deeper and deeper gulf every year.

"It was no free white men that came amongst us, and telling us we ought to be free, that turned our hearts against our masters. No, it was the sale of our fathers and mothers, our children and brothers. It was the dreadful misery of those days when they were lying in the slave-pen, that made us cease to love them.

"Very soon it was found, as the lands were becoming poorer from the constant raising of tobacco on the same fields, that the most profitable thing for a planter was to raise slaves for the market. The people were becoming poorer, but this trade opened to them a new mine of wealth; and, before many years, slave-pens were opened in Alexandria, and hundreds were chained together and sent South.

"Charles, the body-servant of General Jackson, told me that one spring,. after the adjournment of Congress, the general went from Washington to Richmond on horseback. As they rode along beyond Alexandria, they overtook and passed one of these gangs of chained slaves. The general was filled with horror at the sight; and when he passed them he heard him exclaim, 'My God, what a terrible sight!' 'Master,' said Charles, 'what do you think of that?' 'Think,' said the general, 'I do not want to think; surely a day of judgment will come!'

"During these years, when the miseries of the colored people were increasing fast, my desire for freedom grew to be a passion. I thought of it by day, and dreamed of it by night. Many things favored my plan at this time. I was but little at home, but worked on different farms, and in Washington. One year I labored in the city; and after making one hundred dollars for my master, and giving some to my wife, I had fifty dollars left. This I deposited in the hands of a banker by the name of Jones, a good man, who had often em-

ployed me. This money I had intended to use in
aiding me on my way to liberty. During all this
year I had been maturing the plan for gaining my
freedom. I had been learning all I could of the way
to Canada, and had mapped out in my own mind all
the streams and mountains of Pennsylvania and
Maryland. At length, when we were coming to
Christmas, I had all ready for my journey. I had
committed my secret to no one, not even to my wife,
and had been so much occupied with my plans, that
I did not think very much of the sorrow I would
have in parting with her and my children. But I
went home to my cabin on Saturday evening; the
children were never so beautiful, and their ways so
winning. Oh, master, I thought my heart would
break!

"Often, during that evening, I had to leave my
cabin and go out to weep; and then would return
and hug my children, as if I would take them into
my heart, and carry them with me. That night was
one of restlessness and prayer. I had no fear of
being taken; I felt certain I could escape, for I
could be in Canada before my master would inquire for me. But was it right to enjoy a boon
which I could not give to my wife and children?
Was it right to tear from them the great happiness
of their lives? Was it not cruel to subject them to
the insult and wrong which my escape would certainly bring upon them?

"I whispered not a word to my wife of my purpose, and she knew nothing of the cause of my great
distress. I rose early in the morning, kissed my
children, blessed them, bid farewell to my wife, and

9 *

promised soon to return. I crossed the Potomac, went to the house of Mr. Jones in Washington, drew my money, and wandered through the streets until evening. My plan was to commence my journey at night. When it became fully dark, I turned my face towards the North, and crept along through the streets, and for the first time in my life, skulked like a thief. When I had gone beyond the houses of Washington, I had no more fear of being seen. Ah! then my wife and children came up before me like my fingers. I could not see my way — my tears blinded my eyes. I felt their arms around my neck, and their soft faces on my cheek, and their little hands were pressing me back. I wandered, not knowing where I was going, until I found myself standing on the bank of the Potomac, looking over at my cabin. I stopped, and reasoned with myself. Was not this the hour for which I had been planning for years? And now, when all was ready, and the gates open, was I to be so foolish and soft-hearted? Was not *liberty* worth more than everything I had? Could I not, when I had found the way, come back for my wife and children? I talked in this way with myself, master, and resolved to be free. I would not listen to my heart, but would have the satisfaction of breathing the air of liberty, and of being my own master.

' "I turned again towards the North, and when I had gone into the silence of the woods beyond the city, my wife and my children came up before me like my fingers. I tried to be strong: they appeared to look into my face and reprove me. I could not endure it; and I wandered without purpose, until again I stood on the bank of the Potomac looking over at my home. Master, nature was too strong for me. This time I crossed and went to my cabin. It was not yet morning. I never tried it again. This satisfied me that it was not right for me to leave my family. I now took myself more earnestly than ever to my Lord. I learned to read, and obtained greater comfort than ever in the blessed gospel. I was happier than for years, for the conflict in my bosom was ended. I still desired liberty, but committed my cause to my God. But one great sorrow followed on the heels of another.

"First, my wife was seized with a cough and gradually declined, becoming more beautiful and heavenly until she left us. This greatly increased my care and anxiety for my children. My daughters were taken into the house by our mistress, and she was not kind to them. My boy was too small to be sent into the fields to work: I was sent away to labor as a carpenter, and could rarely see my children. I could, indeed, nearly always be at home on Saturday night, and stay over Sabbath: sometimes I was too far away, and I had a constant anxiety about them.

"My daughters were good-looking and smart, and I knew that master was offered a high price for them; and when I thought of their being sold away from me, my heart died within me; and often, master, I have worked all day, and travelled ten miles at night to assure myself that my children were not sold.

"In those times, master, I was often angry, and my heart was very bitter. I thought of the hundreds I had made for master, and I had nothing; and I could expect no kindness or pity from him. I was at times very miserable, and knew not what would have become of me if my Lord had not laid his hand on me and said, 'Hanson, be still, I will help you.' And he did help me. I was never forsaken.

"When I was nearly fifty, my master was taken ill, and continued to be unwell for three years: his disease was dropsy. Sometimes, for a few weeks, he would be nearly well, and then be brought very low again. During those years he was very kind to me, and often sent for me. At one of those visits I found him more unwell than usual; he was breathing with difficulty, and greatly agitated. 'Hanson, you have been very faithful to me, and I have been very unfaithful to you. I promised you liberty many years since.' I said to him, 'Master, have no trouble about Hanson. Think of yourself and what is before you.' 'Oh!' said he, 'this is the thing that most distresses me. I have always intended at some time or other to be a Christian; but while I was promising myself this, I had no thoughts of the difficulties I was daily gathering in my way, and that my procrastination was bearing me, like a ship broken loose, far out to sea; and when I awake I know not where I am. I look up and can see no star, no sun, no beacon light,—all is darkness, pitchy darkness. What can I do? To pray after I have so long sinned is like a mockery; and when I ask for mercy and try to repent, there is so much to be done that I know not where to begin. Can I ask for mercy until in all things I try to make amends for the past? I am hedged about; I know not where to turn. What can I do, Hanson? Looking on the world and into eternity, as I now do, if the choice was offered me, I would gladly exchange with you; I would be born with the colored skin, begin life as a slave, and take all your sorrows, in order that I might have your hope and your Saviour. But, Hanson, I awake too late. Oh! what shall I do? where shall I turn for help?' I told him that our Lord was very merciful; that he had pitied and saved the thief on the cross; that he had healed the most miserable sinners; and that he had spoken the parable of the Prodigal Son to encourage those who awoke to a sense of guilt and ruin, who felt that all they had trusted in had failed them, and all they had leaned on was broken. 'I know, I know,' said he, 'but how can I go to Christ? I have neglected him long; I am full of guilt; I have often, with my eyes open, broken the law of God; I have joined with scoffers, and when I knew that what they and I said was false and blasphemous. The thief never sinned as I have done. I cannot ask for mercy, for I must be honest with God. And when I plead with him to forgive me, I must try to break off all sin and make amends for the past. And where shall I begin? What shall I do with my negroes? If I emancipate them, I injure my family, and they will curse my memory: everything is wrong; every way I turn there is a yawning gulf. I am like a ship-wrecked sailor cast on a naked rock — every way I look I see nothing but death. · O God! I wish I had never been born.' I fell on my knees and prayed God to show mercy to my poor, sinful master. He sobbed aloud, and covered his face with the sheet.

I rose to my feet and left the room, and this was the last time I ever saw him alive.

"A few days after his death, my mistress called me to her room. She said: 'Hanson, you have for a long time desired to be free; your master spoke to me of it on his death-bed, and I promised him to see you, and propose a way by which you may gain your liberty.' She then told me that my master had always liked me, and said that I was true and faithful to all his interests, and in consideration of this she would give me the opportunity of buying myself, and would ask of me only one-half of what I would bring in the market. I replied to this: 'You know, mistress, how long and faithfully I have served you, making for you many hundred dollars, and now I am old, and cannot do much more. If you give me my freedom, I will promise never to be a burden to you or your children; but to raise four hundred dollars I cannot promise. But liberty is so dear that if you insist on the money I will work until I die in order to raise it.' She said I could easily raise the sum; and then, giving me not a word of comfort, with the cold look of one who was enduring a wrong rather than doing a favor, she dismissed me.

"I made a great effort to secure the offered freedom. I went to some white gentlemen in Alexandria, and to Mr. Jones in Washington: they loaned me the money, and I was free. I cannot tell you how deep was my gratitude to God for this great and long-sought boon.

"This event was soon followed by the removal to the vicinity of Richmond of my eldest daughter, who went with her young mistress when she was married and moved there with her husband. My youngest daughter was now all that remained to me. She was a dear, kind child, and would bring far more in the market than I could soon raise; but if I had known that mistress would have listened to me, I would have toiled day and night to procure the money for her purchase. I was hoping that God would incline the heart of my mistress to give me the chance to buy her. But there fell suddenly on me a most terrible blow. On my return one night to my cabin, I heard that my daughter had been sold, and was then in the slave-pen in Alexandria. I hastened to the town, went to the slave prison, and said to the man at the gate, 'Can I see the trader?' He went for the man, who, when he came, treated me kindly. I asked him, 'Is there a young woman here named Lucy, the slave of Mrs. Tyrrel?' 'Yes,' he said, 'there is such a young woman here.' 'Can I see her? I am her father.' 'We cannot permit you to see her without a pass from her mistress.' 'That I shall never ask for; I am her father; I shall see her, but never until I stand with her and mistress in the judgment.' I left the prison a poor broken-hearted man.

"I was now alone in the world. I rarely saw my mistress; she shunned me, and I never sought her. In the course of a year or two she sold her farm here, and moved back to her father's neighborhood. I felt that my age would be cheerless and lonely, and, after some time, married a free woman, who is now my wife. We have lived happily together.

"For years I have been looking for some great

trouble. The people here were far richer and more
extravagant, and appeared to me much less religious,
than those I remember in my youth. They had become cruel, and, without any mercy, had torn asun-
der those whom God had bound together; and a
great wail of sorrow and agony went up in the ears
of heaven from all parts of Virginia—wives sorrow-
ing for their husbands, husbands mourning for their
wives, and parents weeping for their children, and
would not be comforted.

"I knew that a day of vengeance would come for
all this, but I did not expect it to fall on us in the
way of a war between the North and South. I began
to fear some heavy curse when the great gangs of
chained slaves were first sent from Virginia, and
that the day would soon come when the cup of our
iniquities would be full.

" Now all these great and influential families have
been ruined, and many of them are wandering beggars. I was a few days since walking in my garden,
looking down on the country, and the change of a
few months deeply affected me. I looked over on the
house and farm of Mrs. Powell. I remembered the
doctor, her husband, a very smart man, and her five
sons, the most popular young men in the country,
and also her beautiful daughters. Her house was
the resort of many elegant and wealthy people, but
now her sons are in the Confederate Army, her
house is a hospital, her beautiful garden trodden
down, her orchards destroyed, and the fences all
gone.

" There is the house of Mrs. Lee, where, the week
that Ellsworth was killed, one of her daughters was

married, and the house was filled with gayety and mirth; now the grounds are in ruins, her furniture broken, and all the beautiful things she gathered are scattered. There, too, is the place of Colonel. Hunter, his fields open, his barns burnt for fuel, and his house consumed to the ground; and likewise the place of General Lee, one of the finest in Virginia, now used by your troops. His grain-fields and meadows were thrown open, and beaten as the high roads.

"At these painful sights my soul was moved, and I cried, 'O Lord! why has this curse come on Virginia?' And it appeared to me as plain as I ever heard human speech, a voice spoke to me and said, 'O man! knowest thou the land most highly favored of heaven, and where, because God was good, men became desperately wicked, and inflicted the greatest wrongs?' And the voice said, 'Virginia.' Again I heard, 'Knowest thou, O man! the land where human beings were bred as cattle for the market, and where every year thousands of them were sent forth to a fate which they dreaded more than death?' The answer came, 'Virginia.' Again the voice said, 'Knowest thou the land where, in the midst of the greatest blessings, there has been the deepest misery; where most faces were washed with tears, and most hearts torn with anguish; and where the constant wail of distress, inflicted by man on his fellow, was going up into the ears of God?' And the voice said, 'Virginia.' Again the voice said, 'God is just.'

"Then," said the old patriarch, stretching out his arms, and lowering them as if he was relieving his

10

hands of a great weight, "I laid my burden down. And as often as I have mourned since, I have been silenced by that voice, 'Gód is just.'"

Dr. Crawford was moved to tears, and said: "My friend, many have been your sorrows; but you will soon forget them all in the rest of the kingdom of God."

"Oh, yes," said the old man, "I shall understand it all there!"

CHAPTER VII.

Embarkation for the Peninsula — Fortress Monroe — Early Discoveries — Description of the Country and its Wealth — Fight
between the Merrimac and Monitor — Excitement and Terror
at the Fortress.

WE bade farewell to the scenes rendered familiar
and dear by many months of acquaintance and
friendships for life; and on the morning of the 17th
of March struck our tents, gave away the furniture
of our winter homes, and prepared for the march to
Alexandria.

The day was beautiful, with just enough of coolness
to give vigor, and enough of spring to cause all the
birds to sing with the wildest glee, and the trees to
stand with that silent, expectant look they wear on
such days, as if the warmth of the sunshine was
bearing joy to every bud. When, from our camp,
we came to the height over Little Hunting Creek,
the spectacle that burst upon our view was brilliant.
The entire plain and hill-side were covered with
armed men; great columns of soldiers, whose guns
flashed in the light, moved under the eye. Here, on
the right, in the meadows of the plain, were thousands of horsemen, their polished armor reflecting
the sunbeams like hundreds of mirrors. In the
fields, on the left, were many batteries. Here, still
further to the left, stretching from the hills to the

streets of Alexandria, was a long dense column of men, flowing like a dark river, from whose surface arise bubbles, sparkling in the sunshine. In the Potomac lay a thousand craft, of every form and sail. The bands of the various regiments added to the effect by playing the same tune; and often there was a grand burst of harmony rolling over the fields, and quickening every pulse as we listened.

It was a gay and brilliant pageant. But was there no fear that all this would pass away like the dream of the night, and that in a very few months one-half of that army, now so vigorous and hopeful, would be sought for in hospitals or in the grave?

We embarked on the same afternoon, weighed anchor about dark, and steamed down the Potomac. We stopped for the night at Aquia Creek, and the following morning again weighed anchor, and in the afternoon entered Chesapeake Bay; and only in the dim distance could we discern the faint outline of the shore of Virginia. There was, during all this afternoon, looming up in the West and South, a very heavy thunder-storm. This broke upon us before we reached Fortress Monroe; the sea became very rough, and we had to land when the waves were breaking in great billows over the beach. The vessels dashed against each other, cables were broken, and steamers full of men drifted helplessly from the docks.

In the most unpitying storm we landed, and gathered in shivering bands on the shore. There were no shelters, our tents could not be reached, and if they could, there was no spot to pitch them.

Very fortunately, but few vessels could reach the shore, and hence not many regiments were landed. After cowering in the tempest for two hours, at length orders came from General Wool to march the brigade across the bridge towards Hampton, and find encampment. In the darkness, and the storm beating in their faces, with no light but the flashes of the lightning, the men marched more than a mile and a half to an open moor, and there, without tents and without fire, nearly knee-deep in water, prepared to spend the night. Dreadful would have been the sufferings of that night; but there were those who heard of our distress, and pitied us.

The 16th Regiment of Massachusetts Volunteers were encamped about half a mile from the place where we were halted. Some of this noble body of men were on guard when our bewildered and dripping men passed by. When they were relieved and returned to their camp, they roused half their regiment; and in a few moments came to us with large buckets of hot coffee and crackers.

This kindness was of incalculable benefit to us. It was the sympathy of true men and soldiers towards their companions in arms, and cheered us more than the warmth of their offering. But their efforts for us did not cease with this; for they aroused the camp of the 11th Pennsylvania Cavalry, who opened for us their stables, and into these we crept, and were sheltered from the storm. Without the kindly intervention of these two regiments, great would have been the sufferings of that wretched night; many would have risen in the morning from their miry beds, to be borne to hospitals, or left in

10 *

the rear as incurably diseased. This Samaritan charity touched us more deeply, because it was a night when nothing but the call of duty could have forced a soldier from his tent; yet these men came from warm beds, braved the storm, plunged into the morasses and swamps, and found us; nor did they rest until, at two o'clock in the morning, they saw the last of our poor fellows sheltered from the tempest.

I heard a member of the United States Senate, from the West, in his place on the floor of Congress, say: "Sir, the Western men hate the Secessionists, laugh at the negro, and despise the Yankee." I know of some Western men who have a very different feeling towards the Yankee soldiers. We can never forget their bravery in our hundred battles, and their catholic sympathy in our hour of need. I know of no troops in the army who have so just an appreciation of the great interests at stake in this struggle; and who are able, with so much intelligence, to defend our position at the bar of conscience and the world.

After this storm had passed away, we were able to look abroad and weave together, as in a picture of tapestry, the threads of the landscape.

We were now in that region of Virginia of the deepest historic interest. In the spring of the year 1607, three little ships, sent from England, commanded by Lord Newport, sought a landing on our coast. On board of these vessels were one hundred and five men for the settlement of Virginia. At the head of these was the celebrated Captain Smith, a man of rare genius and military ability. Newport had intended to land on Roanoke Island, but a severe storm drove him further north, and he was compelled to enter Chesapeake Bay; and a point which they reached, where they found deep water, put the tempest-tossed emigrants in "good comfort;" hence the name given to the ground on which the fort stands, "Point Comfort." Here a country opened which appeared "to claim prorogative over the most pleasant places in the world." At Hampton they smoked the pipe of peace with the Indian king; and after some days spent in surveys and reconnoissances, on the 13th of May they entered a beautiful river, and, in honor of the English monarch, called it James River, and laid the foundation of the first settlement in Virginia at Jamestown. Thus was discovered one of the finest harbors on the North American coast, which, in connection with its great tide-water advantages, should have made Virginia the first of our States in commerce and wealth.

The depth of the anchorage at Hampton Roads is 59½ feet; from this to Sewell's Point, a distance of six miles, the depth is 25¼ feet; from Sewell's Point to Norfolk, 12 miles, the depth is 23¼ feet; and from Hampton to the mouth of the James River, eight miles, the depth is from 22¼ to 27½ feet. From Chesapeake Bay to Yorktown, a distance of 30 miles, the depth is 33⅓ feet. These are the low tide measurements.

The depth at the entrance of the bay, between Capes Henry and Charles, is 30 feet, thus giving a far more magnificent harbor than that of New York; and all the navies of the world might, with safety, lie in its capacious bosom. This is, unquestionably, one of the most interesting regions on our continent, reminding one of the rich delta of the Nile. Five rivers converge their streams, and pour their waters within fifty miles of each other into Chesapeake Bay, — the Potomac, James, Rappahannock, York, and Elizabeth Rivers. The tide rolls up these rivers one hundred and one hundred and fifty miles, and again up forty or fifty miles in the streams tributary to these, such as the Pamunkey, Chickahominy, Blackwater, etc. The largest steamers and men-of-war have ascended these rivers for more than one hundred miles; and thus can be borne out to the ocean, at all seasons, the productions of the State. These rivers give to Virginia a sea or tidal coast of more than one thousand miles, nearly twice as great as that of New York; and unbounded must must be the surprise of any one familiar with the causes securing, and often compelling, the growth of commercial cities and States, to see here all these advantages thrown away.

Here, where many "golden horns" pour out the rivers of plenty, we only find the small village of Hampton as the growth of two centuries and a half of Virginia commerce. Certainly, if her brain and right hand had not been numbed by a fatal paralysis, a city should have arisen here equal to or greater than New York. And added to all these advantages, the whole trade of the West was at the disposal of Virginia. The difficulties in the way of her securing the passage of the productions of the Valley of the Mississippi to the sea-coast through her canals, and over her railroads, were not to be com-

pared with those to be surmounted by Pennsylvania
and New York. She stretched her arms far west,
and the mountains to be scaled were broken, and
more than one great natural passage-way existed to
the Mississippi and Ohio.

The comparative gentleness of her climate, the
roads unobstructed by snow, her rivers never chained
by ice, her vast fields of coal, secured to Virginia
the vantage-ground in her race for empire and
wealth. But all these were sacrificed and forfeited,
and to-day is her retribution. She, the mother of
States,

"Sits voiceless and crownless
In her silent woe."

The tide-water counties, thirty-seven in number,
are level and flat, not rising more than sixty-five
feet above the sea. Still, there are in them counties
of undulating, waving land. The air is still, and, as
in many parts of the world where there is a vast assemblage of waters seeking the sea, the heavens
hazy, the dews very heavy, and the rains without a
parallel, except in tropical regions. Thunder-storms
arise and succeed each other with a rapidity that
mocks care and safety: the heaviest gloom and the
brightest sunshine chase each other with fabulous
speed; hence vegetable life has a richness not often
seen in our country, and some plants, vines, and
fruits attain to rare excellence.

In consequence of the country rising so little above
the level of the sea, there is in the peninsular and
tide-water counties great quantities of swamp-land.
Many of these could be redeemed, but are now almost
as impenetrable as the jungles of India. But long

tongues of the richest alluvial land pierce these heavy forests, and give a narrow strip of country, three, five, and ten miles wide, and on either side remain the dark forest and bog of primitive times.

The people residing on these narrow strips of fertile land are separated from each other by morasses rarely crossed; and hence live as much out of the world as the inhabitants of small sea islands, and have felt but little of that stimulus imparted to the public mind by travel, education, and railroads. Here, as elsewhere, we found that the old families preferred to drag along in deep poverty, and to dwell in wretched houses, rather than part with the lands which still give them some claim to be ranked with the first families of Virginia.

These tide-water counties afforded the very best lands for fruit-growings. The soil is for the greater part a warm, sandy loam. With this is mingled sea-shells, so that all the well and spring water is highly charged with carbonate of lime (hard). These tide-water lands had been advancing rapidly in value as their true worth became known.

No doubt there is a great source of wealth in the hitherto untouched forest-lands on the banks of the York, Chickahominy, Pamunky, and James Rivers. Many Northern men were engaged in getting out this timber for ship-building and other purposes at the commencement of the war, and were opening a useful and profitable trade. Their mills and stock were abandoned, and they compelled to flee from conscription and imprisonment. But peace and freedom will bear new enterprise and life into these unbroken wilds.

This region will not be for many years, possibly never, so attractive as the higher and valley lands of the State. In summer the heat is oppressive, and in autumn bilious and intermittent fevers are prevalent. The wealthy families leave their homes in July and August, and do not return until the last of September. But the winters are salubrious, and, as a general thing, cloudless.

One great and as yet almost untouched source of wealth, are the fisheries of Chesapeake Bay and the tide-water rivers. In the year 1860 the value of these fisheries to Virginia was $86,000. This is thought to fall far below the truth, for the proceeds of the shore fisheries are supposed to be greater than this alone, the river frontage on single farms on the Potomac renting as fisheries for more than $3000 a year.

The oyster fisheries of York River are full of promise, and will open a great and most important trade in the future. If proper encouragement had been given to planting in former years, the value of these fisheries would have been equal to any in the United States.

The difficult and dangerous disembarkation of our troops at Fortress Monroe, and our subsequent taking the York River as the base of our operations, was simply caused by the terror the Merrimac had excited.

If the army could have been landed at Newport News, and marched up James River to Richmond, there would have been before us few of those obstructions which blocked up our way on York River. We would have found a good road, and, attended

by our fleet, all the supplies of the army would have
been within our reach; and we could have left Yorktown and Williamsburg in our rear, to fall into our
hands at our leisure. It was probably General
McClellan's original plan of operations, to make
James River his base. But true to a prudence that
never braved a danger, he changed his plan after the
appearance of the Merrimac.

The Merrimac was one of the United States vessels of war consumed in the harbor of Norfolk. Her
hull was fished up by the Confederates, clad with
iron, and on the 8th of March she came out of Elizabeth River, attended by two iron-clad steamers, and
advanced steadily towards the mouth of the James
River. Here were lying at anchor two United States
frigates, the Cumberland and the Congress. They
poured broadside after broadside into the Merrimac,
but the shells struck her angular roof and bounded
off. One shell of the Cumberland is said to have
made some impression on the hull of the ironside.
But without firing a gun in return, she kept steadily
on her way, until she struck with her spear the side
of the Cumberland. This vessel careened, filled
with water, and began to sink; but her noble commander refused to strike her colors, or ask quarter,
and the crew worked their guns and fired even when
the water was rushing over the deck where they
stood, and two hundred men went down with her.
The Merrimac then summoned the Congress to surrender. This she refused, but answered by a broadside. To this the Merrimac replied by a terrific
discharge of shell, which tore through the doomed
vessel, cut down many of her crew, and rendered

any further action on the part of her commander useless and fatal: her sails were set and she ran ashore, and in a few moments burst into flames. In this part of the action Captain Buchanan was wounded by a rifle ball, or fragment of a shell.

In the meantime, the Minnesota and Roanoke steamed out from under the guns of the fort for the scene of action. The Minnesota might have accomplished the destruction of the Merrimac by running her down, but before she came within range she ran aground in a position most dangerous. The Merrimac did not attempt the destruction of the Minnesota, which might have been easily accomplished, but remained off Newport News, shelling the batteries and the camps: the presiding genius was evidently gone from his post. Satisfied with this as the work of one day, and possibly for the relief of her wounded captain, possibly for further orders, she returned for the night to Norfolk.

In the meantime, all was consternation in the fort and army. The Merrimac would undoubtedly return to-morrow, destroy the Minnesota, compel the surrender of the hundred vessels in the bay, bombard the fort, and possibly render necessary its evacuation. She might run under the guns of the fort, ascend the Potomac and bombard Washington, and drive President, Cabinet, and Congress from the seat of government. Unnumbered were the predictions of evil, and the hearts of the stoutest failed them; for all the old appliances of naval warfare, which had been so effective in the past, were powerless in the case of this monster. The terrific scenes of to-day only awakened the deeper dread of to-mor-

11

row. Even General Wool talked despondingly of the fate of the fortress, and the deepest gloom pervaded all minds, and none knew where to turn in hope.

There had been, indeed, some newspaper notices of the Monitor, but her destination was unknown. At eight o'clock in the evening of this fatal Saturday this nondescript came into the waters of the bay, unannounced and unlooked for.

Her appearance was so insignificant that she attracted no attention. In a few moments on shore, her commander, Lieutenant Worden, learned of the catastrophes of the day, and the consternation of the night. He immediately presented himself to General Wool, and, like the young David, proffered to meet and conquer the giant enemy. The general was evidently afraid this would be but another act in the tragedy. How could a little vessel of two guns contend with such a powerful steamer as the Merrimac, carrying eight guns of the largest calibre? but as the events of the day had thrown the whole science of naval warfare into original chaos, it might be this pigmy could accomplish something effective in the contest. But whatever the result, General Wool could not reject the proffered aid. The Monitor that same night moved away from before the fort, and took her place near Newport News.

Sabbath morning dawned a fair and beautiful day. The officers and men in the camps seized a cracker, and hurried to the shore; the walls of the fort were black with multitudes who with glasses were peering into the waters for the coming enemy. All the houses around the fort, and along the shore of the bay, were crowded with those who looked with pale and anxious faces for the Merrimac. The shore itself was crowded by a great multitude, waiting for the shock and end. The one hundred steamers and ships were with steam up and sails unfurled, and the sailors at the capstans to elevate the anchors, and be ready in a moment to glide out of danger. As yet but few outside of the fort knew of the arrival of the Monitor.

The expectant multitude had not long to wait; the black smoke in the distance heralded the coming foe. At length her dark hull was seen, and in a few moments the cry ran along the shore, "She is coming! she is coming!" The excitement was intense: children climbed upon the shoulders of their fathers; mothers held up their babes to look on the scene; hundreds of negroes hung upon the branches of trees, and to every mast and yard-arm clung a multitude of sailors. The interest was so absorbing that few spoke: more and more distinct became the nearing vessel, attended, as on the previous occasion, by the two gunboats.

The Merrimac steamed directly for the Minnesota. But suddenly a report from a rebel gunboat at the mouth of James River called the notice of the Merrimac to an unexpected enemy.

The boats started from her side in the direction of Newport News. Now could be seen coming out from the shore a small object like a speck on the waters, "no larger," in the words of my chief informant, "than the head of a floating barrel." All eyes and glasses were now turned towards this new wonder, and a thousand inquiries ran from one cluster of gazers to another. As the gunboats approached the Monitor, there came out from her tower a vivid flash, which was followed by the terrific roar of an one-hundred-and-twenty-pound gun. This satisfied the gunboat; she turned and fled from the Monitor more rapidly than she had advanced.

All this time the Monitor was slowly approaching the Merrimac, which in her turn was advancing on her puny antagonist.

This fresh act was opened by the Merrimac. Two or three of her great guns flashed together, then there was a mighty roar, causing the sea to tremble, the ships to roll, and the houses on the shore to shake. One shell was seen to strike the tower of the Monitor, and fall on her like dust; another struck her flat deck, and bounded into the heavens with a scream that sounded like the wail of agony. In a moment the Monitor returned the fire, and flash followed flash from the guns in both vessels, until the sea was covered with smoke, and in the bosom of the dark pall only the glare of light told the positions of the foes.

After this cannonading had continued an hour, the Merrimac ran off a short distance, apparently to change either her tactics or her position; and after a rest of a few moments, she again turned on the Monitor at full speed, and attempted to run her down. She succeeded in running her prow on the little raft, which glided out from under her powerful enemy unhurt, and almost touching her, poured shell from both of her guns into the hull of the Merrimac. Now commenced the most exciting part of the spectacle; each now began to seek the

weakest point of the other, aiming by every movement to obtain the advantage. It was evident they
had concluded the only vulnerable points of each
were the port-holes, and they waited for the flash
of each others' guns, and one flash was succeeded by
an instantaneous flash from the other vessel. At
length even this was given up; and the Monitor began to run around the Merrimac, and to pour shell
after shell into her stern. This the Merrimac evidently dreaded, and turned and shifted her position
as often as possible, and continued to fire, but not
with the definiteness of aim which had marked the
earlier part of the engagement. It now became
manifest that the Merrimac was weary of the contest, if not injured.

When it became certain that the Monitor was not
at the mercy of the Merrimac, but even superior to
her, the sense of relief was beyond language to express, — a multitude shouted for joy, and tears flowed
down many manly faces.

The contest was still maintained, though the Merrimac commenced retiring towards Norfolk, but
stopping like an enraged bull for another battle.
The Monitor continued to run around her, and pour
her shot into the stern and hull.

After the battle had lasted for four hours, the impression was made, by the appearance and careen-
ing of the Merrimac, that she was seriously damaged.
She slackened her fire, and turned her head towards
Norfolk; the Monitor followed, pouring shot after
shot into her.

Some two or three miles from this scene, lying on
the waters, was a large steamer from Norfolk, cov-

11 *

ered by a multitude of ladies and gentlemen, who, having heard of the triumph of yesterday, came out to witness the burnings, surrenders, contests, and victories of to-day.   In her pursuit of the Merrimac, the Monitor sent a shell at this steamer, which caused her to quit the field with the utmost rapidity. The Monitor chased the Merrimac one mile and stopped, and one of the most remarkable contests in history was ended.

It is said by many that the Merrimac returned to Norfolk on Saturday night, to receive orders from the Confederate Government in regard to what should be the aim of to-morrow.

CHAPTER VIII.

Fortress Monroe — The Ruins of Hampton — The Scene attending its Destruction — The Assembling of the Grand Army of the Potomac on the Plains of Hampton — The Novelty and Splendor of the Spectacle — March upon Yorktown.

In order to catch the best impression of the landscape, I soon found my way to the most prominent building, and one commanding the finest view of the scene.

This building was the Chesapeake Hospital, formerly a female college. This stands on the bay, about one mile to the left of the fort, the most commanding object in all that region. The fort stands on the point of a long tongue of land running into the bay. The walls are, I suppose, fifty feet above the sea: many great guns are in position on these walls, and menacingly frown on any approaching vessel. The fort is surrounded by a moat, but is by no means impregnable. Across the bay, about four miles from the fort, lies a heavily wooded strip of low land. Between this and the fortress are the Rip Raps, where, on a shallow bar, the Government has commenced the erection of a fort; when completed, this will add very greatly to the strength of the position. Afar off, to the left, were seen the white sand beaches and dark, wooded peninsulas; and to the right, the low shores about the mouths of the Elizabeth and James Rivers; as far as the eye could reach, not a hill or swell of land arose to relieve the monotony; at the same time the scene was far from uninteresting, for in the bay were two or three hundred vessels lying at anchor; a hundred little boats were plying from these to the shore and fort; and the sea, always beautiful and rich in wonders and treasures of her own, was there.

But certainly the most striking and never-to-be-forgotten feature of that scene was "Old Hampton." This town lies about two miles from the fort, and we looked upon it in ruins, every house being consumed; but the naked walls of five hundred houses remained like vast skeletons, giving us some faint idea of the beauty, wealth, and enjoyment of the past. Many of the first families of the State resided here, and no place in Virginia was richer in historic legends.

The old English church, one of the oldest in the State, ought to have been spared, as a venerable and sacred relic: now its naked walls utter a protest against that vandalic barbarism which consigned it to ruin. At the time Hampton was burned, General Butler was in command at the fort; our line had extended beyond Hampton; most of the inhabitants had fled, but some remained. After the battle at Great Bethel, General Butler had withdrawn our men from beyond the creek. In order to prevent our occupying the town as winter-quarters, General Magruder sent down a hundred of his men, who, at a given signal, were to set fire to every house in the place. One of the inhabitants, a patrician of wealth, with whom I became acquainted, unwilling to leave the only house he had in the world, remained in the town; and on the afternoon of this day was rejoiced to find a favorite nephew knocking at his door. He had come down from the army to see his uncle and family, and would remain some hours. He recounted to his gratified relative the adventures and escapes of the last few months.

After tea he told his uncle that he had an unpleasant duty to perform, and that was to aid in firing the town; and that his orders were to begin at his house, and five minutes would be given him and his family to flee from the burning place. All was consternation and confusion; they knew not what to take, or what to leave.

And before they had recovered from the shock, the shriek came from many quarters, "Fire! fire! the town is on fire!" and leaving all, they fled; and when they had gone beyond the suburbs they looked back, and saw tongues of flame ascending from every house, wareroom, church, and factory, and streams of fire running from street to street.

A cowering, shivering, and weeping throng of old men, women, and children stood together in the fields; they knew not where to turn. All they had in the world was in Hampton; all the precious things, endearing home memories, the sacred mementoes of the past, all that had been collected by a lifetime of toil, were swept from them in a moment. Their lamentations were heart-rending. One lamented most the loss of the family pictures; they could have given up all, if they had those beloved faces to look on and comfort them. Another mourned the destruction of the holy room where her mother had died, where she had kissed all her children and blessed them, and went up to God. Another wept the loss of the playthings of a beloved child; another mourned, as the bitterest drop in this cup of woe, the vine which she had planted, which, as it wound around the summer bower, was the emblem of peace and love; there her children had played and studied, but now they should never again scent the fragrance of their garden. Others wept because they had no home, and suddenly broken and scattered were all the hopes of their age.

What a vision for the painter would have been that throng of weepers; the darkness and the open fields behind them; the light of their burning homes falling on their faces, and reflected in their tears!

What added to the distress of this hour was that, whichever way the eye turned, fire flashed on them; for the men sent for the execution of this infernal purpose, seized with a frenzy for destruction, set fire to every house and barn on the way as they retreated, and for miles the flames flared up into the heavens, filling the imagination with all the images of terror.

Thus were scattered the families who remained in Hampton, and the city was left a ruined heap.

After some days the grand army was collected in the green fields back of Hampton, and certainly there was never a more imposing and brilliant spectacle. The army consisted of not less than 120,000 men; the troops had been nine months in the field, in various places, and had become almost perfect in military movements and drill.

At dawn the bugles of a hundred camps awakened the soldier to another day; then followed the various bands, with lively notes welcoming the morning, and calling on us to come forth to the duties of the hour. We went forth from our tents, and the morning was indescribably beautiful; the abundant vapors, and the presence of so many waters, imparted the richest splendor to the heavens; the deep crimson of the horizon melted into golden and emerald hues higher in the air, and the horses of the sun's chariot "pawed the twilight into flakes of fire," and then the sun came up to place a crown of gold on the head of every lofty tree of the forest.

The beauty of the morning and evening in this region is more brilliant than I have seen elsewhere in the United States. The sky had the warm, magnificent glow of Italy and the Syrian valleys; and as hue succeeded hue, and one glorious blush of splendor followed another, the spectator was lost in admiration, and knew not which most to admire, the many lights that had passed, or the beauty that remained.

While our encampments were here, the scene was most animating and novel. The presence of 100,000 men, who, from the early morning until the night, are under drill in the fields around, and in every direction one looked bodies of men, great and small, were wheeling, halting, presenting arms, charging bayonets, receiving cavalry, with all the accuracy and precision of machinery, was a rare and wondrous spectacle.

Here a brigade of cavalry, with waving plumes and flashing sabres, dashed across the field. In another direction were all the movements peculiar to artillery practice. On the carriage bearing each piece were seated six men, and two on the horses,— four horses being attached to a carriage bearing a twelve-pounder, and six and eight to the carriages bearing larger guns, and one rider to a pair of horses; a carriage of equal weight, called a caisson, containing ammunition, following each gun. The horses were urged into the wildest gallop, as if rushing into action, wheeling around without the halt of a moment; the men sprang from their seats and unlimbered the guns; the horses were removed, and the gunners went through the pantomime show of loading and firing; and again the horses, with equal haste, were urged to the guns, attached in a second, and with furious speed rushed to another part of the field. Again the men sprang from their seats, the guns were detached, brought into position, and every man stood in his place like a statue, until the command infused into each the energy of one who had only a moment to live.

In another field a long line of three-fourths of a mile, kneeling on one knee, with presented bayonets, was a brigade waiting the dash of an enemy's cavalry. Apparently fastened to the earth, motionless and silent, they reminded one of the armies sculptured on Egyptian monuments.

In another field a brigade, with fixed bayonets, charged upon their enemies; and over brake, and briar fence, and bog they ran with yells on the imaginary foe. The amusement of this spectacle was greater from the fright of the horses of the officers, the wild leaps of fences and ditches, and the panting, sweltering fat officers bringing up the rear.

In another field companies of scouts and skirmishers were being drilled in the movements of that most dangerous but useful arm of the service, — the skirmishers, placed at the distance of fifty feet from each other, the one at the lower end of the line firing on the advancing foe, and rapidly retreating to the upper end, loading as he ran, and again the next in succession, until every man had changed his position.

In another field a brigade that had landed but an hour before were casting their knapsacks on the ground, stacking their arms, and pitching their tents. And in every direction the eye looked, the roads were crowded with freshly arrived troops marching to their encampments, — a thousand banners were unfurled, waving and fluttering in the breeze.

In still another field long lines of horses and mules, stretching for miles, were being ridden and led to water,—the number of ambulances and wagons being not less than 6,000, and the horses and mules for the commissary and medical department alone not less than 65,000. Here hundreds of these animals had broken away from their riders and drivers, and were dashing with fury through the tents of regiments and divisions; and entangled in tent-ropes, they were kicking down the frail canvas, and sending forth the occupants the personification of rage and terror. Here was a brainless soldier mounted on one horse without a saddle, and leading four others by their halters, when the loose animals came careering past, his determined to join in the frolic, and add another feature to the scene. Away they dash, through fields, over ditches, through encampments they whirl, kick, snort, renew the furious plunge; the hat of the rider is left far in the rear, his face the picture of anguish, his hair streaming in the wind, his hands firmly grasped in the mane, his cries of "whoa, whoa, whoa," expressing his utter helplessness.

At another point, the commander of the army, surrounded with his one hundred and fifty aids, all riding upon the gayest and most brilliantly caparisoned horses, reminding one of the brilliant train of the Grand Sultan, increased the novelty, and to *some* the charm of the scene.

The hum of such a multitude, the cries and shouts of thousands, bring to the ear of the listener the sound of many waters.

Such were the never-to-be-forgotten spectacles of the grand army at Hampton. During the two weeks we were here, Nature was in her gentlest mood. The breath of spring filled the air with fragrance, and enrobed every fruit-tree in blossoms; we had but one storm after the landing. It was a delightful season of rest and enjoyment, preparing for the exertions and sacrifices of the future. We left Hampton on the 4th of April, and reached Great Bethel about two P. M. This was the scene of a disastrous battle, fought the 10th of June, 1861. In this fell the lamented Winthrop, as also the equally gifted Lieutenant Greble, both of whom were men of the highest promise. The position is undoubtedly a very strong one, a deep and impassable morass extending above and below; and at this point there is some flow and fall of the streams, and a rather bad ford.

The hills above the creek, possibly forty feet higher than the water, were crowned with earthworks, and a long rifle-pit extending for miles.

As we came near the place, the few troops left here fled towards Yorktown. When we crossed this stream we were in the enemy's land. Our troops had not before been over Bethel Creek. We encamped the first night on the farm of Mr. Russel, at Rose Dale. This we found one of the finest plantations in this region. Russel himself is a timid, soulless man : having no white wife, he lives in the society of his negroes, and has some of the virtues and all the vices of a Turk. But he had a rare eye for beauty, for he had in his house some of the finest specimens of octoroon girls. Every man has some idiosyncrasy — this man's was that he would permit no one to open, or for an hour to occupy, the room of his mother; everything must be kept as she had left it. Several of the officers, with myself, took tea at the house of a poor woman with a family of children, whose husband was in the Confederate Army. She assured us that none of the small farmers, mechanics, and poor people, were in favor of the war, but they had been forced into the service. They could not flee the country, and if they refused to obey the conscription, they were thrown into prison and shot. She said that only the rich slaveholders were in favor of the war, but that her husband had

ever been opposed to it, and, from the time that he
was compelled to leave home, he had constantly
written and sent word that peace would soon be
made; and this hope made her bear up with courage. But now, when she saw our troops, all her
fears were roused, and bitterly she wept and complained of the wrongs that had been done her. The
sufferings of these poor, defenceless, and unprotected
families were of a character to awaken the deepest
pity: the land was swept of fences, grain, horses,
and cattle, and everything they had raised during
the summer. There was none to till the fields, and
no means of protecting what the women and old
men might have planted; and in the peninsula, during the summer, hundreds of families were destitute
and in want. There was nothing left in the country
on which they could live.

In a fortnight after our march to Yorktown, I returned to Fortress Monroe; and in riding through
the country, stopped at the house of Russel to water
my horse. He said that all his property was gone,
and nothing remained for the support of his family
of servants.

We reached Yorktown on the afternoon of Saturday, the 5th of April. The last ten miles of the
road was a continued and unbroken swamp; the
road was corduroy, and over this for miles ran a
river of mud, and along this wretched way stumbled
horse and man: many sank down totally exhausted.

We heard heavy cannonading long before reaching
the open plains before Yorktown. General Porter's forces, and a portion of General Heintzleman's,
were in the advance of us. Several batteries had

commenced firing on some of the redoubts of the enemy, and they briskly answered.

If we had attacked Yorktown on that Saturday afternoon, there is no doubt we should have taken it; for I conversed subsequently with several Confederate officers who had been at the siege, and they all assured me that they had made their arrangements to abandon the town, and, accordingly, had sent away their families, servants, and camp furniture. They expected us to advance that Saturday afternoon, and carry the place by assault; but when they found that we delayed, the officers and troops determined to make the most gallant defence. And soon they obtained large reinforcements, and received instructions to hold us before Yorktown as long as possible.

On the Saturday of our arrival before the place, the rebel officers informed me that they had but 7,500 men for all the fortifications, but in a few days 50,000 were sent to aid in the defence. I have uniformly stated to my friends that our great defeat was before Yorktown, and not before Richmond.

The long delay here, the exposure, fatigue, the fevers generated in the swamps, did more to dispirit the army and waste its strength than five battles. The men lost that buoyancy and hopefulness with which they had left Hampton.

We were thirty days before the place casting up intrenchments and erecting the various works necessary for a successful bombardment.

Around the town are open fields of rich, fertile land, and on these good farm-houses: these places

12 *

were abandoned and the families gone. But in these fields our troops did not remain more than three days, and, because exposed to shells from the enemy's batteries, were removed into the heavy forests around. The woodland was one vast bog, water lying in ponds and pools every few rods. During the thirty days of the siege, it rained and stormed twenty. Thunder-storms succeeded each other with marvellous rapidity, and day and night there was a succession of tempests, and the lightning in vividness and rapidity of discharge exceeded anything we had ever witnessed, reminding those familiar with India of the tempests of the rainy season in that country, as if the entire heavens had become one vast electrical battery.

If our soldiers were on duty digging trenches, on the picket-line, or standing guard, they had to endure all the fury of the storm. If in camp, their tents were beaten down, or the water submerged their beds.

If the night was fair, there were constant alarms along the entire line; the men were called from their sleep to arms, and hurried, at double quick, to the outposts; here, heated and perspiring, they were made to lie down on the wet ground, and soon found themselves chilled to the heart; and on the next day returned to camp wearied and feverish. This was followed by an apathy that crept over the frame and brain like a paralysis, and in a few days there were developed all the symptoms of typhoid fever. And fortunate were those who had nothing to endure but the tortures of rheumatism.

In a short time the sick in our hospitals were

numbered by thousands, and many died so suddenly that the disease had all the aspect of a plague.

Some divisions of the army were subjected to much severer labors than others. It might have been owing to the position they occupied, and the confidence reposed in their bravery. But it gave rise to serious and just complaint.

CHAPTER IX.

Yorktown — Memorials of the Revolution — Antiquities — General Porter's Balloon Ascension and Discoveries — Colonel Samuel Black — His Character.

YORKTOWN was of especial interest to us, because in that place and its immediate neighborhood are found many monuments of the most interesting event in our Revolutionary history. The divisions under Generals Kearney and Hooker encamped on the grounds where had been spread the tents of General Washington and General Lafayette. We daily looked out upon the plain where had been witnessed the combats and struggles which compelled the final surrender of Yorktown to our forces. The old lines of intrenchment, and the mounds of redoubts, lie like a chain across the fields.

The spot where the sword of Cornwallis was surrendered to General Washington, is marked by a stone on the roadside about half a mile to the south of the town. It lies in an open and beautiful field; and as we stood there and looked over the scene, it required no effort of the imagination to bring up the great dead, and to become witnesses of one of those events which have left a lasting impression on the world. Prominent in that spectacle we could see the great, majestic Washington receiving, with the air of one who felt profound compassion for an honorable but humbled foe, the sword of Cornwallis. We could look upon the proud, stern brow of Tarleton, and see by his side the gloomy-faced officers of the British army. Again we looked into the youthful and glowing face of Lafayette, rejoicing not over a fallen enemy, but in the victory of liberty. And alongside of him we summoned up the brave German Baron Steuben, and the courtly Count Rochambeau; and there, gazing on the great spectacle, were many of the heroes of our Revolutionary history, — Knox, Nelson, Clinton, Hamilton. Rarely has the world witnessed anything more impressive and sublime. From this hour opened the great day of our national life.

This scene occurred on the 19th of October, 1781. One of the great actors of this time, to whom the country is most indebted for the final success of our arms, was General Thomas Nelson. He was born in Yorktown, and became one of the most popular leaders in the Revolutionary army. He commanded the militia of Virginia at the capture of Cornwallis. The Nelson House still stands in Yorktown, even at this time exhibiting the impressions made by the shells of the American batteries when the place was held by the English.

Nearer to this are found many interesting antiquities. The ruined English church, one of the oldest on the continent, is surrounded with time-worn and venerable monuments. No walk is more suggestive than one amid the ruins of this ancient sanctuary. With one of the monuments standing in this ground

I was deeply interested. It is quadrangular in form, _
and displays in its inscription the style and thought
of the age. From angel faces on the upper end of
the monument bursts the song, *"All Glory be to God."*
From another angel's trumpet flows the inscription:

"Here lies the body of the Hon. William Nelson,
late President of his Majesty's Council in this dominion, in whom the love of man and the love of
God so restrained and enforced each other, and so
invigorated the mental powers in general, as not
only to defend him from the vices and follies of his
age and country, but also to render it a matter of
difficult decision in what part of laudable conduct
he most excelled; whether in the tender and endearing accomplishments of domestic life, or in the
more arduous duties of a wider circuit; whether as
a neighbor, gentleman, or magistrate; whether in
the graces of hospitality, charity, or piety. Reader,
if you feel the spirit of that exalted order which as-
pires to the felicity of conscious virtue, animated by
those stimulating and divine admonitions, perform
the task, and expect the distinction of a righteous
man."

"Obit. 19th Nov., Anno Domini 1772, *ætatis* 61."

Another monument, of still greater antiquity, is
found amid the ruins outside the walls. There are
around it many broken slabs, and only this one
inscription is legible. The flat stone is adorned
with all the symbols of heraldry, and bears the
words:

"MAJOR WILLIAM GOOCH, of this parish, dyed Octob. 29th, 1655.

"Within this tomb there doth interred lie
No shape but substance, true nobility;
Itself, though young in years, but twenty-nine,
Yet graced with virtues, morall and divine.
The Church from him did good participate,
In counsell rare fit to adorn a State."

No place on our continent exhibits so strongly the evidences of having been often the scene of siege and battle. The crumbling walls, redoubts, and bastions all remind one of some of those ancient cities of the old world whose history runs back into the early shadows of time.

On the morning of the 28th of April we were startled by the cry, "The balloon has broken away; there is a man in it." I ran to the door of the small house in which Dr. Rogers and myself had our quarters, and saw the balloon sailing over us in majestic style. The sun had not yet risen, — the morning was clear and bright, without a cloud. She rose higher and higher in the heavens, until the beams of the sun gilded her like gold. Now we saw plainly a man in the basket, and a cry came down to us, "Oh, what shall I do! what shall I do!" One of our hospital nurses shouted back, "Pull the rope! pull the rope!" The man in the basket commenced pulling up the rope which dangled below. Seeing this, the nurse again shouted, "Pull the valve-rope above you!" By this time the balloon had reached the height of six hundred feet, and was rapidly drifting towards Chesapeake Bay; and as she sailed along, high above the world, was a beautiful spectacle.

But as we looked after her with the deepest interest, we saw, greatly to our relief, that the balloon was descending to the earth, and approaching the tops of the trees, and in a few more seconds she was lost to our sight. Soon several officers dashed along in the direction the balloon had taken, and in the course of an hour they returned, bringing with them the general who had made the perilous reconnoissance of that morning; and from them we learned that General Fitz-John Porter had placed himself in the basket of the balloon very early, for the purpose of watching and judging of some of the movements of the enemy, — the morning was so clear, that there was more reason to expect a good view than one hour later. When above the earth a few feet, the ropes, which had in some way been reached by the nitric acid, broke, and the balloon rose to a thousand feet, and reached a current of air which rapidly bore it out to the bay.

But the pulling of the valve-rope caused the escape of the gas, and soon the balloon began to descend. About three miles beyond us it fell upon the Sibley tent of some officers who were seated at a table eating breakfast. Suddenly there was a crash, — the tent staggered, the ropes broke, the inmates rushed out, and in a second the balloon and tent lay fluttering together; and General Porter, as one who had descended from another world, stepped out in the presence of the officers, and without exchanging words, or waiting for explanations, left the astonished men to their own conclusions. The

THE DESCENT OF GENERAL FITZ JOHN PORTER AT YORKTOWN.

Chap. LI.

general was evidently greatly mortified, and hurried back to his tent, knowing well that the lofty ride of that morning would be the joke of the army for many a month.

During the time of our encampment before York-town, I had an opportunity to renew my acquaintance with an old schoolmate, Colonel Samuel Black, in command of the 62d Pennsylvania Volunteers. At the breaking out of the rebellion he was Governor of Nebraska. He had been, for fifteen years, a prominent politician of his native State, and was, more than most men, familiar with those secret springs which lie far back of every public movement. He was profoundly under the conviction, from the first development of the slaveholders' conspiracy, that if permitted to carry out their plans, they would dig the grave of liberty for the whole continent.

As soon as possible he resigned his office in the West, and hastened to Pittsburg. He was there immediately offered the command of one of the finest regiments ever raised in Western Pennsylvania, which he accepted, and soon after he joined the Army of the Potomac.

We met, for the first time in many years, before Yorktown, and renewed the acquaintance of our boyhood. He was at this time strictly temperate, from principle, and possibly from necessity, never drinking intoxicating liquors of any kind; purely virtuous in all his sentiments, and never uttering, so far as I have heard, a profane word; generous and familiar with his men, always known as the soldier's friend; strict in discipline, he had an almost unbounded influence over the regiments in his immediate circle.

13

In my many conversations with him, I found no officer having a more just appreciation of the causes
generating this rebellion, or who could express so
eloquently and philosophically the views he had been
gradually forming for years, of the consequences
which must follow from handing over the Government, bound hand and foot, to those whose views
were essentially anti-republican.

I was likewise impressed with the conviction that
the colonel was not far from the kingdom of heaven.
His conduct and expressions were those of one who
felt his responsibility to God, and who was determined that his entire life for the future should be
influenced by loftier aims than in the past. He appeared to me to have come at length fully under the
religious impressions received from the example and
teachings of his venerated father. But, alas! while
our plans are long, life is short. He fell at the head
of his regiment at Mechanicsville, on the morning of
the 27th of June, and his loss was amongst the
greatest of that fatal day. If he had lived, there were
before him the highest military and civil distinctions;
and few names of those who, from Western Pennsylvania, have died in battle, will be read in the history to be written with deeper regret, than that one
so gifted perished too early, not for his fame, but for
his country.

CHAPTER X.

Retreat of the Enemy — The Torpedoes left in the Streets, and around Wells — The Sick left behind — The Hospitals created — Night Scene in the Forest — Captain W. Brown.

AT length General McClellan, having completed all his plans for the bombardment of Yorktown, and having brought into position guns and mortars sufficient to throw sixty shells a minute into the place, the whole army waited with intense expectation for the opening of the grand spectacle. But here, as in many other instances, the fruit of many toils turned to ashes as we grasped it.

In this, as in many other cases, when all our plans were defeated by some unforeseen event, was foreshadowed the evident intention of Heaven to prolong this war until we were brought to look the great question at the basis of the controversy in the face. Our disasters and disappointments have educated the people, and disciplined us in patience, self-denial, and firmness.

Having permitted our nation to fall into this sea of trouble, Divine Providence does not design that we should come forth from this baptism without a permanent impression being made on the national character. There were, doubtless, many evils and tendencies to the creation of greater in the license of liberty we enjoyed. We have but to study the lessons of history to learn that no great nation is reared in the lap of ease and peace.

But those nations which have been raised up to give their institutions and laws to the world, were born in the midst of the convulsions of States, and reared in storms and dangers: their institutions, endeared to them by their fathers' and their own sacrifices, became a living people's life, and the best inheritance of their children.

We needed some such calamity as the present war to break down the walls rising between States, and to sweep away, before a common national peril, all those sectional jealousies which divide us. We needed a long national trial, to make us wiser for all time, and to teach us the lesson that no great evil can be grafted on the trunk of a State without its poison being borne to every root and fibre; and that an evil principle left embodied in the laws and constitution of a State will burn like a cancer, and consume like a leprosy.

Well and truly does the Secretary of War discourse on this theme :

"After the close of the war, when men look back to its bloody fields and awful sacrifices, they will be amazed at the insane folly which permitted them to consider the great American Union, with its honorable history, its wonderful progress, its immense power, and its proud standing amongst the nations, as a mere league between petty States, to be dissolved at pleasure; as a thing to be broken into fragments, and to be divided amongst ambitious aspirants, to be made the sport of domestic faction, or of foreign rapacity and domination, changing its form and proportions with every change of popular feeling, and every restless movement of popular discontent. These fatal delusions will disappear forever, and in their place will remain, in the minds of men, the image of a majestic government tried in the furnace of civil war, made solid and immovable by its grand and successful efforts to resist the threatened overthrow of its power.

"Then, with the awe and fear which will be inspired by the tremendous energy put forth to conquer the rebellion, — an energy which will appear only so much the greater and more imposing in proportion to the difficulties and dangers met and overcome, — there will be mingled the better sentiments of love and veneration for a government which reestablishes order, secures protection to civil rights, and restores unimpaired the liberties which have been disregarded for a time in order that they might be permanently saved. To the people of the United States the Union will be what it never was before, and what it never could have been without the sad experience it is now undergoing."

On the nights of the 3d and 4th of May, the enemy evacuated Yorktown and their lines on the Warwick River. But, in order the more effectually to deceive us and to conceal their movements, the firing from their batteries was never so intense and active as on the nights when their entire force was retiring.

Nothing could be more grand than the cannonading of Saturday night. The atmosphere was in a condition eminently favorable for conveying and prolonging the sound. And as one great gun followed

13 *

another, it rolled like mighty thunder over bay, and field, and forest, and echo mingled with echo, and peal answered to peal. The night, the thousand flashes, the trembling of the earth, the stupendous crash, all combined to give an awful sublimity to the hour. But during these nights the Confederates vanished. On Sunday, the 4th of May, at daybreak, our men in the rifle-pits found there was no foe before them; and cautiously creeping up to the very lines of the enemy, it soon became certain that all were gone, and with them had fled our hope of a brilliant victory. Soon our entire army was summoned to the pursuit, and before noon was marching through the renowned intrenchments of Yorktown.

The enemy had planted torpedoes in the roads, around wells and springs, and near the great guns, which, concealed beneath the ground, the capped nipple coming to the surface, were exploded by the slightest touch. Several of our men were killed in the streets and intrenchments by these deadly missiles. They even concealed them in green spots where soldiers would be likely to sit down to rest.

In one case that I heard of, a soldier, taking his seat with his companions on a green knoll, near to a well, saw lying at his feet a pocket-knife. As he picked this up he found around it a small cord; without thinking of the concealed danger, he gave the knife a sudden jerk to break the cord. This was followed by an explosion which blew the soldier into a hundred fragments. Thus, those who entered into Yorktown, and remained any time, were exposed to peril at every step.

The prisoners who had been taken were immediately put to work in unearthing the concealed shells; and no doubt for years to come, among the wonders of Yorktown will be brought to light the torpedoes hidden in the streets. This method of warfare is undoubtedly savage and brutal, and can only react with terrible power on those who take such infernal means to destroy their foes.

We left our encampments on Sunday morning at eleven o'clock, and before noon the entire army was in pursuit of the enemy. We were, however, compelled to leave behind the sick in our hospitals; these were to be removed, at as early a day as possible, to Yorktown. I was ordered to remain, to assist in creating hospitals in Yorktown, and superintend the removing of the sick and wounded of the 63d Pennsylvania, one hundred and five in number. My principal work had been for several weeks in the hospitals. We had connected with our division, General Kearney's, from five to six hundred sick men. The obtaining supplies for these of sanitary stores and clothes, and the attending to their spiritual necessities by daily visitations and prayers in each of the tents, fully occupied me. And when the army started in pursuit of the enemy, all the surgeons of our division, except Dr. Heighhold, of the 105th Pennsylvania, were ordered to join the regiments. We were thus left behind, without ambulances or wagons of any description, to remove our sick into Yorktown as best we could. The suffering at this time was such as I fully believe is endured nowhere but in an army. Hundreds of men tossing and burning with fever were left in camps in the forests, in old houses by the roadside, and in barns, with sick men as their attendants; and that they did not all perish is, indeed, almost miraculous.

The commissary stores being removed, more than half of those sick men knew not where to turn for supplies, the advance of the great army having left everything confused and disjointed in its rear. One of those night scenes I can never forget. There came up a violent thunder-storm on Sabbath afternoon: the tempest continued through that night until Monday night. During this time, Dr. Heighhold and myself were fully occupied with the sick men left in and around the Baptist church on the Hampton road. I was not aware that any men had been left in the camp unable to follow the army, having understood from Dr. Rogers, our brigade surgeon, that the disabled were to be conveyed from the various camps to the hospitals. I therefore supposed that all had been brought in. On Tuesday afternoon I was startled by the intelligence that thirty sick men had been left in our encampment in the forest without nurse or surgeon, and that some of these had staggered to head-quarters and made complaint, and begged for food and medicines. The camp was in the deep forest. The wagons for the removal of the commissary stores, tents, etc., etc., of the army, had cut the roads through the swamp of this forest into a condition beggaring description. Even a horse with a single rider would become imbogged in roots and mud, so as to render his escape perilous or impossible. And if one endeavored to escape from these roads and turned into the woods, the undergrowth was so thick that it was impossible to proceed more than a few feet; but if he bravely

breasted the sweeping branches, and tore his hands
with thorns and briars, there yawned before him one
of those dismal sloughs of uncertain depth, where
snakes, lizards, and small crocodiles welcomed him;
and from the terrors of the swamp the horseman was
compelled to return to the horrors of the road. As
soon as the nature of the case permitted, I went
down to the camp, found the men as reported to me,
some of them very ill. I immediately rode to the
head-quarters of General McClellan, and found some
of the surgeons still there, and some ambulances.
At my request, three of the ambulances were sent to
assist in bringing up the men unable to walk.

It was dark before we reached the edge of the
forest, and even by daylight its entangled mazes were
threaded with the utmost difficulty; but at night
even an Indian would have been at fault. Soon the
ambulances were fast in a morass, the horses kicking and plunging in the wrappings of thorny vines,
and not a road or camp-fire opened before us in the
dismal jungle. But fortunately there was a lantern
in one of the ambulances, — this was lighted, and
I set forth on a voyage of discovery. I was soon
knee deep in water, but went on sounding the
swamp, until I became satisfied that a few steps further might eventuate in my sudden departure from
the Army of the Potomac. I then crawled upon a
rotten stump, clinging to vines, swinging from root
to root, and from stump to stump, now on a crumbling log, now clambering amid the brushy branches
of a fallen tree. I found my way across the pond,
and when I reached firmer ground I shouted aloud,
hoping the men in the camp might hear me, know

my voice, and come forth and answer. The drivers of the ambulance shouted back. I found my way around the waters, until I became satisfied who it was that replied to me, and then set forth anew.

After exploring the circumference of many sloughs, trying the strength of a thousand vines, disturbing innumerable lizards, and wandering I knew not how long — for anxiety to attain the end I was in pursuit of, left me without any idea of time — after many calls and shoutings, there was heard a voice in reply. This was one of our sick men, who heard me, and was answering. I soon reached them, and now arose a new difficulty. The sickest men were not able to walk, and they must be removed that night, while we had the ambulances, for to-morrow these would be gone. We therefore took them up in our arms, having called all who were able to give the slightest assistance; and staggering, sometimes falling, often halting to shout and discover the position of the ambulances, working our way along paths that mock description, we had at length the satisfaction of hearing the response to our calls; and before midnight the cases requiring immediate attention were safe in the hospitals, but some of them never to go forth again.

Amongst those left behind us at Yorktown, on the advance of the army, were Captain William Brown and Lieutenant Anderson of the 63d, and Lieutenant Powers of the 105th Pennsylvania. These officers were under my care until their removal to other places. On the 6th of May the parents of Captain Brown came from Pittsburg to take their son with them, if possible. After consultation with many physicians, and taking the best advice possible, his removal was deemed expedient, if not best for his recovery. He bore the trip to Fortress Monroe well, and rather improved on the steamer to Baltimore, and everything gave hope that he was recovering. The party reached Harrisburg on Saturday night, and resolved to remain for rest over Sabbath. Here the most unfavorable symptoms returned, and on the following Wednesday night he died.

Thus was taken away from us one of the most promising young men in the army. Singularly pure and correct in morals, kind and generous in spirit, conscientious in duty, the most affectionate of sons, his death was felt as a great loss by his company, and irreparable to his parents.

Lieutenant Anderson never recovered his strength, but after a return to his regiment for a few days he was again compelled to enter a hospital, and ultimately was borne home to Western Pennsylvania to die.

CHAPTER XI.

THE enemy had retreated from Yorktown to Williamsburg, a distance of fifteen miles. On the
highway leading from one town to the other, for
many miles we passed through the abandoned encampments of the enemy. Their destitution of all
the comforts of the camp was manifest, — without
tents, they had dug holes in the ground for shelter,
constructed villages and cities of booths, boughs of
trees being woven together, affording a protection
from the sunshine and the wind, but giving little
from the rain. The road was filled with broken
wagons, abandoned ambulances, and all the *débris*
of a retreating army.

A very heavy rain-storm fell on us during the
night of the 4th, — this had to be endured as best
we could. On the following day, the 5th, the storm
continued with even greater violence, until the
wagons of the army, containing commissary stores
and ammunition, sank so deeply in the mud, that
for miles the whole army train remained motionless,
and it became impossible to move forward our sup-

plies. About two o'clock in the afternoon of Monday, a very heavy cannonading commenced in our front, about two miles east of Williamsburg. General Hooker, leading the advance, found the enemy posted at Lee's Mill. After a few minutes' engagement they retreated, falling back into the forest. General Hooker advanced, and found the enemy more strongly posted. Now commenced the action of Williamsburg. We had to pass over a narrow strip of land, — on either side were creeks, and their flats and swamps, and between these marshes was a narrow neck of land, along which we were compelled to march, in order to reach the open fields in front of Williamsburg.

Fort Magruder, constructed by the enemy, commanded this road, — hence the fierceness and long continuance of the battle, our army having to debouch from so narrow a way. The enemy brought up 15,000 or 20,000 men to oppose Hooker's division of not more than 8,000 or 9,000. This general here exhibited that pluck and indomitable courage which have since won for him the highest position in the American Army. For hours he resisted the overwhelming odds, and held his own. It remains one of the mysteries yet to be explained why he was not reinforced in the early part of the engagement, — why was he left to struggle alone ? As soon as possible, however, Kearney and Heintzleman pushed forward to his support; and now Kearney performed one of those brilliant feats which made him the model soldier of his division. In order to disclose to his troops the concealed position of the enemy, and to exhaust their fire, he announced his

14

determination to ride in front of the enemy's lines. Surrounded by his aids and officers he dashed out into the open field, and as if on parade, leisurely galloped along the entire front. Five thousand guns were pointed at him, the balls fell around him like hail, two of his aids dropped dead at his side, and before he reached the end he was almost alone. He secured by this hazardous exploit what he aimed to accomplish, the uncovering of the enemy's position, —then riding back amongst his men he shouted, "You see, my boys, where to fire!" His forces held their own until Hancock, by a flank movement, compelled the retreat of the enemy within their works.

All the soldiers and officers of this portion of the army not only spoke of Hooker and Kearney as displaying, on that day, the most brilliant soldierly qualities, but likewise commended in the highest terms the coolness, discrimination, and courage of General Heintzleman.

During the night of the 5th the enemy left their works, and commenced their retreat towards Richmond, carrying with them most of their guns, and abandoning but few by the way. But that night in the history of the Army of the Potomac is never forgotten by the soldier. After many hours of ceaseless marching and battle, they found themselves, having been run at double-quick many miles, exposed to a most unpitying storm, standing in many places knee deep in the water, without food and without fire, and all night under arms. They remember this as the hour of the greatest suffering in the Peninsular campaign.

On the following morning our army marched through Williamsburg. I have often heard our soldiers speak of the ghastliness of the spectacle, as they saw along the road, and over the field of battle, hundreds of dead strewn in every direction, trampled on, mangled, half-buried in mud; great numbers of wounded still lying on the field, beckoning with the hand, and pleading with piteous moans for help; hundreds of dead and dying horses lay scattered through the field; while broken carriages and abandoned guns added another feature to the scene.

And here was one of those never-to-be-forgotten things which a soldier bears in his heart as the mementoes of battle,—lying in the road, with upturned face, as if gazing into the heavens, was a dead soldier, the lower half of his body buried in mud. The storm of the night had washed his face; it was strikingly beautiful, like that of a lovely woman; a smile as of the sweetest peace lingered on the face of death. That calm, angel-like expression in such a scene struck every passing soldier with wonder. Hundreds stopped and looked,— many said that he died dreaming of his mother, that his last moments were cheered by the presence of angels. I have heard many soldiers speak of this as one of the most affecting incidents of battle.

I have before said that I was not with the army at the time of our advance on Williamsburg, but remained in charge of the sick, and to see to their removal from the hospitals in the field to Yorktown. When this work was completed, on the 12th of May, I started in pursuit of the army, and on the evening of that day reached Williamsburg. This I found to be one of the most interesting towns in Virginia. Captain John Smith laid the foundation of James-town in the year 1607; and this was, for upwards of eighty years, the centre of influence and authority in the colony. But in the year 1697 the principal officers of the government removed to Williamsburg, which is four miles from Jamestown. Of Jamestown nothing now remains but the tower of an ancient church, and some broken walls. Williamsburg was chosen as the capital of the colony on account of the greater healthfulness of the atmosphere. It contains some of the most interesting historic monuments in the State; amongst others the college of William and Mary. This institution was founded by King William and his Queen Mary, and endowed by them with a thousand acres of land, with duties on fur and skins, and one penny per pound on all tobacco ex-ported from Maryland and Virginia. What adds to the interest of this institution is, that many of the most distinguished of Virginia's sons, such as Wash-ington, Patrick Henry, Jefferson, and Madison, were educated within its walls. The building itself, and many ancient monuments about it, and houses of the olden style, give to the place a peculiarly Eng-lish aspect. On a beautiful square fronting the col-lege stands the statue of Lord Botetourts, one of the colonial governors; and though considerably muti-lated, it still presents a fine specimen of sculpture. He appears in the flowing robe of his day, with a short sword by his side. The inscription on the pedestal of the monument reads:

"The Right Honorable Norborne Berkley, Baron de Botetourts, His Majesty's late Lieutenant and

Governor-general of the Colony and Dominion of Virginia. Deeply impressed with the warmest sense of gratitude for his excellencies, prudent and wise administration, and that the remembrance of those many public and social virtues which so eminently adorned his illustrious character might be transmitted to posterity, the General Assembly of Virginia, on the 20th day of July, Anno Domini 1771, resolved, with one united voice, to erect this statue to his Lordship's memory. Let wisdom and justice preside in any country, and the people must and will be happy."

Of the old capitol in which Patrick Henry began his brilliant career as the great orator of Virginia, nothing now remains but a few scattered bricks. It was in this same building that Washington, after closing his career in the French and Indian War, was complimented by the Speaker of the House of Burgesses for his valor, and for the honor he had conferred upon his native State. Stammering and confused, Washington stood in the presence of the venerable aristocracy, and was greatly relieved by the adroit exclamation of the Speaker: "Sit down, Mr. Washington; your modesty is equal to your valor, and that surpasses the power of any language that I possess."

The first newspaper published in Virginia was issued at Williamsburg, in the year 1736. It was a sheet twelve inches long and six inches wide. This was continued until the commencement of the Revolution.

In the year 1671, Sir William Berkley, the Governor of Virginia, thanked God that there were no

14 *

free schools and printing presses in Virginia, and hoped that these should not be known for a hundred years to come; and, accordingly, put down the first printing press established in that State, which was in the year 1682.

Of the old State House nothing now remains. It was accidentally burnt at the close of the Revolution.

Amongst the most interesting monuments of the past, I found the old English church, where lie entombed many of the early governors, judges, and military captains who lived and died prior to the Revolution. This church had been occupied as an hospital; the seats torn up, and beds, cots, and stretchers extended over the whole building; and across the floor in every direction had run streams of blood. Into this had been gathered, after the battle of Williamsburg, great numbers of the wounded and dying of the rebel army: outside of the church, on the grounds amidst the monuments and tents, the wounded had all been placed, and every spot was baptized with blood, and even on the white slabs were the traces of human suffering. Those that survived the first few days were removed by our surgeons and officers to the college and other buildings of the city.

In this graveyard and the church are some of the most ancient monuments seen in the State. One of them, a slab in the wall of the church, struck me as being peculiarly rich, and therefore I transcribed it.

"Near this monument lies the body of the Honorable David Parke, of ye County of Essex, Esq., who was of the magistrates of the county, eleven years, and sometime Secretary of the dominion of Virginia. He dyed ye 6th of March, Anno Domini 1679. His

other felecityes weare crowned by his happy mar-
ridge with Rebecca, the daughter of George Evelyn,
of the co. of Surry, Esq.   She dyed ye 2nd day of
Jan., Anno 1672, at Long Diton, co. Surry, and left
behind her a most hopeful progeny."

There were great numbers of Confederate officers
and soldiers lying in the college and in the churches
of the city. „Our own wounded men, except those
whose condition forbade the hope of recovery, were
generally removed, having been taken to Yorktown
and Fortress Monroe. But from motives of humanity many of the Confederate wounded were permitted to remain by our government, their negroes attending them, and very often being nursed by their
mothers and sisters.   The majority of the wounded
were from South Carolina and Alabama. I received
here the impression, which subsequent events confirmed, that the troops from Alabama were amongst
the bravest and most humane in the Confederate
Army.

I found one Herculean specimen of the South-
west, a non-commissioned officer, in the college hospital, attending a wounded and dying brother. This
brother, shot through the lungs, he had borne in his
arms from the field of battle, and rather than leave
him had become a prisoner. As soon as he found
that I was a clergyman, he begged me with tears to
go to the side of the wounded man, prepare him to
die, and pray with him. I did so, and received very
satisfactory replies from the dying brother, and found
that it was no new thing for him to think of God and
the destiny of his soul. At his own request I prayed
with him, and he urged me to return to him during

that day. The gratitude of his attending brother to our surgeons and officers was unbounded. He said he knew not how he could ever lift his gun against us again.

In other wards of the college, I saw many officers and soldiers of the Confederate Army, attended mostly by our surgeons and nurses; and they uniformly expressed their astonishment at the generosity and humanity with which they were treated. I could not but contrast, subsequently, the cruel treatment and close confinement of our surgeons when taken prisoners, with the full license of activity and enjoyment given to the Rebel surgeons when prisoners at Williamsburg. They were permitted to go where they pleased within our lines: to wander without restraint in the streets: they boarded wherever they wished, kept their servants and horses, and nothing was withheld from them that was thought to be essential for the comfort and recovery of their wounded.

I heard of not a single case of inhumanity; they had full liberty of speech; and the secession ladies of Williamsburg treated our soldiers and officers with indecent rudeness, and yet there was no utterance on our part of violence or revenge. I heard of but one act of brutal violence, inflicted on a widow and her daughter by a colored servant of one of the New York regiments. When caught, he was compelled to dig his own grave, and was shot while kneeling in it.

The scenes described to me by eye-witnesses of the departure of many families from Williamsburg, when they became aware of the retreat of their army from Yorktown, were deeply affecting, and worthy of the pencil of the painter. Families without horses or carriages, impelled by the fear of one or two members of the household, arose and fled to the streets, and were seen in scattered groups all along the highways. The young helping the aged, mothers and fathers bearing little children in their arms, the elder children carrying little bundles of such things as they could bear, and the slaves unwillingly assisting in the flight. Where carriages or wagons could be obtained, they were busily filled with the things that were thought to be most useful, and in the wildest haste they hurried out of the place to a spot of imagined safety.

Old persons were seen in the way, who, having been conducted by their slaves a short distance, were abandoned; and mothers and children fled until darkness and weariness arrested them. Many of them expected that our soldiers would perpetrate the greatest outrages, and commit murder in every house they entered. One lady, the wife of a Rebel officer at Williamsburg, who had spent years in the North, exerted all her influence to induce the citizens of Williamsburg to remain in their homes, assuring them "that she much more feared their soldiers than the Yankees;" telling them that she was not afraid to ride along through the entire Federal Army. These assurances influenced many of the more respectable families to remain, but probably more than one-half of the inhabitants fled.

The city of Williamsburg itself, with its old aristocratic dwellings and antique structure, its public buildings, its English look, with its houses embowered with vines and roses, is one of the most charm-

ing places in the Old Dominion. The country around
it is in a high state of cultivation, and **very** beautiful,
strikingly in contrast with the dismal regions through
which we passed coming from Yorktown. I delayed
longer at Williamsburg on account of the danger
attending travel in the van of our army. Guerilla
bands swarmed along the roads, ready to shoot down,
without a moment's warning, any unprotected officers or soldiers. I left on Wednesday morning, the
14th of May, and travelled along the road leading
to New Kent and Richmond. I went in connection
with a large train of ambulances of Sedgwick's division of the army, which were ordered to follow our
forces and pick up the wounded and sick that might
be found by the way. This day we travelled over a
country much superior to any part of the Peninsula
I had yet seen, except a tract of land lying around
Hampton and Williamsburg. Most of the families
had fled from their homes, and their houses were
occupied with our sick men, who had dropped out
of the ranks by the way. At these houses we invariably halted, and removed our disabled soldiers to
the ambulances. In one of these houses was lying
Colonel Wilson, of Beaver, Pennsylvania, very ill
with typhoid fever. The family of this house, however, had remained and were very kind, rendering
it unnecessary and certainly inexpedient to remove
him. Two weeks subsequent to this he died, an
officer of much merit and true patriotism.

I had as my companion in travel Doctor B., of
New York, a very young man, who, from one of the
most aristocratic families, was now enduring the
severest trials and dangers of the army. He had

been partially educated in Europe, and had spent three or four years in a German university. Our conversations of the day brought out the fact, that though so young there had been bitter passages in his life.

"Do you think, doctor," said he, "that it is ever right to kill a man, except in self-defence?"

"Yes," I replied, "if he is the enemy of your country, and as such appearing on the field of battle, he forfeits his life."

"But," said he, "is it right to kill a man that slanders you, insults you, and takes every means to lead to a quarrel, that he may shoot you?"

"No," I replied, "the law of the Great Master is, 'Resist not evil, but whosover shall smite thee on thy right cheek, turn to him the other also,' 'Love your enemies,' 'Bless them that curse you,' 'Do good to them that hate you.'"

"Well," said he, "that law may do very well for men like you, but if not in fact, in thought and feeling, it is constantly violated by the world. I feel more interested in this, because I was so unfortunate as to have myself a duel in Germany. The man was a miserable brute, and far exceeded me in strength, and took every measure in his power to kill me or drive me from the University as a coward and a spotted man. I fought with and killed him, and my conscience has never troubled me for the act, and I would certainly do it again. I repeat every Sabbath morning, as I go to church with my mother, the prayer of the Episcopal service, 'O Lord! have mercy upon us, miserable sinners;' and amongst all my sins that rise up at such an hour, that does not appear. I regret that I had to kill the scoundrel, but it was his fault, and not mine. He had made up his mind to take my life, and God helped me to take his; he went to his own place, and I am in mine; and I hope I will be no less faithful to my country, no less honorable and virtuous, because I was so unfortunate as to kill a bad man in a duel."

I replied to this: "The man whom you shot, doctor, was undoubtedly one of those gross, cruel monsters whom we often meet, but whom, vile as they are, God permits to live; and I do not think that any insult can justify you in taking the life of a fellow-creature. You know that our passions oftentimes blind our reason, and silence our consciences; and because you feel no remorse, you ought not, therefore, to rest assured that God does not hold you guilty of that man's blood. No doubt, at some point in the controversy you greatly sinned, and will find, in review of the whole case, and more especially as you summon up the principles that then governed your life, that you have reason to use the penitent petition of David: 'O Lord! deliver me from blood-guiltiness.'"

"Well," said the doctor, heaving a deep sigh, "I have not felt it yet, but if it is necessary that I should, I hope I shall before I die."

Here the conversation on this point ended, and we soon found it necessary to shelter ourselves in a house by the roadside from a violent thunder-storm; and here we found an old lady and her son, the only occupants, with the old story of negroes gone, horses stolen, fences burnt, and cattle driven away.

We reached New Kent Court House about dark.

The storm continued for many days, until the roads became impassable; and at every movement we made we had to halt for hours, until the pioneers covered the entire road with the trunks of trees. We encamped, after leaving New Kent, for some days on the Pamunky, at New Cumberland, about ten miles from the White House. From New Cumberland the whole army marched to Baltimore Cross-roads. Here we halted and encamped, waiting for the falling of the streams, the bringing up of supplies, and the repairing of the York River railroad.

15

CHAPTER XII.

WHILE we were in camp at New Cumberland, on the Pamunky, Colonel Hays resolved to send me back to Yorktown to report the state of the sick men whom we had left behind, and to bring up such as were fit for duty. I went down in a Government steamer, and found, when I reached Yorktown, that the mortality had been far less, from the serious character of their sickness, than I had been led to apprehend.

The sick in the Army of the Potomac, at this time, was certainly not less than 15,000 men; the wounded in battle were not fewer than 1,500. Of the sick and disabled, between 5,000 and 6,000 had been brought into Yorktown; the others were taken to Fortress Monroe and Newport News. Even before leaving Yorktown some of our regiments had suffered incredibly from sickness; and in the advance on Williamsburg some had left half, and often two-thirds, of their members behind in the hospitals. The surgeon of the 92d New York Regiment, Dr. Mansfield, to whom many thousands of the sick of the army are under the deepest sense of gratitude, told me that his regiment left the city of Albany, on the 1st of March, 1862, 850 strong, and now it could bring into the field only 196 men. I found that wherever there had been causes in the regiments to dishearten the men, from the loss of officers, or the absence of discipline, they were much more liable to sickness than in those regiments where the spirit of the officers infused life and unity into the whole. There had been wrought, during my absence from Yorktown, a very great improvement; the streets had been cleaned, the rubbish burned, the pools drained, the houses whitewashed, and a great number of contrabands were constantly at work to clear away everything calculated to generate disease. The presence of such a wise and active officer as General Van Vleit was manifest in every department. The sick had been kindly and assiduously tended by such surgeons as Drs. Greenleaf, Mansfield, Heighhold, and Munson. Miss Dix was likewise there, ministering with a thousand charities to the relief of those whom many pitied, but few could reach. I found that some whom I had left apparently dying had so far recovered as to be out of danger.

During the time that I was there, there occurred one of those singular things attending the breaking up of society by war. Passing by the old jail of Yorktown, I heard the plaintive wail of many voices singing as in some funeral service. I saw standing at the windows a group of officers and soldiers looking in and listening. As I approached, the throng made way for me, and I drew near the iron-barred window and looked through. Within I saw forty or fifty negroes, men, women, and children, some leaning against the walls, others crouching, and others seated on the floor.   All were united in singing one of the hymns which belong to the sacred literature of the negro.   The leader of the company, a man about forty, perfectly black, gave out the hymn, which he sang in a plaintive minor, until all voices joined in a full, generous swell on the chorus. In all the slave assemblies for worship I discovered that though the leader might be a young man, he always assumed the tremulous tones of an old patriarch, — the solemn plaintiveness of age entering into all the negro's conceptions of eloquence and piety. With a richness of melody I had never heard excelled, they sang their celebrated hymn :

> "O! I want to die, and go home to heaven
>   In the morning."

This brought up vividly to me some aged African, going forth from his cabin in the morning, listening to the thousand melodies of field and forest, scenting the fragrance of nature, looking with admiring eyes on the myriad gems and diamonds glittering on grass and leaf, seeing the glow and beauty of the heavens, and feeling the sunshine falling into his face as if gently kissing him, — in such a scene lifting his eyes to heaven, and turning into song the meditations of the moment:

> "I long to go to heaven in the morning."

Heaven, as an endless morning; where the flowers would ever breathe out their odors of sweetness; where the sun would never smite him; where the glory and beauty would never fade; where he should

be young again, the eye bright, the hand strong, and
the knee never tremble ; where he should ever join
in the chorus :

> "Oh! it is the morning of the Lord!
> It is the morning of the Lord!" *

After this song was sung, they all kneeled on the
floor, — the leader prayed in language which appeared to have been very intelligible to his fellow
slaves, for it brought forth a multitude of cries of
"Hosanna! Praise the Lord!" and many were the
tears that rolled down those sable faces. Often in this
prayer the meaning was lost in the strangest and
most incongruous association of Scripture phrases
and scraps of hymns. After the prayer was over I
spoke to the leader, and asked him why they were
in prison, what crime they had been guilty of? He
told me they had been guilty of no crime; that they
were charged with shooting our pickets; "but,"
said he, "massa, it not us."

I then inquired further, and learned from the officers near me that some of our men had been shot on
the roads and in the forests between Yorktown and
Williamsburg; that some white men had directed
the attention of our officers to these negroes; and in
the houses they occupied were found some broken
swords, shattered guns, and bayonets. These slaves
had been left behind by their masters on plantations
near to Williamsburg, on York River, — and after
the battle of Williamsburg the soldiers of our army
had gone to their huts to purchase milk and butter,

---

* Appendix.

15 *

and had advised these almost naked negroes to go forth into the battle-field and pick up the shovels, blankets, and overcoats which had been thrown away, and also to gather up the abandoned muskets, which might at some future day be valuable to them. The negroes, guided by the soldiers, went into the field, and collected various articles; and without knowing how to load or shoot a gun, having never shot one in their lives, some malicious persons had suspicion directed to them; their houses were searched, and guns found; hence their transfer, until the circumstances could be investigated, to the jail at Yorktown. And here the poor, ignorant creatures, thinking that they had no defenders, and concluding that some morning they would all be led forth to be shot or hung, were making deliberate preparations to die.

I assured them that, if innocent, they had no reason to fear; that our officers would be as just and as merciful to them as to white men. "But," said I, "is it possible that you could be guilty of so great a crime as shooting our men, when they had never done you any harm, and were your friends?"

"No, massa," they all exclaimed together, "no, no, massa, we no tell which end ob de gun bullet go out; no shoot a thing as big as massa's big barn; massa neber allow shoot gun, or carry knife, 'scept one broken blade. No, massa, de oberseers dey kill your men; they lie in bush to shoot de soldier."

I then assured them that, if innocent, they would soon be acquitted, and sent back to their homes. They smiled and looked cheerful for a moment, but the gravity soon returned; and feeling "dat white man bery uncertain," and that they had better make use of the day given them, they recommenced their hymns, and poured forth more prayers for peace in death. What became of them I never learned; but they were, doubtless, acquitted, or I should have heard of their condemnation.

When I returned from Yorktown I found that the army had removed from Cumberland Landing to Baltimore Cross-roads, about eight miles from Cumberland, and five miles from the White House. I landed at the White House, and found more than a hundred vessels, transports, and steamers lying in the river at this place. No one who is not familiar with a great army can have any conception of the vastness of the expenditure of labor essential to feed it.

The White House, standing on the elevation of fifty feet above the waters, is of especial interest, because the property of the Rebel General Lee. It has likewise some romantic interest. Here General Washington met, in the year 1758, Mrs. Custis, who afterwards became his wife.

I landed at the White House, on my return from Yorktown, under the impression that our entire army was in the immediate neighborhood. Here I learned that General McClellan had removed his head-quarters four miles on the Mechanicsville road towards Richmond; and after making diligent inquiry of a thousand persons, I could learn nothing definite or satisfactory in regard to the position of General Kearney's division. I went to various distinguished officers, and received from them the most contradictory "beliefs" as to where was pitched the

head-quarters of General Heintzleman's army corps.
Knowing the danger of plunging out into a great
army, and that I might go to and fro with as much
uncertainty of finding my division as has a wandering Arab in the desert in search of his tribe, I resolved to go to General McClellan's head-quarters;
but arrived just in season to see the general and his
staff depart for Mechanicsville. I determined to follow, and after reaching head-quarters, learned of
General Williams that General Kearney was upon
the left wing of the army at Baltimore Cross-roads,
and would cross the Chickahominy at Bottom Bridge,
and that I was fully fifteen miles from my regiment.
And here I may pause for a moment to bear testimony to the uniform courtesy of this excellent officer, who bore into the army and never lost the ur-
banity of a true gentleman, and the patient kindness
of a Christian.

I found shelter for the night in a farm-house; as
usual, there was a weeping woman, whose husband
was in the Rebel army, with half a dozen small children, a home without comforts, and negroes all gone.
In the same house lay sick a Hungarian captain of
General Sykes's division, who had been brought in
during the day very ill with a fever; and far away
from his native country, he recounted to me the battles he had fought for liberty in his own land; and
he expressed his great fear that he might die in a
hospital, and not have the honor of meeting death
on the field of battle. He had all the air of a man
of gentle blood, and was evidently of superior culture. Having devoted his life to the cause of liberty
in the whole world, when driven out of Hungary

he drew his sword in defence of those principles which he had been educated to revere.

I satisfied myself, while here with the right wing of the army, that there was far less sickness amongst these regiments than in those of the left wing.

There came up before dark one of those tropical thunder-storms which cause almost all the soldiers to remember the Peninsula as a land of flood and fire. On the following day, after long and weary wanderings, and being lost innumerable times in swamp and jungle, I reached General Kearney's division at Baltimore Cross-roads, and found the army in motion towards the Chickahominy. On the following Sunday we crossed this river at Bottom Bridge. This renowned stream, in most places, has scarcely any perceptible flow, but spreads itself out in wide swamps, and flows around innumerable islands, but here and there is contracted into a stream from fifty to seventy yards wide. The country through which we passed had many very fine farms and magnificent dwelling-houses; and these, generally abandoned, were in the course of a little while filled with the sick of the army. Some of the most aristocratic families in Virginia had their homes in this section of the Peninsula. The fields were covered with excellent wheat, now in full head, the corn was knee high, and the fruits were ripening on some trees in the orchards. But in the progress of the army the fences were all broken down and consumed, — a single night of encampment converted beautiful plantations into a desert.

The lands beyond the Chickahominy were poor, and more exhausted than any we had passed over.

The general aspect of the country was that of a land which, by poor cultivation, had been worn out, and was finally abandoned to the pine, the briar, and the stunted oak.   It is a peculiarity of that part of Virginia over which the Army of the Potomac passed, that the pine comes up abundantly on all the exhausted fields, and soon overshadows them, so that a ray of light seldom penetrates the gloom.   This is the effort of Nature to restore what man has destroyed.   The pine and the cedar are rarely found in the original forests of Virginia, but spring up in consequence of the abstraction, by tobacco, of certain vital elements in the soil, and these can only be restored under the leafy shadow ; and therefore Providence plants the million pines which kindly shelter and enrich what man has impoverished.   Thus is frequently seen in Virginia on one side of the road the original forest, extending many miles without a single pine-tree, and on the other side a heavy forest of dark evergreens, in which not a single tree of any other description is permitted to grow.   This is accounted for on the principle I have mentioned, — the pine covers the exhausted fields of a former generation.

We reached the banks of the Chickahominy on Saturday morning, the 24th of May; and while our men were standing in an open, muddy field, waiting for the order to advance, there came upon us one of those thunder-storms which deluge the Peninsula, and turn the entire country into a vast swamp.

The army was ordered, on Sunday morning, to advance beyond the river.   We had expected that the enemy would await us in strongly intrenched positions on the heights beyond the bottom of the river; but on our advance they removed their guns, and retired to Richmond. The order for striking our tents came to us very early on Sabbath morning. As it was evident that we could not have any religious services, I went to Colonel Hays and requested permission to ride back to Baltimore Crossroads, a distance of ten miles, and report the condition of the sick men whom we had left there. This was most cheerfully granted. On my way I had to pass by the head-quarters of General Kearney. He was standing at the door of the house he occupied. I saluted him.

"Where, chaplain, where?"

"To the rear, general, to see after the sick men we left behind."

The sternness of his face relaxed in a moment. He advanced a step. "All right, sir, all right, call and report to me on your return."

I bowed, and rode on. Previously to this time I had had no acquaintance with the general. I could not tell how he knew me to be a chaplain, except from the peculiar clerical gravity of my horse, which never so lost his dignity as to put on any war-horse prancings or curvetings, but who preferred a quiet and even tenor, and frequent friendly halts for greetings by the way.

The perils of this journey are incredible to one who has not been on the Chickahominy at this season. The nature of the country, the narrowness of the causeways, and the density of the forests, compelled the army to move over the roads, however bad. The bogs, sloughs, and sluggish streams had been covered

with logs and branches of trees, but these had been
torn up and thrown into all the bristling positions
of a *chevaux-de-frise* by our heavy wagons and artillery. In some places, as far as the eye could reach
there was an endless succession of horrors. Here a
great gully lay directly across our way, and invited
us to fathom its unknown depths. On the left a
broken wagon, whose fore-wheels had entirely disappeared, gave us warning that there were no sound-
ings in that neighborhood; on the right a dead
horse standing upright amid the roots of a stump,
the mud covering all the back part of his body, told
us of the dangers there. In the bog before us there
were various objects, so encased in mud that it was
impossible to tell what they were, — they might be
logs of wood, heads of horses, feet of mules, or bodies
of men.

After an incredible struggle my panting, trembling horse stood with his fore-feet on the slippery
bank, and his hind parts gradually sinking out of
sight. There was great danger that he would be
added to the monuments of that scene; I encouraged
him to another effort, and after two or three falls on
his knees he reached the top of the bank. Before
us now stretched a long river of mud; the timber
used in corduroying was afloat, and rolled beneath
the feet of my horse; sometimes he would fall between these, and then there was the greatest danger.
Dead horses and mules were lying, some half buried
and others floating, every few rods. One poor horse
was still alive, so covered with mud that his color could
not be told; he had fallen down, and unable to go
further, had been shot by his brutal driver. The

blood was trickling down from the wound in his head, and staining the mud; but his sufferings had not extinguished the gnawings of hunger, for the poor animal was biting little pieces of the bark of a tree beside him.   A little further on a sutler's wagon had been engulfed, the goods thrown out, and they were in such a condition that no one stopped to pick up the sweet cakes, tobacco, and cheese.   All the *débris* of an army was there, broken boxes of crackers, abandoned tents, ambulances, and wagons.

After passing through these heavy forests, I emerged into the green fields at Baltimore Cross-roads.   At all the houses for miles around, and in the barns and stables, had been left our sick men. As yet there was no provision made for sending the sick of the army to the White House.   I rode to the place where I saw tents in the field, and learned that the sick were to be gathered from all these places and sent to a particular house.   On re-pairing to this house I found a young surgeon, having under his care some three or four hundred patients. The men were extremely despondent, the place was lonely and out of the way, the army having gone, and they felt like those abandoned on a desert island. The hospital was in one of the large country houses, surrounded by a great number of outhouses, built without any definite plan.   In these houses, and in tents and barns, were lying the sick, in all stages of disease.   During the day all those who had been scat-tered over miles were gathered in.   I returned the same day a part of the way, taking the long bridge road, which carried me almost to the pickets of the enemy, but I escaped the dangers of the army road.

16

The following morning I reached our encampment
beyond the Chickahominy, and was gratified to learn
that we were within ten miles of Richmond.   I could
not find the head-quarters of General Kearney, and
therefore reported to General Jamison the condition
of the sick of his brigade left behind, and requested
that he would take measures to send back nurses
and hospital stores.

Very soon after General Jamison rode to the head-
quarters of General Kearney, and reported to him
my statement.   In a few moments an orderly came
into our camp, bearing a request from General Kearney "that Chaplain Marks should report himself at
his tent."   I confess I rode to his head-quarters with
many misgivings, for I had not reported, as commanded, to the general himself.   When I came up
to his tent door, I was ushered into his presence by
an orderly, — his face was frowning.

"How is it, sir," said he, "that you did not report
to me in person?"

"Excuse me, general," I said, "I did not think
my report of sufficient consequence to authorize me
to trouble you with it; and I designed, as soon as I
could find your head-quarters, to report to you in
person; but in the meantime meeting General Jamison, I reported to him the condition of the sick in
his brigade."

"Well," said he, "you reported that sick men in
my division were lying in the woods and in tents, a
long distance from any house, without any medical
attendance or nurses, and no one had looked after
them since we left: is that so, sir?"

"Yes, sir."

"Why, sir, did you bring back a report so calcu-lated to demoralize and dishearten the army?"

"I reported to none but General Jamison, and that with the purpose of having sent back to them medicines, nurses, and hospital supplies, and, if it was best, to go back myself."

"Well, sir, why did you not remain there, and bring in all those sick men? how did you dare to come away and leave them?"

"Sir," I replied, "I saw the last man brought in before I left; every man from the fields and woods was in the hospital."

"Well, sir," relaxing a little, "you must obey orders. Say nothing about this in camp, chaplain: everything relating to my sick men touches my heart. I'll have occasion for you again. Chaplain, now go; but hereafter obey orders."

I bowed and left the tent. From that hour General Kearney was my warmest friend, and invariably treated me with the greatest kindness.

On the next morning I received an order from the general regularly detailing me to take charge of such sick in the hospitals as had to be removed to the White House, and to take measures to obtain for them in all the hospitals such sanitary stores as could be reached.

The expectation began to be universal, that at the very first hour possible an advance would be ordered, and therefore preparations were made to send away all the sick in the hospitals on the field; and on the Monday previous to the battle of Fair Oaks the order came down from head-quarters to move all the sick of the camp-hospitals to the White House.

The arrangement was made to send the sick of Kearney's and Hooker's divisions to Meadow Station, about one mile east of Savage Station. The surgeons were generally satisfied with seeing the sick placed in the ambulances, and sent with them no nurses and often no food. They were brought to the station, and placed upon the porticoes and under cover of the building: a great number arrived, and soon under every green tree were lying sick men. Many of these were in the delirium of fever, giving commands, standing guard, marching on the enemy, and talking to their friends at home. Others were apparently in the last stages of sickness. Many were constantly crying for water, many begging for medicines, and others beseeching me to write to their friends. To all these it was necessary, in various ways, to give attention. The porticoes around the station were from four to six feet above the ground; and there had to be a constant care lest the trembling, staggering men, or those tossing with fever, should fall and be seriously injured. We had expected to be taken from this place in two or three hours, but the cars on this road were in such demand to transport troops, ammunition, and forage, that the conductors refused to halt long enough to place the sick men on board. Hence we remained two days at this station. The sufferings of the men the first few hours after their removal were very great; the fatigue, the joltings on the rough roads, the anxiety, all increased their miseries, and caused many to pray for death.

In the course of two days we had them all removed to the White House. At this place, in one of the great fields, was pitched a city of hospital tents. The location of these was most ill-advised; for the ground was swampy, the water lying much of the time upon the surface. Many of the tents were without floors, and the men suffered much from dampness. This locality was the more inexcusable, for there was an excellent position for the tents around the White House: here the grounds were high, well drained, and covered with grass, and the whole surface protected by shade-trees. No more genial and delightful spot could be selected near the Pamunky than the grounds around General Lee's house. But for some unexplained reason a boggy field was chosen for the hospital tents, and guards were stationed at every gate of the White House, allowing no one to enter the premises.

In one of these journeys from hospital to hospital I came across a garden near an abandoned farmhouse, not far from Dispatch Station, and discovered under the shadow of the evergreens, in the now open ground, several fresh graves. These were of soldiers who had died of fever; and their companions had marked on a neat board, put to the head of each, his name, regiment, and time of death; and sometimes the words which followed were: "He died in hope;" "He rests in peace;" "He sleeps until a better morning;" "He fell asleep far from home, but in the Lord."

About this time I received the following letter from General Kearney, which I introduce here as an illustration of his watchful interest and care for the sick of his division, expressing as it does sentiments

16 *

of humanity which add to the glory of one of the bravest of our commanders.

[Copy.]

"Hd.-Qrs. 3d Division,
"Fair Oaks, *June* 15, '62. }

"Dear Sir : — I return you my grateful acknowledgments for your noble and energetic conduct in behalf of our poor sufferers of this division.

"From long experience in the field no one appreciates more sensibly the service you thus render to humanity and to our cause.

"If there has been one point, more than another, where I have hitherto laboriously, and conscientiously, and successfully fulfilled my duties as an officer, it has been in my solicitude for the sick and disabled. I am thankful to find in you a strong coadjutor; and when I am a little more free to separate myself from the cares of being on the spot to command in case of attack, I will ever be found a constant visitor of the hospitals.

· "Most respectfully, your obdt. svt.,

"P. Kearney, Br.-Gen'l.

"The Rev. Dr. Marks,
"Chaplain 63d Reg't Pa. Vols."

CHAPTER XIII.

Battle of Fair Oaks — Dash of General Longstreet on General
Casey's Division — Severity of the Contest — Severe Losses of
some Regiments — Scene on Saturday night at Savage Station
— Conversation with the Wounded and Dying — The Battle of
Sunday Morning.

I WAS returning from one of my journeys to the
White House, on Saturday, the 30th of May, when
the battle of Fair Oaks commenced. We had become accustomed to daily cannonading, to skirmishing, and picket firing; but this had a continuous
roar, and the heavy, crashing ring of a great engagement.

When I reached Despatch Station I learned that
a battle was then in progress. I stopped at our
encampment, but found that all of General Kearney's troops had been hurried up to the scene of
conflict.

I ran up the railroad towards the field of battle.
It was now three P. M.; and at Meadow Station, one
mile east of Savage Station, and two and a quarter
from Seven Pines, I began to meet the wounded
men, who, with broken arms, shattered fingers, and
flesh cuts, were wandering to the rear without any
definite purpose. They were mostly of General
Casey's division, and being disabled, when relieved

by Generals Kearney and Hooker they were at liberty to seek safety and surgical aid.

They uniformly represented that their picket-lines were not more than one-fourth of a mile in advance of their camp, and extended to the long swamp which stretched for miles on both sides of the railroad along our front, and that their pickets had been advanced as far as possible, most of the men standing in water, or on tufts of grass and briars above the bog.

That suddenly, while they were at dinner, the pickets commenced firing, the enemy having stolen up close to them, and followed the retreating men into the camp, and in a moment the cannon and musketry of the Rebels opened upon them; every way they looked long lines of their foes were rushing out of the woods into the open fields, and with wild, Indian-like shrieks were running towards them. Some of the regiments stood their ground around the camp until half of their number had fallen, all the horses of the batteries were killed, and the captured guns turned upon them; and even then they fell back but one hundred rods, and rallied in the bushes, and against overwhelming odds held the enemy in check.

And here, for three hours, less than 5,000 men held back 20,000; for the force of General Casey, at the commencement of the action, was not more than 6,000 men, and 1,000 were, in the first attack, placed *hors de combat;* and thus crippled, the division had to sustain this unequal contest for so long a time.

Many of the Confederate officers whom I met in

Richmond, and before it, uniformly spoke in the highest terms of the bravery of General Casey; and said that his troops fought as well as they had ever known fresh and undisciplined regiments, and that they met from them a far more vigorous resistance than they had anticipated.

They said that the position of General Casey was one of the greatest peril. Thrown in advance of Hooker and Kearney three miles, if they threw against him a large force it was almost impossible to reinforce him in season to prevent defeat. That they had expected to cut his division to pieces, and before reinforcements could possibly arrive, drive back the shattered regiments, to bear with them consternation and panic.

But so far from this being realized, the unyielding firmness of this division prevented their cutting through our left wing, capturing a part, and demoralizing the whole; for it held out against them until reinforcements came up. I was glad to hear them vindicated, and relieved from those charges which were so unjust and painful.

The first night after a battle is always full of indescribable horrors, men in their struggles throwing themselves into every position, the cries of those alongside of them complaining of the touch of their shattered limbs, others shrieking for water, many praying for death, and some begging a kind hand to lift them up once more.

During the entire night the wounded were brought in, until they covered the grounds around the house of Mr. Savage, and filled all the outhouses, barns, and sheds. Lying alongside of our wounded were many Confederate soldiers and officers; and to the honor of our men be it said, I heard no words of anger or reproach, but the rebels were uniformly treated as kindly as the Union soldiers.

All night the surgeons were occupied in amputations; and, in the circumstances, they found it impossible to look after those whose condition demanded immediately, to revive them, food and stimulants. Wounded men suffer greatly from cold, and shiver as in winter, or with an ague. It was therefore essential to lift them from the damp ground, and cover them as far as possible.

In the course of the evening twenty or thirty soldiers from different regiments, who had borne in upon their shoulders their wounded comrades, permitted me to organize them into a corps of nurses. Colonel McKelvy, than whom no man was more active for the relief of our men, furnished twenty bales of hay, a thousand blankets, and permitted me to draw on the Commissary Department for coffee, sugar, and crackers to an indefinite amount. The nurse-soldiers soon spread down this hay, and many a shivering, wounded man, when lifted from the damp earth, and placed upon the soft grass bed, with a blanket spread over him, poured out his gratitude in a thousand blessings. When this was done we followed with hot coffee, and found our way to every suffering man. Everywhere we were compelled to place our feet in streams of blood: one spectacle of anguish and agony only succeeded another. The mind was overwhelmed and benumbed by such scenes of accumulated misery. Where there was so much to be done, and where we could do so little, the temptation was to hurry away from such painful spectacles, and remember them only as the visions of a frightful dream. Great must be the cause which demands such a sacrifice. Here and there over the grounds were seen through that night a circle of lanterns waving around the tables of amputators. Every few moments there was a shriek of some poor fellow under the knife. And one after another the sufferers were brought forward and laid down before the surgeons on stretchers, each waiting his turn. And then again one with face as white as marble, and every line telling that he had passed through a suffering, the utmost which human nature could endure, was borne away and laid down for some kind-hearted man to pour into his lips a few drops of brandy, to lift up his head, and give him the assurance of life and sympathy. There a brother knelt and wept over a dying brother, and his voice, broken with sobs, begged me to come and pray that his brother might be able to see Jesus and depart in peace. There a father held up in his arms a dying son, and was receiving his last message to mother, sister, and brother; here a group of sympathizing soldiers stood around a dying companion who was loudly bewailing his early death, and that he should never see again his native hills. There four or five were holding in their strong arms one whose brain, having been pierced with a ball and deprived of reason, was strong in the frantic energy of madness; here a beckoning hand urged me to come, and at the sufferer's request sit down by his side, and tell him what he must do to be saved. Then was whispered a story of disobedience, of crime that now stung like a serpent and bit like an adder. Another begged me to come early in the morning, and write a line to father or wife. Others entreated that they should not be compelled to submit to the knife of the operator, but that their limbs might be spared them, for they felt sure that under the surgeon's hand they should die. Others begged that some board might bear their names and be placed at the head of their graves.

If I turned from these scenes on the open ground and entered into any of the houses, spots of blood stained the steps and the stairs. In the halls were lying alongside of each other many of the wounded and dead. The rooms were crowded with sufferers, broken and shattered in every conceivable way by the enginery of death. From the mouth of one was running a stream of blood; another was upheld in the arms of a friend and gasping for breath, and the deep and unnaturally bright eye told that all the energies of life were summoned to the struggle. One lying on the floor told by his loud snore of the injury done to the brain, and that he, in all probability, would never open his eyes; and another begged for help, that he might change his position and relieve the suffering of his shattered thigh.

"Night of nights! who can tell thy tales of woe?"

At one place where a wounded soldier was panting his last, I was summoned. He begged me to pray for him, and taking from his finger a gold ring, he asked me to send it to his wife, who had given it him on the day of their marriage, and now he wished it to be restored to her. In a few moments the last battle was fought, and the soldier was asleep. On examining the ring I found underneath the wrappings of a thread the initials "J. S. to C. B." This had been done to preserve the letters, and was the careful act of human love, anxious to preserve a sacred memento. In another group of sufferers I found a little boy apparently not more than twelve years of age; the long hair thrown back from a beautiful forehead, enabled me to see by the lantern light a very childlike face. His right leg had been amputated above his knee, and he was lying motionless and apparently breathless, and as white as snow. I bent over him, and put my fingers on his wrist, and discovered to my surprise the faint trembling of a pulse. I immediately said to my attendant: "Why, the child is alive!"

"Yes, sir," said he, opening his eyes, "I am alive; will you not send me to my mother?"

"And where is your mother," said I, "my child?"

"In Sumterville, South Carolina," he replied.

"Oh! yes, my son, we will certainly send you to your mother."

"Well, well," said he, "that is kind; I will go to sleep now."

Sabbath, June 1st. — It was understood that the battle would be renewed this morning; and with the first dawn of the day I saw Generals Keyes and Heintzleman leave the head-quarters of the latter at Savage Station. They rode, surrounded by their aids, across the field leading to the Williamsburg road. I had heard, during the night, that an hospital had been created about a mile from the Station towards the battle-field. I started to find it, and in a

17

short time reached the house, in and around which
were lying a multitude of our dying and wounded.
Several surgeons were there, amongst others Dr.
Rogers, to whom all accorded the praise of being
one of the most successful and humane of operators,
and Dr. Heighhold, one of the most active and humane surgeons in the army. Ambulances were here
removing the disabled to Savage Station. Mingled
with the great number of wounded were many dead,
who having been brought in, did not survive the
night.

Amongst the badly wounded was Joseph Bynon,
of Alleghany City, Pennsylvania, a young man of
the most generous nature, universally popular in
the regiment, and the hope and staff of a widowed
mother. He was lying on a blanket near the house,
wounded in the bowels. I asked him about his sufferings. He replied that he did not suffer much;
that he was faint from loss of blood, as he supposed.
I saw from his pulse that he had but a few moments
to live, and said to him :

"Joseph, are you willing and ready to die ? I am
afraid you cannot live."

"Well, doctor," he whispered, "I should like to
live ; I love my mother ; this will be a great sorrow
to her, and I should like to do something for my
little nephew and niece. But there is another life,
and I know I shall find my mother there. I feel
I have been a sinner ; in many things I have done
very wrong ; but ever since the conversion I experienced in Camp Johnson, I have tried to follow my
Saviour, and now I die trusting. My mind wan-
ders ; I find it difficult to think and speak ; in pray-

ing to God I may not say the things that are right; do, doctor, lift up my hands and clasp them together, and pray for me; I will follow you."

I lifted up the hands crimsoned with his own blood, and pressing them in mine, commended him to the Merciful One, who for us all had suffered the bitterness of death. He repeated word for word, prayed for his mother, and then said: "Oh! Lamb of God, who taketh away the sin of the world, take away my sin; into Thine hand I commend my spirit!"

He then left his blessing for his mother, his thanks to her for the toil and affection of the past, and thanking me for what I had done for him, he stopped exhausted, but his face became as tranquil as that of a little child. While I was yet talking with him, the rattle of musketry commenced near us, and in another moment a shell came shrieking over us. Instantly there was the call of "Men, to arms! fall into line!" General Heintzleman ordered his men to march through the orchards and enter the forest. The firing became more brisk, and was coming closer. All the stragglers, servants, ambulance drivers, some of the surgeons, and all the nurses, commenced a wild, pell-mell retreat. There were still many wounded men lying around; they begged not to be abandoned and left to the enemy.

Joseph Bynon called me to him, and said: "Doctor, do n't leave me."

"No, Joseph, you shall be removed before I leave."

I ran out to an omnibus then driving past, and commanded the driver to stop and take in all he

could carry. After much persuasion he drove up to
the gate. Just then Mr. William Grey, of Taunton,
Pennsylvania, drove up apparently as calm as in the
quietest march, and placed in the three ambulances
all the living lying at this spot. Joseph Bynon
died before he reached Savage Station, and was
buried under the shade of the apple-trees in the
orchard.

Our men were in line of battle about one hundred
yards in advance of this house, in the edge of the
forest. It was now about seven A. M. The firing
was very brisk and steady all along our front lines,
but having none of the regularity and continuous
roar of battle, but lively skirmishing. While I was
aiding the wounded into the ambulances, I heard
loud shouts to our right, and turned to look for the
cause. I saw coming out through the forest from
the railroad a large body of our troops. This was
General Sumner's corps, which had crossed the
Chickahominy on the previous evening, and reached
the right of our wing in season to prevent our right
flank being turned, and consequent defeat; and
now, with the true instinct of a loyal and brave commander, he was bringing his men to the scene of the
greatest danger.

I felt certain, when I saw this magnificent corps
move along with the steady step of veterans, that
the day was ours. As regiment after regiment passed
in front of our lines, with waving banners and music,
they were hailed and cheered with the loudest shouts.
They turned up the Williamsburg road, and were
immediately followed by General Heintzleman and
his corps. For a few moments there was the ominous

calm which often precedes battle. Taking advantage of this, I ran up along the Williamsburg road in pursuit of the army, and in a few moments reached our breastworks, which extended along our entire front from the Chickahominy to the White Oak Swamp. Our batteries were in position, and on the breastworks themselves were planted many field-pieces. Within the intrenchments was a long line of men, as far as the eye could reach, every man bending on his knee and resting his gun on the embankment, silent and motionless, intently looking for the enemy. The gunners stood around the cannon, equally alert and watchful.

In front of this line of intrenchments were open fields, extending two miles on each side of the road. The open ground in front of us was probably about one-fourth of a mile wide, and then again was interrupted by forests. On the opposite side of this field the enemy was posted, under the covert of the woods. After I had passed out of the intrenchments, and gone beyond the first field batteries, I saw the troops of General Sumner's corps and those of General Heintzleman, under General Hooker, march into the field, deploying to the right and left, and with a steady quick step they commenced advancing on the enemy. Before they reached the centre of the field, their march became double-quick: continually firing as they ran, they dashed forward on the enemy. Occasionally I could see a gap in our lines following the thunder of some field-pieces, but in a moment this was not perceptible, and the men were marching on as brisk as ever. Very soon our troops reached the edge of the forest, and I trembled in apprehen-

17 *

sion of the sanguinary contest; but nothing could resist the energy and determination of our soldiers. The struggle was but for a moment, and the tide of battle rolled into the forest, and our front line was lost to the view, except an occasional gleam of arms that came out from the openings amongst the trees. Then the din, and the clash, and the roar went up into the heavens more distinctly from the field beyond. By climbing into the trees we could see the enemy pushed back into the swamps, and gradually the rattle of musketry ceased: we heard only the cannon firing on the retreating foe. There is no doubt of the truth of the statement often made, that the enemy on this day were thoroughly defeated, and that it was possible for us to have taken Richmond. The Rebel soldiers rushed into Richmond, heralding their defeat and spreading alarm, thousands of them throwing away their guns in their flight; and if we had pushed vigorously forward we could have been in Richmond before night. General Johnston had been severely wounded the previous day, and the enemy acted without concert or plan.

General Heintzleman afterwards told me that when it became evident that the day was gained, and the Confederates in full retreat, he had already given command to advance until the works of the enemy were taken. But General Kearney reminded him that his only reserves were General Couch's and General Casey's divisions, which had lost large numbers on the previous day, and were considerably exhausted and dispirited; that he could receive no reinforcements in season from the right side of the

Chickahominy, and if our army should receive a check, the peril of its position would be great. This induced the general to order the halt of our army. As often in our lives, we were wise too late; and thus ended one of the most hotly contested and severe battles of the Peninsula. Our loss was estimated at 7,000 killed and wounded; the loss of the enemy is known to have been greater, probably 10,000. In no battle did our troops show more unflinching determination, and in none were their endurance and courage more thoroughly tried.

I subsequently passed all over this field, and saw nowhere, in any battle-scene of the Peninsula, the signs of a more terrific conflict. Our troops and the enemy were often, during Saturday afternoon, within a few feet of each other, in the midst of the pine slashings and swamp forests, and in their stealthy advance would suddenly find themselves looking in each other's faces; and then would commence one of those exciting and sanguinary scenes not often witnessed, except in Indian warfare. Men skulking behind the nearest tree, or crouching down sheltered by a stump, singling out an enemy, taking deliberate aim, and if one dared to display his hand, or cap, or shoulder, instantly there was the crack of the gun of his foe. Often did our men, in such positions, take off the blouse and gently lift it out on the end of the ramrod; this would draw out the enemy's fire; then the blouse would fall as if the man was shot; this would embolden his foe to look up and reveal his position for a moment, and then his own gun flashed, and possibly his enemy was forever harmless. Hundreds of such scenes occurred. Some of our troops engaged in this contest have told me that the face of the foe that fired at them for an hour was so distinctly daguerreotyped on the mind, that they would know the man for years wherever they should meet him. No man can pass over the scene without amazement. The balls must have fallen in an incredible number at the point on the battle-field where General Kearney's men so hotly contested every inch of ground on Saturday afternoon. In the swamp slashings to the right of the Williamsburg road are signs of a terrific conflict; all the fallen trees are pierced and torn with musket-balls, grape-shot, and shells. A small sapling tree of about twenty-two feet in length, and about the size of a man's arm, I singled out as the one on which to count the number of balls that had struck it. I numbered twenty-five musket-balls as having pierced one side of the tree alone. The marks of this contest were so numerous on the standing trees and stumps, and in the slashings, that my astonishment was that any one could have escaped with life. It appeared to me that not even a small bird could fly

"Unscathed where fell this storm of bullets."

Many of our brave men did indeed fall in this conflict, — but three out of five escaped without a wound.

Our soldiers ever spoke with the greatest admiration of the coolness and bravery of Generals Heintzleman, Hooker, Sumner, Kearney, and Couch. General Hooker on this day more than sustained the reputation he had obtained at Williamsburg, as possessed of that clear-sightedness, and courage, and prophetic prognostication of the position and movements of the enemy, which have since placed him at the head of the Army of the Potomac. General Kearney showed himself equal to every emergency, dared every danger, and risked his life in the most hazardous positions. His men seemed to be capable of performing anything under his eye, for their confidence in his courage and military sagacity was unbounded. I have often heard the men speak at the camp-fires of his unruffled coolness during both of those days; and they tell of General Heintzleman the characteristic story, that in the midst of the thickest of the fight on Saturday afternoon, a New York colonel, who had been absent from his regiment on picket-duty, came hurrying up to the general with two companies, and earnestly inquired where he would find his brigade. "That, colonel, I cannot tell," said the general; "but if it is fighting you want, just go in, colonel; there is plenty good fighting all along the lines."

Of Colonel A. Hays (now General Hays) General Heintzleman, in his report of the battle, spoke in the highest terms. He likewise had been separated from his regiment by detail duty, and when he snuffed the battle afar off, rushed to the front with the eagerness of a war-horse, and instantly commenced collecting the loose, straggling soldiers, wandering without officers, and organized them into a corps of upwards of three hundred men. Animated by his eye and voice, they followed him with shouts into the thickest of the fight. I mentioned before that I had taken my position on one of the advanced redoubts in the field, and was here looking with emotions that I can never describe upon the contest, and again witnessed another illustration of the remarkable quickness and acuteness of General Kearney, who, though I was at some distance from him and his staff, saw me in a moment. He was seated on his celebrated grey. He turned his horse and came within speaking distance, and said:

"What, sir, what, you here?"

"Yes, general," I replied.

"What brings you here, sir?"

"My regiment is here," I replied, "and I wanted to see the battle."

"This is no place for you, sir," said he. "Go to the rear, sir, to Savage Station, and report to me. All the men of my division that you find there wounded or dead, attend to them, sir, and I will thank you. Are you ready to report of the men that you took down to the White House?"

"Yes, sir," I replied, "I saw them all in their hospital wards before I left."

"That's well," said he. "Now go back and see to the poor fellows at Savage Station, and you will do a great deal better than to stand here and be killed."

I then told the general that I had spent the entire night at Savage Station attending to the sick and wounded.

"Well," said he, "report everything to me."

I bowed, descended from my elevation, turned my face from the field, and stopped only when the tumult of battle seemed to swell up with great force. One remarkable thing I noticed on this field and

many others. There was a class of battle thieves
who picked every dead man's pocket, and many a
wounded man's, before he could be reached by his
companions or borne to the rear. There is, no doubt,
a class of men with both armies who suspend fighting,
and creep and crawl from one dead man to another.
One thing was certain, that however numerous the
dead on the battle-field, before their friends could
return to them their money and their watches had
been taken.

This battle was very fatal to many of the finest regiments in the army.

General Berry's brigade of brave Michigan troops
suffered greatly, but fought with fierce determination unequalled in any subsequent engagement. The
105th Pennsylvania, the celebrated "wild cat" regiment, lost 255 men, — more than one-half of those
brought into action, but contributed much to hold
the enemy in check and prevent the execution of
his plan of piercing our line, and thus hurling the
broken fragments into James River and the Chickahominy.

It became plain on Saturday afternoon that, cal-
culating upon the swell of the Chickahominy consequent upon the very heavy rains that had recently
fallen, the enemy had thrown his whole force on our
left wing, basing his operations upon the hope that
the high waters of the river would prevent our right
wing reaching us; that the swollen waters would render impossible the passage of artillery, and sweep away
the bridges ; therefore General Johnston seized this
moment to annihilate our left wing, and to accomplish
this brought out and hurled on us all his available

forces. When the battle had vigorously begun, General Sumner, with the true instinct of an old warrior, comprehended the whole move; and gave orders for the advance of his corps across the Chicka-hominy. By incredible efforts he succeeded in urg-ing over before night all his men, and bringing with him several pieces of artillery.

After General Sumner had crossed the river, he had no other guide to the scene of battle but the cannonading; but hurrying up he succeeded in reaching the field in time to prevent Johnston sur-rounding our left wing, and thus saved our honor and the Army of the Potomac. For the four divi-sions composing this wing of the army would cer-tainly have been overcome by vastly superior num-bers, though they had fought with the bravery of Spartans.

Before night separated the combatants, we knew with certainty that we had to contend with the en-tire force of the enemy; and there should not have been a moment's hesitation in ordering across 50,000 men from our right wing; but the issuing of this order was delayed four hours, and a night march became impossible. Before morning the Chicka-hominy had rapidly risen, the bridges were afloat, and the passage of the right wing became impossi-ble; and that delay prevented our triumphant en-trance into Richmond on the 1st of June.

During this day, the Sabbath, there was a con-tinuation of the scenes I have previously described in the tents and on the open ground at Savage Sta-tion. A great number of the wounded, however, were sent to the White House, to be placed in various steamers which had been sent up the Pamunky for the purpose of receiving them.

The endurance of our wounded men was truly noble. They all appeared to think that the cause was of far more value than their lives. Many of them were very cheerful, though so severely injured as to die in a few days afterwards.

Many most touching incidents occurred in connection with these scenes, the wounded showing the deepest sympathy for those whom they thought in a worse condition than themselves. There were many instances of their refusing the cup of coffee or toddy, in order that it might be given to a greater sufferer. Many of these cases made upon my mind the deepest impression I have ever received of the primitive dignity and glory of human nature. One young man, Thomas Coats, sergeant of the 63d Pennsylvania, who was most painfully and mortally wounded, his right thigh being shattered, displayed a patience, a fortitude, and a submission that were really sublime. Three times we bore him up, racked with suffering as he was, and conveyed him to the cars, and each time were we doomed to be disappointed, for the cars were filled up by those who were stronger and better able to help themselves. The disappointment, the pain, the harrowing scene, he bore without a murmur or a frown; and when we parted, with a countenance as placid as in perfect health and full of hope, he bade his friends and companions farewell, with no expectation of ever meeting them again. How many such young men have fallen, who, if they had lived, would have been

18

centres of ever-widening influence and pillars in society!

We had taken two or three hundred prisoners;
these were assigned a certain district of the picket
garden. The officers were respectable-looking, intelligent men, and very willing to defend their cause.
The soldiers were poorly clad, dejected looking, and,
with rare exceptions, very ignorant; but apparently
no less gratified than amazed at the kind and the
abundance of the food. They had been led to expect the most cruel treatment from the Yankees, but
now they confessed that they were a great deal better
off as prisoners than they had ever been as soldiers.
But they were very anxious to know their fate:
"Were they to be sent to prison, tried for their lives
and hung, or sent away to some distant country?"
Occasionally some of these prisoners were sent with
our men to dig the graves of the dead, and at such
times there occurred some of the most amusing and
interesting conversations I ever listened to. Some
of the Confederate soldiers were able to paint in
strong colors the character of the Yankees who had
found their way South; their tricks, meannesses,
and sharp transactions. They complained of negroes
tampered with, of books and tracts put into the
hands of those who were inciting to insurrection, of
hostility to slavery, of wagons sold made of rotten
wood, of carriages without iron, of swindles in every
department of business and trade, of violated pledges
and compacts. They had lost all confidence in us,
and did not wish to live under the same government. They wished a gulf dug as deep as the centre of the earth, over which we could never pass to

them.- To this and much more some shrewd New
Yorker or New Englander who had been down
South, would reply, and picture the miserable condition of Southern society, the vices and cruelties
of the aristocracy, the ignorance, indolence, and
misery of the masses. "As for swindling, they
were so stupid and withal so vain that they tempted
every keen operator to pluck them, to quicken
their wits and give them some sense. As for
cheating, the whole South broke up every ten years,
and robbed the North of hundreds of millions. And
as to stealing, the Yankee never was born who
could come within a hundred leagues of Floyd. As
for getting along without us, they might as well attempt to fight without powder, or walk without feet.
What had they that we did not give them? Our
teachers taught all their schools; their houses were
built by our mechanics; their fields were cultivated
with the ploughs and hoes made in our shops; their
railroads were created by our capital; their calicoes,
cloths, shoes, and stockings were made in our fac-
tories; our ships bore to foreign parts their cotton;
we baked their bread for them and put the butter
on it, and sent it down to them hot for breakfast.
Do without us? Yes, it will be a poor do. When
we were all the time helping you, you could scarcely
get along. If we just take you at your word, the Indians and Negroes will take all the South."

Then another Southerner would have his story
of griefs and wrongs. These conversations, so far
from embittering the men towards each other, molli-
fied their manners and spirits: they comprehended
each other's position, and the respect of each for his

opponent was evidently increased. And to the honor of our men be it said, I never saw any of that bitterness and malignant hate so often exhibited on the other side. I do not believe that one Confederate soldier had the least cause to complain of neglect or cruelty.

I have spoken of a number of surgeons who at this time distinguished themselves by surgical operations of the rarest skill. Of this number were Doctors Page and Hall, of Boston, Doctor Bliss, of Michigan, and Doctor Swinburne, of Albany. The latter gentleman had been sent to the army by Governor Morgan to minister relief to the wounded soldiers of that State, and to give them the benefit of his eminent surgical abilities. To a most unflinching hand he added the gentlest heart, always sparing when there was the least hope for a shattered limb, and by a thousand acts of kindness endearing himself to a multitude of sufferers. I shall have occasion to speak of him again in connection with the seven days' battles. I can never cease to feel grateful to Doctor Bliss, brigade surgeon of General Berry's brigade. He was sleepless and unwearied in his attention to the wounded, took every measure in his power for their relief and encouraged every one who would in any way minister to the comfort of those under his care.

This was the more commendable, for there were surgeons who were too indolent or thoughtless about their wounded, and made no effort to obtain beds or covering, and were apparently indifferent to the many wants of the men suffering from exhaustion and pain.

The value of a physician in such circumstances is more in securing a faithful and constant care on the part of the nurses in seeing that the patients are washed, their wants instantly attended to, their food suitable and frequent, and the stimulants administered and not drank by others, than in bandaging or amputations; for while one wounded man requires that the broken limb should be cut off, five require constant care lest they die of exhaustion and nervous prostration.

In the course of a week all the wounded whose removal was possible were taken in the cars to the White House, and thence transferred by boat to Fortress Monroe and Northern cities. The most of them never returned,—one-fourth were maimed for life, one-fifth, after lingering for days and weeks on couches of pain and suffering, passed from earth forever, leaving desolate a thousand homes; and by many a stream the broken harp of hope was hung on the willows, and the song began in gladness ended in the sobbings of despair.

On the Tuesday after the battle of Fair Oaks, I saw General Casey's division marching to the rear of the army. The day was one of continuous storm, the roads were covered with water, and the streams that ordinarily were but little brooks ran like rivers; and on such a day and in such a condition of the country this division was remanded from its encampment in front and sent back six miles to the rear. And during the continuance of the tempest these soldiers were seen gliding along on the edge of the forest on the Williamsburg road, endeavoring in the bushes to escape the swamps of

18 *

the field and road. Worn down with exertion, exhausted and sick, some had fallen out of the ranks, and were lying down in the mud and water, or were seated on stones. These soldiers had none of the free, manly look which ought to sit upon the countenance of every American in the army; but they were dejected, and doomed, without a hearing, to the most ignominious insult.

I looked then with profound indignation on the scene; and every time I reflected upon it, my astonishment has been increased that any American general should dare to inflict such an act of injustice and inhumanity. They were sent back into the swamps of the Chickahominy without tents, and exposed, on one of the most inclement days I ever saw, to the fatigues of a long march, and to the disastrous consequences of exposure and disgrace.

After the action described in the previous chapter, it was perfectly evident that our entire army should have been removed for safety and for success to James River. The battle of Fair Oaks made it plain that one wing of the army might be defeated before the other wing could be brought up to its aid; and that widely extended as was our front, it was impossible to collect our forces in time to prevent the success of a combined attack of the enemy upon any vulnerable point. Much would likewise have been gained by removing our troops from the malarious swamps and muddy camps we then occupied to a higher ground and an open country. Such a change of base appears to have been contemplated by General McClellan, and at one time resolved on, but deferred in execution until it was forced on us. We now commenced making regular advances as in siege, by throwing up earthworks and redoubts.

On these one-third of the army was daily employed, and the works constructed from the 1st to the 21st of June will remain for ages the monuments of our industry and perseverance. All these works were constructed under the fire of the enemy: there were frequent skirmishes along the line, and shell and round-shot fell during all working hours amongst our men. Still the work went on, and great mounds were thrown up, and vast embankments created, which will excite the astonishment of future travellers.

During these weeks no day passed by without some sanguinary scenes being witnessed; and wounded men were brought in nearly every morning to the hospitals. Everything combined to exhaust and diminish the effective force of our army. Our troops were day and night doing fatigue duty, which either means hewing down the forest, or digging and shovelling in the intrenchments; or they were on watch, frequently called to arms, ran out at double-quick through ponds and lakes to our front; then, added to all, the heat of the day was tropical, the sun smote with a power that withered and blasted our strength. From all these causes and operations, the sick of our army during these twenty days increased at a fearful rate. I have no doubt that one-half of the left wing was prostrated and unfit for duty before the commencement of our retreat. I knew some regiments that had left Hampton 1000 strong which could not now bring into the field 250 men; and in less than two months, from the daily increase in the number of the sick, our entire army would have melted away.

The sufferings amongst the sick were of the most acute and painful character. They were tortured with constant thirst, generally with intense pain in the head, and frequently with delirium. The camp diseases, such as dysentery, diarrhœa, and miasmatic fevers, are very painful and exhausting. The hospitals had to be created on the field in the immediate neighborhood of our camps: often these were rude cabins, without floors and without beds, and generally speaking destitute of any of those comforts that go to alleviate sickness at home. No wonder that many soldiers gave themselves up with stoic indifference to die.

My employment at this time was, as before, the superintending of the removal of the sickest men of the division from the field-hospitals to those that had been created by the orders of General Kearney in various farm-houses.

CHAPTER XIV.

General Stuart's Cavalry Raid—Wild Commotion on the Pamunky—Hospital at Carter's House—Arrival of General
Franklin's Troops—Mr. Alvord's Labors.

On the evening of the 13th of June I went to the
White House on one of my semi-weekly excursions,
for the purpose of seeing after the condition of the
men in the hospitals, reporting the same to General
Kearney, and obtaining supplies of medicines and
sanitary stores. The day had been oppressively
warm. I was invited on board the steamer Commo-
dore by the surgeon in charge; and during the evening we were alarmed by the firing of cannon and
musketry, and the intelligence that the enemy had
taken possession of Tunstall's Station on the railroad, and had attacked our troops on other parts of
the line. Instantly the signal was given for the various vessels at anchor at the White House to fall
down stream. The whole night was one of the
greatest commotion and alarm. This was the celebrated raid of General Stuart, in which he, with
1800 cavalry, swept round our entire rear.

On the following day I saw several of our wounded
men, and learned from them that they had been on
duty at Tunstall's Station; and that the enemy had
attacked and overpowered them with vastly superior

numbers. A few moments before the arrival of the
train bringing down a considerable number of officers, and sick and wounded men from the army, the
enemy had placed obstructions on the railroad track,
and was determined to capture the train. The first
indication that the conductor had of the presence of
the enemy was a number of officers standing on the
track, and waving their swords for the train to stop.
There was a momentary check until the engineer
comprehended the truth, and then he put on all
steam and dashed forward with the greatest speed
he could command. The Confederates now poured
a deadly fire into the cars, wounding many of our
men. A hundred guns were aimed at the engineer,
and though struck, he did not forsake his post, but
rushed on, sweeping the Rebels and the obstructions
out of the way, and safely reaching the depôt.

When the wounded and dead were brought in on
these cars, and the many officers and soldiers sprang
out to tell the story, the scene of excitement beggars
description. Hundreds of negroes, running back to
their miserable shanties, gathered up their little
effects; sutlers packed their goods, and hastened
them to the vessels that were about slipping their
cables; numbers of officers ran to and fro to gather
men to repel an attack; others were busy securing
the papers and goods of their departments, and issuing orders which no one obeyed. And any observer
could see how easy it is for a few men, acting in
concert, to scatter ten thousand acting without a plan
or head.

Colonel Ingalls, at the head of the commissary department, acted with the greatest coolness; and in

case the enemy had made an attack, would have saved to the country three-fourths of the supplies and public property accumulated there, which was estimated, including the military and commissary stores, and shipping, at $5,000,000.

The enemy, however, after being foiled in capturing the railroad train, gathered up such horses and guns as he could find, rode to Baltimore Cross-roads, and encamped for the night. We had a hospital near to this place, and to this General Stuart and the principal surgeon connected with his staff rode over. Their conduct was humane and gentlemanly, the surgeon coming in, indeed, and borrowing a small quantity of medicines, the general not permitting any of his officers to enter the house, saying he did not wish to alarm the sick men. He placed guards around the premises, to prevent any of our men leaving during the night and communicating with our army. Though General Stuart said he did not wish to alarm our sick men, yet that night was fatal to more than one. It is easy, in a certain stage of the typhoid fever, when the whole nervous system is at the lowest depression, to destroy a patient by an alarm or shock. Of the sick in this hospital was one noble young man from Indiana County, Pennsylvania, Ralston Hoover, who died that night. He had been sick three weeks, and was thought to be recovering, and was deemed at this time to be out of danger. In his pocket, after his death, were found some of the most touching and beautiful letters from a child sister and a little brother, telling him how much they missed him, how they longed for his return, how they counted the days until he might come back, but, above all, telling how proud they were of their soldier brother. And they never heard a drum beat nor a fife play without thinking of him, and feeling glad that they had one noble brother to fight for his country. Poor children! I read these touching and eloquent letters at his grave, and could not but add my tears to theirs, with deep regret that one who had such a home would never return to gladden with his presence the hearts of those that loved him.

About this time General McCall's division, and other troops from the Rappahannock, under the command of General Franklin, were landed at the White House, and added some 15,000 fresh troops to our effective force. I saw this division when landed; and in the march up to the railroad to different positions I could not but look upon them with considerable satisfaction, for their condition was so much better than that of the army which had been breathing the pestilential air of the Peninsula for three months.

I have before mentioned the hospital in Captain Carter's house. This was about one mile north-east of Savage Station, and a half mile from the railroad. Captain Carter was evidently a man of taste and enterprise. Around his house were blooming roses and magnolias, and everything about the place gave evidence of refinement and cultivation. The outhouses and barns were not, as in most Virginia plantations, miserable tottering sheds, but painted and well inclosed. Near to this house was one of the finest springs I have ever seen, overshadowed with oaks and mulberries. It rushed out as if laughing with joy to escape from the dark imprisonment of caverns, but stopped to twine its arms lovingly around the roots of the magnolia and to kiss the hyacinth and lily.

This spring was a fountain in the desert to hundreds. Many a fevered and staggering soldier made this the first request of the morning, that we would permit some nurse to help them to the spring, and when taken there they would wash their burning hands and cool their throbbing temples in the waters; and then seated with their backs against the trees, they would linger for hours, hearing the sweetest music and seeing every moment new beauties. They were dreaming of distant scenes. Such a spring was near the old homestead; and father, mother, and sister might be this moment walking around it, and they could see their faces. Or just such a spring flowed by the door of their home in the mountains, and over pebbles just as white and shells like these; and they could hear the voices of their children, and see the pale, anxious face of one dearer than all. Such spots and scenes have an amazing power in soothing and quieting the sick when despondent, shattered by weeks of pain, and the future all dark. Such a place, whispering of the ceaseless benignity of Providence, brings to the heart the relief that the harp of David threw over the troubled King of Israel.

To this house of Captain Carter was sent about 150 of the sick of General Kearney's division. I was sent by Colonel Hays to take charge of them. A physician of the 105th Pennsylvania, Doctor Smith, visited us once or twice a day. His hospital

19

was about one half mile from us on the railroad.
Here likewise were 180 men.

There had been brought to Meadow Station on
Friday evening, the 27th of May, about 100 men,
mostly of Hooker's division, to be sent to the White
House on the cars.

But before this was possible the enemy were in
our rear, and those poor suffering men, without
physicians and only three nurses, were left without
food, and they knew not where to turn or to whom
to appeal. Their surgeons were more than occupied
with the demands made upon them in the field;
and there was no one to look after these men. Sent
away, they hoped they might be safe, but if not
they could not help them. Their generals and regimental officers were every hour needed at their
posts. And hemmed in, changing position, fighting
every day, there was no man that could be spared
to hunt up the sick and see to their removal. I say
this to relieve many minds of the apprehension they
have, that a number of our sick and wounded were
cruelly neglected. That there were physicians who
manifested great heartlessness, and who, when detailed for special service in hospitals and in removing the sick, were inattentive, stupidly indifferent,
and even drunken, is, to the disgrace of human nature, true; but let us not demand of surgeons more
than is possible. Some of them manifested the highest moral heroism, and became martyrs to their humanity. If the Roman soldier who saved the life
of a citizen was honored with an oaken chaplet,
surely many of our surgeons deserve the gratitude

of the country, and especially of the men whom they saved from perishing.

The days which intervened between this and the commencement of the final struggle, are marked by few incidents or events of great interest. But in the meantime the heat of the sun had become tropical, the dense forests preventing the free circulation of air, and the fields being white and beaten : the sun smote us as if every ray was a drop of fire. This, together with the daily fatigue labors on the intrenchments and redoubts, and the night duties of the watch, began to tell most disastrously on our men. The sick increased by hundreds, and all the hospitals were crowded.

At this time my labors were entirely in the various hospitals connected with our division, and amongst the wounded men left at Savage Station. I had the invaluable aid of the Rev. Mr. Alvord, of Boston, who was in the army as agent of the American Tract Society, and who gave his time and his horse and wagon for the carrying of supplies of clothing, food, and sanitary stores to our sick. I never appealed to this kind and noble man in vain, but invariably, however impassable the roads, however deep the swamp and flood, he would harness up his carriage to convey to the sufferers the supplies obtained. New England has sent many generous and excellent men into the army, but for none does she deserve more of the gratitude of the country than for the Rev. Mr. Alvord.

Everything began to wear the appearance, to my eye, of despondency in the army. Rumors came to us daily of the great increase of the Confederate forces, while ours were evidently rapidly diminishing. And it appeared to me that even in head-quarters "coming events were casting their shadows before;" and everything betrayed the absence of that vigor which is given by hope and distinctness of plan.

CHAPTER XV.

Commencement of the Seven Days' Battles — Second Battle of Fair Oaks, on Wednesday, June 25th — Battle of Mechanicsville, on Thursday, June 26th — Battle of Gainesville, on Friday, June 27th — Scenes amongst the Wounded at Savage Station — Narrow Escape of Rev. Mr. Dickson — Mr. Brunot, of Pittsburg — Dr. Swinburne, of Albany.

ON the 25th of June commenced the combined advance of our army. General Heintzleman was commanded by General McClellan to advance the entire front of the left wing, and this movement was successfully accomplished. This is sometimes called the second battle of Fair Oaks. Up to this time there had been quite friendly relations between our pickets and those of the enemy, often exchanging courtesies, trading tobacco, and passing from one line to the other the *New York Herald* for the Richmond sheets.

This was the first of those grand and never-to-be-forgotten contests called "The Seven Days' Battles." We had been for many days in a state of intense expectation, for everything indicated that all was now ready for an advance on Richmond. It was therefore determined, as the first step, to push our lines from one-half to a mile in advance of our present position.

19 *

The accomplishment of this task was committed to General Hooker.

In front of General Hooker's encampment was a thick entanglement of low pines, vines, and ragged bushes, full of ponds and marshes. This wilderness was about five hundred yards wide, and beyond this an open field of half a mile in width; and in this field were the rifle-pits, earthworks, and redoubts of the enemy. The plan was to drive the enemy from the forests and field, and establish our lines where his then were. The attacking column consisted of Grover's, Sickles's, and Robinson's brigades. General Kearney was sent to protect the left flank, and the 19th Massachusetts, Colonel Hicks, was ordered to advance and protect the right.

The three brigades mentioned advanced slowly, but steadily, into the thickets, and some distance within met and drove back the enemy's pickets. This was soon followed by a rapid and incessant firing, until in a few moments the forest was a scene of furious contest, and the ominous quiet was succeeded by the terrible din and clash of arms, and the roar of cannon and musketry. Soon nothing could be seen for the heavy cloud, rising up and twisting itself amongst the trees, hanging over the forest as a pall; and then streams of fire, like angry lightnings, would flash out from amongst the trees; and anon an orderly would rush from the gloom, covered with dust and blood, with garments torn, carrying reports or hasting for orders.

In half an hour the skirmish extended along the entire line, and Kearney's and Hooker's divisions were engaged in the liveliest action; and soon, from the arrival of fresh troops on both sides, the engagement assumed the magnitude of a battle.

Our troops pushed steadily forward, and in less than an hour drove the enemy out of the forest into the open field, over which they fled and sought protection in their rifle-pits. Here our men raised the shout of triumph, which was taken up by brigade after brigade, and borne through the army.

General Grover was about to order an advance on the enemy in their defences, when our troops were halted by an order from General McClellan. From some misapprehension of the actual condition of things, he ordered General Hooker to retire from the field of victory, and return to our original positions; but when the commander-in-chief came upon the scene of action at a later hour, he ordered our troops to advance and reoccupy the woods and fields they had taken, and before night the enemy was driven out of the rifle-pits, and from the fields, and we had gained a victory which cost us 640 of our best men in killed and wounded.

About six o'clock the enemy came out in force and attacked General Robinson's brigade. He made a most resolute charge, led by a very brave regiment of Georgians, but was met by men equally as brave, was driven back, and left 300 men dead on the field.

In this attack Lieutenant Cochran, of Franklin, Venango County, Pennsylvania, received his death wound, — living some hours, and giving to those who stood around him on that night most comfortable assurance that he went up from the field of carnage into the bosom of our Lord.

During the entire night our men were under arms, and every few moments there was an attack upon some part of our line, as if they were determined to win back what they had lost; but all these were only feints to fully occupy our attention, and to prevent reinforcements being sent to our right wing.

At the time of Hooker's advance upon the enemy, on the 25th, we were full of hope that this was the beginning of a grand series of actions which would, in a few days, carry us victorious into Richmond. On the 25th we were successful, and hoped that the next day we would overcome half the objects lying between us and the Rebel capital. Thursday, the 26th, came on so still and motionless, that the very trees seemed to be asleep, and the breath of the morning was without freshness. In the very earliest hour we heard on our right, upon the Chickahominy, the roar of battle. This was the long-continued and hard-fought battle of Mechanicsville, — where our troops, placed upon the Beaver Dam, and under the protection of some beautiful catalpa trees, defended their position during the entire day, and expelled the enemy. The attacking force was 60,000; the number of our troops 35,000. At night tidings were brought in, cheering our hearts, that Porter had achieved a brilliant success.

At this moment a new scene opened in the drama, and a new actor appeared upon the stage. On Wednesday night General Stonewall Jackson reached the camps on the north side of Richmond. Thursday found him deploying his army upon the rear of our right wing, compelling the evacuation of our positions before Mechanicsville, and a retreat during the

night to Gaines's Mills. Friday morning came on, and
so slowly do our illusions disappear in the presence
of truth and reality, that though we discovered the
firing was much nearer to us than on the previous
day, yet we did not entertain any distinct apprehension that the enemy was coming closer to us, and
that the whole army was already in retreat. On this
day was fought the battle of Gaines's Mills, in which
Porter's division so bravely struggled against overwhelming odds.

During this action a dear friend, the Rev. William
Dickson, chaplain of the 12th Pennsylvania Reserves,
ran a perilous journey, which I suppose he has no
desire to renew. He was in an hospital, attending to
the wounded men. The hospital house being in the
shadows of a ravine, the enemy, in order to outflank
us, were pushing several columns up the ravine.
Soon the officers, hurrying back from the points of
attack, shouted to all in the hospitals to flee, for the
enemy was at the door. Mr. Dickson ran up the hill-
side, and looking down the ravine, could distinctly
see the gleam of the enemy's guns; but on the summit he heard the cry, "Lie down; you are right in
our way." And at the moment there was a roar
from one of our guns, and a shell shrieked by him;
and knowing that the guns are fired in line, one gun
succeeding another, he marked the flash, ran a few
steps, then halting waited for the next thundering
crash, and then again halted, and thus ran with
safety the gauntlet of two batteries. And as often
as they cried to him, "Out of the way; you'll be
shot," he replied, "Fire away; I'll take care of my-

self," a coolness only gained by being often under
fire.

During this day 600 or 700 wounded men were
brought in from the battle-fields to Savage Station.
For some unknown reason the wounds were not so
severe as in the previous engagements. Many were
struck in the feet and arms, and the flesh wounds
were more numerous than at the battle of Fair Oaks.
But again were renewed the painful, excruciating
scenes of suffering that paralyzed and benumbed
the faculties of the most benevolent. It now began
to be apparent to us that a retreat from our present
position was inevitable, and that we must fall back
upon the Pamunky or James River. The former
was the course that the enemy expected us to take :
the retreat upon James River, however, was chosen
by General McClellan. The right wing of the army
passed the Chickahominy in safety during Friday
night, bringing with it nearly all our guns.

On the evening of Friday, the 27th, General McClellan changed his head-quarters from near the Chickahominy to Savage Station ; and the wounded men
brought in from the field, and couriers arriving at
head-quarters, made us aware of the fact that our
right was in full retreat across the Chickahominy ;
and now, if not before, the peril of the army stared
us in the face. We knew that Jackson was in our rear,
sweeping down the Pamunky, and would, in a few
hours at most, cut off our communications with the
White House. Broken squadrons of troops, and dusty
and wounded officers, were arriving during the entire
night, increasing our consternation. Groups of men
were seen collected together discussing, with anxious

faces, our probable destiny and fate. In spite of all that could be done to avoid inquiry, and to throw us on a false scent, our real condition began to make itself sensible to every mind and to blanch a thousand cheeks. Every way we looked there was destruction and death. Cut off from the base of our supplies, in a country surrounded by our foes, embarrassed by thousands of wounded and sick men, with all the avenues of escape closed up, the prospect before us was most gloomy and appalling.

During the entire night all was hurry and confusion. Officers arriving in haste and departing in even greater haste; orderlies quickened by imperious commands to hasten to every part of the army. Consternation reigned everywhere; the uncertainty in regard to our future movements palsied every one. The gloom of this night was greatly increased by the constant arrival of ambulances bearing the wounded, of others borne in on stretchers and the shoulders of their companions, and again, as at Fair Oaks, all the open grounds around the house of Mr. Savage, all the floors of the barns and stables and outhouses were covered with a ghastly multitude, bleeding, groaning, and dying.

Saturday morning was ushered in with a quiet unusual and almost unnatural in the Peninsula—not a gun was fired. This was owing to the fact of the enemy looking for us on the banks of the Chickahominy, and not anticipating our retreat on James River. General Stoneman had been detached with two regiments of infantry and one of cavalry to amuse and deploy the enemy in the direction of the Pamunky: this succeeded. We had been twelve hours marching to our new base before the enemy became aware of our plans. During Saturday our immense baggage train, between 5000 and 6000 wagons, was dispatched along the Williamsburg road, followed by the ambulance train; and during the day Generals Porter, Sykes, and McCall, with their divisions, passed over the railroad, taking the direction towards Williamsburg. Our communications with the White House were not cut off until ten o'clock on Saturday morning; for we had already sent down a train of cars filled with wounded men, and another train was laying at Savage Station with 500 wounded men, waiting the signal to start, when the telegraphic wires suddenly ceased working. I was in the telegraphic office when this was announced by the operator. Our worst fears were now realized. It was certain the enemy was in our rear. The train moved down the road three or four miles, to learn, if possible, the condition of things at the White House; but failing to hear anything satisfactory, it returned to the station; and for several hours the poor, broken, maimed men waited and hoped, and rejected the offer of friendly hands that proposed to remove them from the cars, and place them on beds upon the ground.

We waited in a state of the most gloomy expectation for tidings from the White House, still hoping and praying that our fears might be unreal. In the meantime everything wore an aspect the most sombre.

The wounded had increased to the number of 2000; the sick lying in the various hospitals in the camps and country-houses were brought in and

lifted out of the ambulances, and placed on the
ground; the drivers departed, and without nurses,
physicians, or comrades, they were left in that scene
of misery. Hundreds of these, as I passed along,
beckoned to me, or uttered a low, beseeching cry,
"Doctor, we are not to be left here, are we?" "Is
there no water, doctor?" "Our wounds have not
been dressed for three days." "We have had no
medicines." "I have no blanket, doctor, and suffer
greatly with the cold."

The number of surgeons who had been detailed
for service here was much smaller than was absolutely necessary for so many patients demanding care
the most constant and watchful. For such is the
great draft upon the nervous system, that a surgeon
can perform but few capital operations in a day
without complete prostration and danger to his life.
And I soon discovered that a surgeon cannot breathe
the atmosphere poisoned with the exhalations of disorganized flesh and blood, without very soon suffering from an exhaustion which appears to palsy every
vital power. And after being for weeks with the
wounded, and dressing a multitude, I learned to be
more merciful in my judgment on physicians in hospitals; for I have been often compelled to turn away
from many who came to my tent door, and begged,
with tears, that I would wash and bandage their
wounds, and destroy, with chloroform and spirits of
turpentine, the maggots that tormented them. But
sick and fainting from breathing an air so offensive,
from sights so ghastly, from groans and shrieks of
pain which the most gentle hand must wring from
the sufferer in dressing his wounds, I have fled from

20

what I could no longer endure. I now began to comprehend the cause of the intense craving for stimulants, especially for brandy and whisky, on the part of surgeons: the exhaustion was thus repaired, and they were able to endure what would have been otherwise impossible.

All of Saturday was spent in the most wearisome and distressing uncertainty. There were a thousand rumors of things most improbable: but we were prepared to believe anything, however extravagant, for we were like sailors who, by the sudden wreck of their noble ship, were cast into the sea, and on broken fragments borne they knew not where, and in the terror of the hour compelled to anticipate the greatest misfortune.

As yet the generals and prominent army officers kept to themselves the purposes of the future. The soldiers were made to think that they were marching to guard the bridges of the Chickahominy. The whole weight of our disaster did not fall on us to-day. During the day great numbers of wounded who had fallen near the Chickahominy were brought in. Many that had been wounded beyond the stream, in the battle of the previous day, had been left behind in the night retreat; and after incredible hardships and dangers, had dragged themselves to the banks of the river, found some one that pitied them and helped them over, and now were brought into the hospital. The tragic scenes and hairbreadth escapes of that night would fill a volume of as interesting story as was ever published.

We had now at Savage Station about 2500 wounded men. They were lying in the various houses before mentioned. Mr. Savage, like an oriental, appeared to have built a house for every birthday and for every child that came to him, and now a man of gray hairs, he was surrounded by a village. Into all these houses the wounded were borne, and besides these places of shelter there were pitched fully 300 tents; for every tent were fifteen or twenty men. To three tents there was assigned a nurse; and, again, a surgeon to every four or five tents. These hospital tents being arranged in streets, every surgeon had his own ward, which might include 100 or 150 patients. There were six or eight surgeons, mostly brigade surgeons, to whom was assigned the task of amputations. Besides these we were so fortunate as to have with us at this time Dr. John Swinburne, of Albany, who had been sent to the Army of the Potomac previous to the battle of Fair Oaks by Governor Morgan, anticipating that his services might be of benefit to the soldiers of his State; and after having displayed his pre-eminent surgical abilities on that occasion, he was again sent, and arrived just in season to be the greatest of benefactors.

Of this man I cannot speak in terms of too high praise. He was thoughtless of himself, forgetful even of the wants of nature, untiring in his labors, uniting to the highest courage of man the tenderness of a woman, and the gentleness of a child. In that terrible hour, when other surgeons were worn out and exhausted, no labor appeared to diminish his vigor. After days of toil and nights of sleeplessness, he was as fresh and earnest as though he had stepped forth from a night of quiet sleep; and while others became impatient, and had to escape from those scenes and seek repose, he operating for hours at the time, found relaxation and refreshment in going from tent to tent, counselling the surgeons, advising the nurses, and speaking words of cheer to the wounded and the dying.

Dr. Swinburne was left in charge at Savage Station, and so long as our army was near us, we had physicians for each of the wards; but on Saturday many of these were ordered away to join their regiments. Dr. Smith, of the 105th Pennsylvania, at the hospital on the railroad, of which I have spoken, was one of the physicians ordered to his regiment, in consequence of which all the sick in these hospitals, — the Meadow Station, Railroad house, and Carter's house, —were left under my care. It was my custom to spend several hours each day at Savage Station. The demand for my labors, however, was not so great before we became prisoners as afterwards, because there were several chaplains, whose regiments were near, who were enabled frequently to visit the hospitals.

I often met, going from tent to tent, the Rev. Mr. Guilder, of the 40th New York; the Rev. Mr. Barnes, of the 26th New York; the Rev. Mr. Fuller, of the 16th Massachusetts; the Rev. Mr. Glen, of the 103d Pennsylvania; and the Rev. Mr. McAdams, of the 57th Pennsylvania. There were, doubtless, many others who faithfully discharged their duties, and spent much of their time in ministering to the comfort of our suffering men.

Greatly for the relief of the wounded, there had arrived, some days previous to the battles, the Rev. Mr. Reed, of Washington, District of Columbia, who brought with him hospital stores and sanitary goods contributed by an association in New York. These were faithfully used, and were of unspeakable benefit. To Mr. Reed had been assigned a considerable number of nurses and assistants, and thus the charities of distant benefactors were borne to every tent. Every two or three hours these nurses were sent to the sickest and most exhausted men with nourishment, such as hot broth and milk toddy; and thus the dimly smoking flax was not wholly quenched, and the bruised reed not broken. Mr. Reed showed himself, through all this time, to be a true man; and never was a benefaction more like one sent from heaven.

There was likewise another, a layman, a man whose name will be held in everlasting remembrance by a multitude whom he fed, clothed, comforted, and prayed with,—Felix Brunot, Esq., of Pittsburg, Pennsylvania. He came to us as the representative of a benevolent association of that city, and brought with him as assistants a number of young men. Some of these were students, sons of wealthy parents, who were prompted by the purest benevolence to come to the army at this critical hour. No man could have appeared amongst us more eminently fitted for the time than Mr. Brunot. With a piety most unaffected and sincere, with a heart overflowing with sympathy, with a kindness that never wearied, he went forth from tent to tent, ministering to each as charity would dictate, and as the circumstances demanded. He had likewise brought with him large stores of such things as were needed in such a time as this. Amongst the events that we look upon as

20 *

indicative of the kindly providence of God, was the sending to us for this hour such men as Mr. Brunot and his fellow-laborers in his work of love; and they voluntarily remained, to endure the dangers and miseries of captivity.

There had been at one time, on Saturday morning about nine o'clock, very heavy firing; but the Confederates, fully assured that our army would fall back on the Pamunky, made no effort on Saturday to cross the Chickahominy. But we knew that this quiet was only for a day. In the meantime, though one enemy did not appear, another did.

Death came to many; and the poor fellows that had died during the night were every morning seen lying on stretchers outside the tents, and as soon as possible borne away to the place in the orchard where all our dead were interred. They were folded up in their blankets, gently let down in the grave, their overcoats placed over them; and if a chaplain was present a prayer was made, and dust to dust, he was covered from our sight forever. Very often some friends would carve on a board the name, company, and regiment of the deceased, and the place of his birth. A large number of the noblest men of our army lie around Savage Station, and to a thousand hearts the spot is sacred, for their dead are there.

It was one of the saddest scenes of those battle days to meet in the evening some one who spoke strongly of his hopes of life, of return to his home, and how soon his mother or wife would have him well, and in the morning return and find his place empty. He had died in the night: we would step out from the tent, lift the blanket from the face, and

there, cold and silent, was the companion of yesterday. Death often impresses a most noble look on
the brow, as if the dying one had caught glimpses
of the grandeur of the Infinite, and it left its impress
in the majestic solemnity of his face. Often did I
find the face singularly placid and composed, and
much more beautiful than in life.

During the entire day of Saturday the various regiments and columns of the right wing marched by
Savage Station, taking the Williamsburg road for
the James River. The advance was very slow, for
beyond our own line we knew nothing of the enemy,
and therefore there were frequent halts of our army
for throwing out skirmishers and scouts. In a region of almost impervious swamps and forests it was
easy to entrap an army into an ambuscade, and therefore the necessity for the greatest caution. In this
region invaluable aid was given to us by the negroes.
They were our only guides in the entangled mazes
We had not the slightest knowledge, from previous
reconnoissances, of this forbidding region. This
greatly increased, therefore, the disadvantages under
which we advanced and struggled, and threw a deeper
gloom over the army; and the question was often
asked: "Why had not all this country been fully
explored? Why not all these roads long since felt
by our cavalry? Surely somebody has been asleep!"

CHAPTER XVI.

SUNDAY, *June 29th.*

Consternation and Alarm in the Hospital — Scene at Savage Station — The drawing in of our Pickets — The Destruction of our Military and Commissary Stores — The Burning Train — The Grand Appearance of Sumner's Rear-guard — Battle of Savage Station.

SABBATH morning dawned upon us, one of the clearest and warmest mornings of summer. All that could arise were up with the earliest light, for we knew this was to be a day of important events, and were very uncertain of beholding the setting sun.

I went from room to room, prescribed for the patients, ordered breakfast, gathered the nurses, and gave them the instructions for the day. At the same time I sent out two of the nurses to report the appearance of affairs about us, and if anything could be seen of the enemy, or if our troops were visible.

They soon returned, reporting that several regiments were drawn up in line of battle near us, and that the officers of our army had recommenced our removal from the hospital, for it might be in a few moments in the midst of a battle-field. For the enemy was crossing the Chickahominy below us, and would most certainly advance upon our troops through the ravines leading up from the valley, past the house we were in.

I went out into the fields, and saw the long, dark lines of Meagher's Irish Brigade drawn up on the bluffs overlooking the river. I saw most distinctly the tents of the enemy in the open fields on the opposite heights, and heard the sound of axes and hammers at work cutting a road and constructing a bridge.

In a few moments Colonel Burke, of the 63d New York, rode up to the gate of the hospital, called for me, and strongly urged the removal of all the inmates, as the probability was now almost a certainty, that in a few moments the enemy would rush up and plant their batteries in the field about us, and the house and barns would be seized by one party and the other alternately as the places of rallying and defence. He said he had been instructed by General Meagher to warn us, and urge our removal.

I answered the colonel that we were without ambulances; that every one had been ordered away; that we had not one wagon, and were without horses, except my saddle horse and baggage pony; that we had not more than six men well enough to help the others away; and for these to remove one hundred and fifty sick men, some of them in a dying condition, was simply impossible. We would have to remain and trust to God, as we had done before.

The kind-hearted colonel was unwilling to leave us in a condition which he deemed so desperate, and he lingered several minutes, trying to counsel and devise some way for our escape. He said he would send men, if possible, from his regiment; but every man was needed at his post, and if he did, he could not take the responsibility, for the place to which he bore our men might be the spot of the severest carnage. But he urged me to ride up to head-quarters, to state our condition and the prospect for a battle around us, and urge, with all the eloquence possible, our instant removal. I thought it due to him and the men of whom I had charge, to follow his advice. I rode with all haste to Savage Station. As I approached it, I beheld the long lines of army wagons and ambulances stretching for miles, slowly retiring in the direction of James River. When I reached General Heintzleman's tent, I found everything foreshadowed an immediate removal; generals were there for council and commands — orderlies hurrying backwards and forwards in the wildest haste — surgeons, commissaries, colonels, crowding for directions and help. Now comes in a captain, with clothes torn and sword bent, with the tidings that the wagon train was hopelessly locked, and the troops were unable to proceed; then comes another, reporting that the enemy was crossing the Chickahominy at the Grapevine Bridge, and might be soon upon us. Another, that Jackson and his troops had taken the White House, and destroyed stores and transports. Another announced that the woods were full of scouts and spies of the enemy, who were stealing across in small squads, and even now capturing sick officers and small parties who had strayed into the by-roads. All these announcements created a fresh commotion, and orderlies were despatched with messages, and officers with commands.

The general issued the orders with all the calmness of one familiar with the greatest dangers. He listened most kindly to my statement, and told me that nothing could be done to help me; that all the wounded at Savage Station would have to be left behind, and that General McClellan had ordered all the ambulances to depart unencumbered; that four or five thousand wounded and sick men would so embarrass the army that escape might be impossible; and that much as it was to be regretted, it was a matter of stern necessity to leave our wounded in the hands of the enemy.

I asked him what he deemed my duty under the circumstances; that I could not now see Colonel Hays or General Kearney, and felt uncertain what, in this posture of affairs, they would desire me to do.

He replied: "I cannot advise you. If you remain, you will become a prisoner; no man can tell you what you may have to endure; you will lose all. You have no commands holding you here, and if you please to go with the army, no one ought to blame you."

I had hoped he would order me to remain, for to leave the men under my charge I felt was dishonorable and cruel, and with them I had resolved to stay, live or die; but I wished to be defended in my position by the command of such a man. I left the general's tent, and soon found my friend, Mr. Brunot, and learned that he, with that true, unflinching, and martyr-like devotion to the cause which he deemed to be right, which pre-eminently distinguished him, had resolved to remain and share the sorrow and captivity of those who had poured out their blood for their country.

I was strengthened in my purpose by this heroic resolve, and rode back through the forest to Carter's house, for the first time fully realizing the fate before us, and thanking God that it was my privilege to aid and comfort men who had borne greater hardships, and braved greater dangers, than I had been called to meet. When I reached the hospital, the lines of our forces were still standing under arms, facing the valley, and each moment expecting the appearance of the enemy from the forests on the stream.

I had as soon as possible the officers and men assembled under the shadow of a mulberry tree in our back grounds. All the sick who could walk, or be assisted, were likewise brought down.

I read to them a short portion of the New Testament, and then explained to them the actual position of things; that our army was retreating towards James River, and that our division had already started; and I advised such of them as felt they could walk a few miles to fall into the retiring columns; that some kind-hearted driver might permit them to ride, or that with the troops, if they should faint, some way would be provided to carry them on; that even if they should have to stop every few rods, it would be better than to fall into the hands of the enemy. I entreated the stronger to help the weaker; that God would send his angels to strengthen and defend them, if they, like the good Samaritan, lifted up and aided those who were ready to perish by the way; that the stores should be opened, and every man provided with all he needed.

I likewise told them that I had now no apprehension that the enemy would cross the river below us, for they were crossing one mile higher up; to take their time, and pack up what they thought they could carry; if they could bear their guns, to take them; they might be better to-morrow, and able to strike another blow; and that I hoped they would remember their safety was not in any human arm or defence, but in the watchful care of that God in whose hand was their breath and all their ways; if they fell down exhausted, to pray to Him; if they could not rise again, and were left alone, to lift their eyes to Him to whom the dying thief looked and hoped, and died in peace. If they fell into the hands of the enemy, to trust God, and even their enemies should be made at peace with them; and if taken captives, not to be ashamed of their cause, but to defend it boldly. "Do not let the enemy think that our soldiers are without consciences or principles. They are rebels and traitors, but you are the soldiers of law, and the representatives of the principles for which our fathers fought; and do not forget that a prisoner does not part with all his rights, and though deprived of his gun, he is still at liberty to defend his government and her constitution."

Those who were too ill to think of making the effort to escape I advised to endure patiently their fate, and to remember that there were thousands of their brave companions-in-arms that were in a worse condition than themselves; and that lying at Savage Station were many of these that had to be left behind, but to bear calmly what was one of the inevitable calamities of war.

We then sang together the beautiful hymn commencing,

"Jesus, my God, I know His name."

21

I then prayed with them, and committed each one and their families to Him in whose sight they were of "more value than many sparrows."

After the service was concluded, the agitation that had reigned in all minds was evidently stilled, and each felt that we were safer, because we had invoked the Divine protection; but the inquiry began to run from lip to lip: "Doctor, what are you going to do? Are you going to leave us? What will become of us, if you forsake us?" I soon relieved their apprehensions on this score by telling them that I would never leave them; and I was more than compensated for all the suffering that followed by the gratitude and blessing of many.

While I was yet speaking, Mr. Douglass, one of the nurses in the hospital over which Dr. Smith had presided, came to me and said that more than half of the patients in that hospital had left in pursuit of the army, and that the remainder desired to come over and place themselves under our care. He went back, and in a few moments, on stretchers and in the arms of their companions, the sick were brought to us; and soon after Mr. Luke, the hospital steward, and Sergeant Temple, came in, having followed the army some distance, and finding the woods full of the enemy, had returned. I was again urged by officers and men to go up to Savage Station, and ascertain the state of things now, for possibly there might be some change. I could find at least what would be the best road for them to take in retreat. I went again to the Station, and learned from my friend, Colonel S. McKelvy, that the order had already been issued for the destruction of all remaining ammunition and commissary stores. He then informed me that the long train of cars, forty or fifty in number, was being loaded with shells, kegs of powder, and cartridges, and that in a few minutes the work of destruction would begin. I could see, mounting above the trees, the flames from the vast commissary stores at Fair Oaks Station.

I entreated Colonel McKelvy to permit me to place in the cars a barrel of coffee, twenty boxes of crackers, a bag of rice, three or four barrels of potatoes, and three barrels of dried apples. This he had done himself, and ordered the engineer to run down the road as far as Meadow Station and the Railroad house, and throw off for us these articles, and such other things as were likely to be in demand.

This was done, and thus was secured to us the food that preserved our lives for a fortnight. When I returned to the hospital at Carter's house, our troops had been removed and concentrated around Savage Station; but as they were marching away one of the colonels rode up to the gate and said he was withdrawing his pickets, and that it was highly probable the enemy would be there in less than half an hour, and urged all to make their escape. As I approached the house through the fields, I beheld a long, scattered line of the patients staggering away, some carrying their guns, and supporting a companion on an arm,—others tottering feebly over a staff which they appeared to have scarcely strength to lift up. One was borne upon the shoulders of two of his companions, in the hope that when he had gone a little distance he might be able to walk.

One had already sat down fainting from the exertion of a few steps; some had arisen from the first rest, staggered forward a few steps and fell in the road, but after a few moments in the open air, and stimulated by the fear of the enemy, they could walk more strongly. Never have I beheld a spectacle more touching and more sad. They retired one by one across the fields, and were lost in the forest; and of all that throng of sick and wounded men not more than five or six fell into the hands of the enemy; the rest struggled forward until they reached the army, and borne on by a living stream, knew not how they were carried forward.

Of the number that left us on this day were several officers, and amongst the rest Colonel Kirkwood, of the 63d Pennsylvania, who had for two weeks been confined to the hospital with typhoid fever; and when he resolved to escape he had to be lifted on his horse, and attended by his colored servant left us to find, if possible, his regiment. But after going out into the forest, the black boy was frightened at the appearance of some Confederate soldiers near them, and at once fled, leaving the colonel unable to guide his horse, and at the mercy of the enemy. Just at this juncture one of our nurses, by the name of Scott, of the 57th Pennsylvania, who had gone some distance with his comrades to help them, was returning, and seeing the colonel, generously went to his assistance, led his horse, and held him on until he saw him safe in the bosom of the army.

I returned to Savage Station, taking nurses with me for the purpose of securing such articles as would be needed at the hospital, and would otherwise be destroyed.

About noon the work of destruction commenced, and no language can paint the spectacle. Hundreds of barrels of flour and rice, sugar and molasses, salt, and coffee, were consigned to the flames; and great heaps of these precious articles in a few moments lay scorching and smouldering. A long line of boxes of crackers, fifteen feet high, were likewise thrown into the mass; and the workmen seemed to have a savage and fiendish joy in consigning to the flames what a few days afterwards they would have given thousands to obtain. The scene was altogether unearthly and demoniac. The men, blackened with smoke and cinders, were hurling into the fire boxes of goods, tents, fragments of broken cars, and barrels of whisky and turpentine; and then would be hurled into the burning mass boxes of ammunition, and explosion followed explosion, throwing up fragments of shells into the heavens, and the flames mounted above the tops of the loftiest trees. The ammunition was not so easily disposed of, and shells, kegs of powder, etc., were placed in the cars.

The engine attached to this train was ready at any moment to spring on the track; each of the cars was set on fire, and when the flames began to wind around the wooden structures the train was put in motion. Being a descending grade it was soon rushing with the wildest fury, and every revolution of the wheels added to the volume of the flames, until the eye ceased to see the structure of the cars, and only beheld a terrific monster, which,

21 *

like some huge serpent of fire, had come forth to add a new feature of horror to the scene. On and on it rushed, with a tread which caused the hills to tremble. I could not think of anything as a suitable representation of a spectacle so grand, but that of a thousand thunderbolts chained together, and wreathed with lightnings, rushing with scathing fury and the roar of the tornado over the trembling earth. In a few seconds the engine, cars, and wheels were nothing but one long chain of fire, a frightful meteor flashing past us.

The distance from Savage Station to the Chickahominy is about two and a half miles. I had placed myself on one of the eminences near our hospital, from which I could command a fine view of the railroad and the coming train. I knew that the long bridge over the river was burned. It plunged past me like some vast monster from a sea of fire. On it thundered until there was a stupendous crash, and far up in the heavens were thrown burning fragments of the cars. This was instantly succeeded by the explosion of innumerable great bombs and kegs of powder. Now a great shell dashed into the air with a wild and angry shriek — this burst and left behind a flash of flame; and again another darted forth and tore with fury through the branches of forest trees; and bomb after bomb sprang from the fiery mass, hissing and screaming like fiends in agony, and coursing in every direction through the forests and the clear heavens. Crash came after crash for many minutes; and again some great shell exploded under the waters, and threw far up a jet of the stream, to which, as it fell in drops and spray, the light of the evening sun gave more than the splendor of ten thousand diamonds.

Rarely, I believe, has there been a spectacle of greater wonder and grandeur. Such was the momentum of this train, that when it reached the chasm it sprang out fully forty feet, and the engine and first car leaped over the first pier in the stream, and there hangs suspended one of the most impressive monuments of the Peninsular disasters.

I spent most of this day at Savage Station. I wished to be near the great centre of intelligence, and learn, if possible, what was to be the fate of our army. During these anxious hours we were at one time comforted by the report that General Burnside had landed on James River with large reinforcements, and was then marching to our relief. But this, on reflection, was dismissed as fabulous; and we turned again to look our real condition in the face.

About three o'clock in the afternoon General Heintzleman, surrounded by the officers of his staff, mounted his horse. The officers and soldiers who still lingered with their companions, now prepared to leave. And many a manly cheek was wet with tears as they bade farewell to those whom they never expected to meet again. Fathers had to drag themselves away from the couches of their sons; and after they had gone a few steps, would return to look once more, and to renew the oft-repeated instructions to nurse and surgeon. There were many sad partings. Up to this time the disabled had not known that they were to be left behind; and when it became manifest that such was to be their fate, the scene could not be pictured by human language. Some wounded men, who were left in their tents, struggled through the grounds, exclaiming they "would rather die than fall into the hands of the Rebels." I heard one man crying out, "O my God! is this the reward I deserve for all the sacrifices I have made, the battles I have fought, and the agony I have endured from my wounds." Some of the younger soldiers wept like children; others turned pale, and some fainted. Poor fellows! they thought this was the last drop in the cup of bitterness, but there were yet many to be added.

The surgeons who were on duty in the hospitals joined their regiments, and not more than one-third of those who had before been with us remained. The names of some of these are found in subsequent pages; and it gives me great regret that I have not the names of all those who remained, thereby incurring all the sufferings and losses of captivity.

More than one-half of the nurses left us and joined the long procession of sick and wounded, which was greatly increased by the straggling mass of men who had lost their regiments. Some nurses who might have gone remained with the sick and wounded, to endure privation, want, and incessant toil. I wish I had their names. I would invite all the towns and villages of which they are citizens to honor them as deserving more than a wreath of laurel.

About four o'clock we saw moving over the plain opposite to us the last of the ambulances and wagons, retiring in the distance, and the light of the evening sun was reflected in dazzling brilliance from the guns of the departing regiments. Here and there was a horseman galloping through the the dust; but the great throng of dashing officers, of plumed cavalry, of regiments with waving banners and music, had passed away like the dream of a brilliant tournament. We were not, however, yet quite abandoned. Opposite to Savage Station, looking north, is a large plain of several hundred acres. On the furthest line of this is the Williamsburg road, and beyond is a dark pine forest. The field gradually ascends from the station to the road. On this field were standing in line of battle 20,000 men under General Sumner, the rear-guard of the army, left to hold in check the enemy until our troops were safe beyond White Oak Swamp.

General Sumner commanded his own corps and part of Heintzleman's and Franklin's. For hours they stood in this open field, waiting the approach of the enemy — thousands of them still and motionless as statues. Now and then a soldier would start out of the dark line and come down to the station for water, bearing his own and his comrades' canteens. And when he returned all were as silent and motionless as before. Seldom have I seen anything in my life more impressive and morally grand than that presented by this rear-guard of the army. Regiment after regiment, and division after division, filed by them, — long trains of wagons and ambulances passed through the ranks, but they moved not. All faces amongst them wore the expression of heroic sacrifice. The fate of the army was in their hands, and they were determined it should be saved; and there was no flinching when they were left alone without supports and reserves. Never was there assembled a nobler body of men, and rarely was there a sublimer spectacle.

About five o'clock, P. M., we saw rising up in the field towards the Chickahominy a great cloud of dust. Very soon afterwards there burst upon us the thunder of artillery, and from the upper rooms of the Savage House we could see the approaching columns of the enemy.

The first balls discharged from the enemy's guns fell amongst our wounded men, and the pains of one poor sufferer were at an end. Dr. Swinburne immediately sent forth a flag of truce, saying that the house was an hospital, and the grounds around it were crowded with wounded men. General Jackson expressed his regret, and had the direction of his guns changed. Then commenced a magnificent artillery duel. Shell met shell in the heavens from the contending cannon, and battery responded to battery, until it was one continued and unceasing roar of the mightiest thunder. For an hour not a musket was fired,—the lines of the army remained motionless. Suddenly the whole mass of the enemy's forces sprang forward with wild yells and screams like Camanche Indians, and hurried past us into the open field in front of our troops. At this moment it appeared to me I could see long streams of fire, like serpents' tongues, dart from our many thousand muskets, and louder than the roar swelled up the shout of defiance. Beaten back by this leaden storm, the enemy wavered and retreated a few steps to the railroad. But soon after troops coming up behind them, pressed the front line once more into the field.

Again there leaped from ten thousand guns the fiery blast, and yell answered yell. Now the whole field was so covered with the pall of battle we could see nothing but the vivid flash from the cannon, like the lightning darting out of a cloud, and the muskets in the hands of our men pointed towards us, still vomiting forth streams of flame. For a moment there would be a pause, a lull in the battle, to be succeeded by the instantaneous discharge of five thousand guns; and then, as if the contending hosts had been stung to frenzy, the rage of the contest was redoubled. The clash of arms was occasionally interrupted by the coming into the field of fresh regiments, cheering their companions with loud shouts. The dullest ear could perceive the difference between the voices of our men and those of the enemy. Ours shouted in clear, ringing, and manly tones, while the enemy's sounded like the scream of the panther and the yell of the savage.

At one time in the conflict there was the simultaneous discharge of two thousand muskets, as if men had fired in each other's faces. It was a moment I shall never forget; the thought of the crushing, the piercing, and the agony; the life-blood gushing out; the strong arm palsied, and the bright eye darkened forever; the many souls appearing the same instant before God,—all brought to the heart overwhelming emotions, as if in a moment I had lived years. This I afterwards learned was occasioned by two regiments, the 5th Vermont and the 11th Alabama, finding themselves within ten feet of each other. In the cloud of battle and shades of the evening, neither were certain of the character of the other: both withheld their fire. Some of the officers of the Vermonters were anxious to fire and charge, but the colonel could not give an order that might be fatal to friends and brothers. He therefore advanced in front of his regiment, and called out aloud, "What regiment is that?"

For a moment there was no reply; when there was the response, "What regiment is yours?"

"The 5th Vermont."

"Then," cried the Rebel commander, "in God's name take it, fire!"—and the men, looking into each other's eyes, placed their guns against each other's bosoms and fired. How many of the enemy fell I know not, but I understood two hundred of the brave Vermonters were left on the field. Some of these I afterwards saw, and from them received this account. The battle continued to rage with unabated fury until about half past eight o'clock; then the firing gradually slackened, the cannon of the enemy ceased to reply to ours, and the discharges of musketry from their side became more and more distant, and at random. Now and then the battle would for five or ten minutes burst out afresh, some portion of the Confederates retiring from the field would wander near our lines, be attacked, turn on us and rally for a moment, and then flee. At nine o'clock they were all gone, and not a sound arose from the field and forests but the groans of the dying, and the calls for help. This was one of the most desperate conflicts of the Peninsula.

The force of the enemy must have been far greater than ours, for I learned from their officers that fully fifty thousand men were dashed on our rear-guard.

But nobly and grandly were they repulsed; and when the final cheer of victory arose from our columns, and regiments in forest, rifle-pit, and field answered each other, and the great shout of triumph could be heard for miles, there was not a solitary derisive cry in answer. The victory was complete; well did our rear-guard fulfil their trust, and hurl back the forces which were pressing from behind to throw us into confusion, and secure the capture and destruction of a large part of our army. The repulse of that evening enabled our columns and baggage trains to place between us and the enemy the difficult and, in most places, impassable slough, White Oak Swamp. The retreat under such circumstances, in the presence of two armies, each of equal strength with our own, was most hazardous. We had for our vast wagon and ambulance trains, and parks of artillery, but one road; and along this narrow passage-way, thus encumbered, our entire army had to retire, and if our rear had been defeated and pressed by an active enemy, the result must have been fatal to thousands.

But to General Sumner and the gallant men whom he commanded is the gratitude due of holding in check an enemy double our strength.

The anxiety which he felt during the progress of the battle can never be told. During the early part of the engagement we could see clearly the movements of the troops in that portion of the battle fought in the open field; but as the cloud became dark and night came on, we could see nothing but the blaze of musketry and the fiery burst of cannon. But still we felt certain that our men held their own, for there was no change in their positions, and we

22

could hear distinctly the commands of our officers. But as the strife thickened, and the thunder became more appalling, all hearts stood still: the devout prayed, the timid wept and hid themselves, the pulses of the wildest excitement bounded in the veins of the true soldiers; and great was our relief when it became certain that our forlorn hope had sustained itself and beaten back the foe.

From some of the officers of our army who were in the columns marching towards White Oak Swamp, I have heard that the roar of battle as it came from the rear was majestic. The night was unusually calm, not a breath of air stirred the trees, and all nature around them was asleep; but from one spot came the sound of the most terrible tumult, as if, while the whole world slept, on one point had been let loose all the elements of destruction and terror. A dark cloud rolled up in the heavens, angry flashes of light darted over its face, the earth trembled, and there came out of the bosom of the forest the voices of the most terrible tempest.

I heard it stated at the time, amongst the incidents of this battle, that the enemy had driven column after column, after his usual manner, to break our centre. Here was General Burns, with clothes and hat pierced, and face covered with blood: — the general still rallied and cheered his men. At length two companies, concluding that all would be killed who remained there, commenced deliberately marching off the field. General Burns expostulated, entreated, commanded them, all in vain. At length, taking off his torn hat and throwing it down, he besought them not to disgrace themselves and their general. This last appeal was successful, they returned and fought more desperately to wipe out the cowardice of a moment.

Never was there a more impressive spectacle than that presented by this retreat of the "Grand Army." This vast body of men, well trained, fully equipped, and equalling in courage any army which the world has ever seen, eager for the fight, asking but for generals to lead them on to victory, was, after having almost knocked at the door of the Rebel stronghold, retreating in haste — at the command of one man — who, however distinguished for ability in one department of military science, in every hour of danger was a child, and in every great emergency was oppressed with conscious incapacity. After the enemy was repulsed at the battle of "Savage Station," General Sumner sent to General McClellan for, as he expressed himself, "orders to push the enemy into the Chickahominy." General McClellan's reply was, that "the rear-guard would follow the retreat of the main body of the army." On the reception of this command, the greatest consternation and displeasure reigned among both officers and men. Many openly rebelled—they wished to sacrifice themselves in any way, rather than by a disgraceful retreat. But at length order reigned, and the rear-guard took up their line of march, slowly toiling through mud and marshy plains, and the grey light of dawn found them safe beyond the White Oak Swamp. Many most interesting incidents occurred during this forced march. I have heard of the lady and little child, an infant of but a few months, whose smiles shed a radiance upon all around them; and the tired soldiers were nerved to fresh endurance of the weary march by the presence of these delicate ones, who shared their hardships and fatigue. They were the wife and child of General Richardson, of Michigan — a brave and noble officer — who afterwards died of wounds received at the battle of Antietam. His wife had spent much time in camp with him, and was looked upon as a good angel by the soldiers who had been favored with her gentle ministrations. Ex-Governor Wood, of Illinois, was present on this occasion, and though only a civilian, greatly assisted the officers by his counsel and cheering advice. Many times when the long train of wagons seemed hopelessly locked, did he, by a word fitly spoken, untie the Gordian knot, and set them once more in motion. At other times his venerable form, with snowy beard and hair, could be seen riding through the ranks, encouraging the faint-hearted, and shaming the cowardly by sharing all their dangers and privations; and such was his influence, that, under his eye, none complained, but marched solemnly on, grimly determining to wipe out this disgrace by future victories.

During the night General Sumner withdrew his batteries and troops unmolested, and before the enemy was apprised of it, was five miles on the way to James River.

I have never seen any official report of our losses in this battle, but I heard that General Sedgwick lost in his division six hundred men. He occupied the most dangerous and fatal part of the field. I presume our killed and wounded were not less than one thousand. Most of the last were gathered up by ambulances, and brought into Savage Station, but numbers were found on Monday and Tuesday by the enemy, and sent to Richmond.

It may not be inappropriate to say here that no small part of the praise for the successful retreat of our army is due to General Sumner. Like an iron wall he breasted the foe at Savage Station, when he stood between the enemy, flushed with victory and confident in our continuous defeat, and our exhausted and desponding army. Again, on the next day, at Glendale, he infused his invincible courage into all his command. The disposition of the troops at the battle of Malvern Hill was known to have been made by him; and, in the absence of General McClellan, General Sumner, during most of that memorable day, commanded the army. The energy infused into every corps and company, and the bold confidence which sprang up in the bosoms of worn, exhausted, hopeless men, displayed the presence and power of a master spirit.

22 *

CHAPTER XVII.

MONDAY MORNING, *June 30th.*

Silence of the Morning after the Battle — The Rebel Soldier reconnoitring — The Surrender of the Hospitals — Refusal of German Marines to surrender — German Soldier at Meadow Station — Peril of Chaplain Sloan — Conversation with a Confederate Officer, Captain Taylor, of New Kent.

IMMEDIATELY after the close of the battle of the previous evening, a violent thunder-storm had come up; and so suddenly did this burst upon us, that for a time we thought it was a renewal of the battle. This served to purify the air, and was refreshing to the wounded lying on the field.

The morning came to us cloudless and calm. Very early I went forth to discover the actual condition of things. I advanced to the highest point in the field, and looked down on the main road, the railroad, and a dark pine forest. There was no sign of the presence of the enemy. Our army had disappeared; and in field and forest, where a few hours before had been a most terrific tumult, and the voices of thousands shouting in defiance or triumph, not a sound came forth, not a soldier moved along the roads; the tents were silent, and the fields deserted. The scene reminded me of the sublime vision of the prophet: "I beheld, and lo! there was no man, and all the birds of the heavens were fled; I beheld, and lo! the fruitful place was a wilderness, and all the cities were broken down."

While I was asking myself, "Who shall next appear on this stage?" I perceived an object that instantly fixed all my attention; this was a Rebel soldier about forty rods from me, creeping along towards the railroad; very fortunately he did not see me. I was standing in the open field; he was crouching under the branches of the trees, and after the manner of a scout, was creeping from point to point, then stopping and minutely surveying the scene. I followed his example, and with a step of furry softness hastened to a neighboring fence, and there watched him; and from this point of concealment, I observed his movements with the deepest interest. After disappearing, and again appearing, he was finally lost to my eye. I hastened back to the hospital, fully assured that we would know the fate reserved for us in a few moments. I had the nurses aroused, breakfast served, the rooms cleansed, and the house put in order, for I knew not but that Captain Carter might be one of our visitors.

About seven A. M. we saw in the distance a troop of cavalry. They had come out of the forest; and on seeing our house were halted for orders; their swords were drawn, and with a wild dash, leaping ravines and fences, they rode up to our gate.

As soon as we saw them in the distance, I had all the men called to come within the house: this command was obeyed before given.

When the cavalry drew up at the gate, the officer in command shouted aloud:

"Who is in command here?"

I was standing on the portico, and stepped out and answered, "I am in command."

"You are a surgeon, are you not?"

"No, captain, I am a chaplain, but in command of this hospital and the one at Meadow Station."

"Ah," said he, "and how many men have you?"

"At both places, about two hundred and thirty," I replied.

"Are any of them able to travel?"

"Not one; all such left us yesterday."

"Have you any personal property here? for all you have shall be respected. Is that your horse?"

"Yes, sir, and the pony."

"Well, they shall not be disturbed, and nothing that you have shall be taken; but all the arms and the clothing of the officers who have left are ours, of course."

He then alighted, came into the house, spoke very kindly to the men, and went from room to room, assuring the sick that they had no reason to fear; they should be well treated. But such was the agitation produced in some cases of extreme nervous debility, that I was apprehensive of the worst results. One young man was with great difficulty revived from the shock.

In a few moments the dragoons were seated around the table in the· background, chatting in the liveliest way, drinking coffee, and eating such food as we could provide. They were loud in their praises of Jackson, and spoke in the highest terms of his bravery and piety; they recounted the brilliant feats performed by them in the last few days; and all united in assuring us that our entire army was bagged; that Jackson, Longstreet, and the Hills were in our rear and left flank, Magruder and Huger in front and on our right flank, and that escape was impossible; that they expected to have to fight another battle, and then the Grand Army of the Potomac would live only in history and song.

In answer to my inquiries, they assured me that the force under Jackson was about 35,000, and that 40,000 troops had arrived in Richmond within a few days from the army of Beauregard; and that they supposed their entire force was 150,000. They expressed great surprise when I told them that our army had not more than 70,000 effective men; and that Porter's corps, 35,000 strong, had in the first day's engagement defeated and driven back 60,000, and in the second day's fight had been overpowered by double their numbers.

They predicted a speedy peace, but most solemnly affirmed that a return to the old Union was, under any circumstances, impossible. "No," said they, "if you were to get down on your knees to us we would not come back." The leader of this band was a Texan, and evidently a kind, generous-hearted man. I subsequently saw him in Richmond, where he alighted from his horse, and came a considerable distance to shake hands, and to inquire if he could aid me in any way. Before he left, he gave me a paper, authorizing me to exercise full authority in the hospital, to retain all the stores on hand, and commanding all officers and soldiers of the Confederate army to respect these orders; and for our protection he left a sergeant of the 16th Mississippi, of the name of Houeb.

After they left us small numbers of soldiers came to the hospital several times, asking for bread or water; they were humble and polite, requesting permission even to enter the kitchen. I found from conversation with many of these that more than two-thirds of them could not read; they were very ignorant and very dirty; some clothed in a light, linsey-woolsey grey, and others in butternut brown. As a general thing they knew nothing of the causes of the war, but supposed they were called to repel us from going South, taking their negroes, and giving all the lands of their country to the slaves. They acknowledged that our troops were very different from what they had anticipated; they found them far braver than they had been led to believe. "Some of your men," said they, "fought like tigers, and when defeated did not run, but turned at bay, and fought as men who had made up their minds to die. We knew that the Illinois and Indiana troops were desperate fellows, and could generally beat us, for they are stronger men than ours, but we had not expected such hard play from the Yankees." Then they talked for two hours, and were perfectly at home with us.

After they had gone I took the guard who had been left for our protection, and walked over to Meadow Station. Here again I found that the shock arising from the presence of the enemy had seriously imperilled the lives of some who were in a fair way of recovery. Seated amongst the sick soldiers on the porch under the shadow of the trees were many of the Confederates, engaged in animated discussions, and each magnifying his exploits.

While here I learned that twenty marines, mostly Germans, had that morning come up along the railroad from below the White House, determined to find out what had become of our army. They had by some means passed through the enemy's lines, and on reaching Meadow Station stated that on the way they had not seen a soldier, but when they came to the station they met several Confederates. They refused to surrender, drew their pistols and cutlasses, turned back and deliberately walked down the rail track. What became of these brave men I could not learn, but supposed they reached their vessel in safety, for I never heard of their being taken prisoners.

I can never forget the pluck of a German soldier whom I found lying on the porch of the depôt, very sick. I spoke to him and felt his pulse. He had been brought in that morning from some one of the deserted camps, and did not know me. To my questions he was indisposed to answer. I brought him some medicine and wine, and when I told the nurse to lift him up and administer the restorative, the German shook his head and turned away his face, and said, most decidedly, "No good, no good; I'se no take your medicine; you the enemy of my country, and shot my broders: no take your medicine."

I saw in a moment he took me for a Rebel surgeon. I took off my hat, showed him the U. S. on the front, and told him I was his friend and brother.

He looked intently into my face, and exclaimed: "Tank Gott: I takes him, doctor, I takes him all."

I then and in all my subsequent visits looked upon this man with the deepest respect, for he was a soldier from principle, and loved the right more than life. The noble fellow improved. I afterwards saw him in Richmond, and hope he still lives.

This was a day of the deepest anxiety and gloom. Every Confederate officer and soldier whom we met said that General McClellan was perfectly entrapped in the swamps and surrounded by his enemies: his escape was impossible. They were smiling and joyous, and told us the war was over. The North could never raise another army, and after the capitulation of this we would see the perfect folly of attempting to subdue the South. At Savage Station I found that all our officers and surgeons were despondent and nearly hopeless in regard to the escape of our forces: all they could hear was from officers on the other side.

There had been left with us 200 or 300 Confederate soldiers as a guard. They were not cruel or insulting, and were very soon on the best of terms with the Yankees. There was between them and our men a most striking contrast. They were in complexion as dark as Asiatics; sallow, with long black hair hanging over their shoulders, and without any nervous restlessness; but the moment they were off duty sinking into oriental languor; "the sweet doing of nothing" was the highest enjoyment. Even if a knot of them played cards, it was indolently and carelessly done; and often their English was an African patois, and needed an interpreter. But our men were restless, and even when on duty trod the ground with impatience, gathering into bands for smoking, discussing questions, cooking, digging up roots, and running from one part of the grounds to another to see every new arrival. This endless tumult, bustle, and hurry, but, above all, the ten thousand questions asked, distressed and annoyed the stagnant Southerners, and they would often beg the Yankees to take themselves off and let them rest.

During the afternoon we were at work removing the stores of provisions from the railroad track to the hospital. I had all the nurses engaged in bearing these across the fields on their backs and on stretchers, and in various ways we were securing what had been spared for us.

During one of these trips we observed a company of horsemen riding swiftly towards us. When they approached within fifty yards of us, I saw the young men around the captain throw the strap of their carbines over their shoulders, placing their guns over the pommel of their saddles, cock them, and moving slowly they drew near. I thought the action was strange and threatening, and commanded the men to drop their loads and sit down on the grass. I advanced in front. When the captain came within ten paces of us, I saw him turn and wave his hand to his followers. They uncocked their pieces, threw the strap over the neck, and came up to us.

The leader bowed, and introduced himself as Captain Taylor, of New Kent, and the commander of a company in the celebrated Stuart cavalry. He was much of a gentleman, asked me when we were taken prisoners? how we were treated? how many sick we had? After he had satisfied himself, he asked me if I was not a chaplain? I replied that I was.

23

"I thought so," said he. "Do you know Chaplain Sloan?"

I told him I did not. (I subsequently saw Mr. Sloan at Harrison's Landing.)

"Mr. Sloan," said he, "once preached for us at New Kent; we thought a great deal of him. My mother and myself and wife were members of his church. These young men," said he, "were all students in the classical school he superintended at New Kent. He was a very valuable and useful man amongst us. At the commencement of the war he left us and went, as we understood, to Philadelphia. But we afterwards heard that he had become a chaplain in your army, and we all took a solemn vow that wherever we should meet him we would shoot him; and when we first saw you we supposed that you were Mr. Sloan, and you may have observed the young men cocking their guns; this was when we took you for him. And now," said he, "I am very glad that you are not Mr. Sloan, for it would have troubled me all my life to have shot him." I told him my pleasure at not being Mr. Sloan was fully equal to his in not finding him.

He then went on conversing, with the manner of one who had thrown a mighty load off his soul. He evidently did not relish the thought of being the murderer of Mr. Sloan, and sincerely hoped that he might never come in their way. He then told me that he had left his family, mother, wife, and children, at New Kent; and the families of most of the men about him were in that same neighborhood, and that their anxiety had been intense when our army advanced to New Kent. "But," said he, "we have been fifteen times in your rear, and know all that was done by your troops; and to your credit, I must say that your men behaved well. They did not rob the families nor molest them, and I have not heard of a single case of violence. We have heard, indeed, of your taking pigs, turkeys, and chickens; this is what is to be looked for in an army; but we have not heard of a single case of violence or insult to families; that speaks loudly for the discipline of your army."

I told him "I thanked him for that drop of comfort. I knew that the officers aimed to restrain the troops, but sometimes men broke over all discipline."

"Your men," said he, "behave well, but don't fight like our men."

"Pray, captain," said I, "where did your men show any superiority to ours?"

"Why, I think, in every battle yet fought, and nowhere more than at Williamsburg. We fought you with our rear-guard; we had no expectation of being able to do more than hold you in check until the main body of our forces were out of harm's way. But when your generals were so easily checked, this emboldened us to hurry back reinforcements, and attempt greater things; and I do believe that if we had resolved to make a final stand at Williamsburg, we could have bound you there another month, and then the heat and fever would have finished the work we began."

"Captain," I replied, "you know that the battle of Williamsburg was mainly fought by one division, General Hooker's. Generals Kearney and Hancock rendered very essential aid, but it was almost night when they reached the field. We had not so many men in that battle as you had, and yours were all the advantages of position, intrenchments, and strong earthworks, and we had to debouch into the fields in your front, over a narrow neck of land. You had every advantage that men should ask; the storm was drenching and disheartening; our artillery was engulfed in the mud; yet, notwithstanding all these things, General Hooker, with the aid of three or four regiments of General Kearney's, held his position for five hours, until, by a flank movement of General Hancock, you were driven from the field. In the strength of your intrenchments, you ought to have held out against fifty thousand men."

"Well," said he, "we have thought that one of our men was equal to four of yours: that may have been slightly too large; do you not think, in all honesty, doctor, that our men are greatly superior to yours in military qualities?"

"No," said I, "our men are fully equal to yours, and in many respects superior. We are cooler, will endure more, suffer greater hardships, and fight more unflinchingly than yours."

"Well," said he, smiling, "you have never shown those qualities yet; but I hope, for the honor of the American name, you may in the future. We have had several battles on the Peninsula: in which of these do you think you were victorious?"

"Were you at Savage Station last night, captain, in the battle?"

"No, we were on the left. But what of it?"

"Why, simply this: that you were most thoroughly whipped, and if you had been there at the conclusion of the firing, you would have seen our columns standing where they did at the commencement of the fight; and of your men, there was not one in the open fields, and all your artillery was removed or silenced."

"And how many men do you suppose General Jackson brought into action?"

"I do not know, certainly, but suppose from forty to fifty thousand. —Well, sir, we had but twenty thousand, all told; and men who have been under arms for twenty-five days, who, during all this time, were enduring the severest toil and exhausting duties, and yet they repulsed twice their number of fresh troops; and in the engagement of last night your men pursued their usual tactics: they crept into ravines, hid behind fences, and skulked like Indians into forests. No, captain, you have asked my opinion, and I have given it to you. Your men, as a general thing, are not equal to ours."

He laughed, and said: "Doctor, I have provoked this; we will not be likely to agree, but I don't think less of you for answering and defending your soldiers with spirit. But do you not think that your cause is fatally defeated, and the independence of the South certain? We have just come up from the left of your army; we consider the escape of General McClellan hopeless. We have seventy thousand in your rear, and fully as many in front; and entangled in the forest and swamp, how can you escape? It was understood when we left that General McClellan had sent an aid to General Lee, to arrange the surrender of his entire army."

"You may believe it, but I will not; if twenty
23 *

thousand men could beat back your army last night, I feel sure that seventy thousand will do more than that to-day."

"Well," said he, "there are some things which even brave men cannot do; you cannot drag your cannon through swamps; you cannot move your trains through forests so deep and dark that the light of the sun never reaches the earth; you cannot bridge rivers in the face of a powerful and victorious enemy; we know all this country well, and I assure you the escape of your army is impossible."

"Well, captain, you will find that when you press such men as ours to the wall, they will defend themselves with a desperation which will end in your defeat. Even now, the roar of the battle is the proof that we still have an army."

In the meantime the men on both sides had become quite familiar, and were fully exchanging views. The captain bade me good-bye, and hoped we might meet in better times.

CHAPTER XVIII.

MONDAY, *June 30th.*

March of the Army from Savage Station — Guns left behind —
Frequent halts for return of Scouts— Movements of the Enemy
— Crossing White Oak Swamp — Uncertainty of every Step
— The relief— Night firing — Position of our Army on Mon-
day — Battle of White Oak Swamp — Exciting Scenes.

I HAVE before mentioned that General McClellan
left Savage Station on Sunday morning, June 29th.
Most fortunately for us, up to this time the Confederates were under the impression that General Mc-
Clellan would most certainly retreat by the way of
the Pamunky, and retire towards Yorktown; and in
order to prevent this they sent strong bodies of
troops to the north side of the Chickahominy, and
did not become aware of our real purpose until noon
of Sabbath.

The march of our army was of necessity slow.
We had an enormous train of more than five thousand wagons, and but one narrow road. The woods
on both sides were swarming with enemies. There
was entire uncertainty in regard to everything before us; our foes might be massed in force beyond
the White Oak Swamp. The roads had, therefore,
to be carefully felt, and scouts were sent in advance,
and who as they returned and reported that to a cer-

tain distance the way was clear, the order was then given for the advance of a mile or less. In this way the army slowly moved on, until it disappeared from the cultivated fields and was buried in the wilderness; and all our artillery and guns were saved but one siege piece, of which the carriage broke, and the gun had to be abandoned.

Before night came on there was felt by all the general officers the most profound uneasiness. The crash and thunder of battle in the rear; the roar of cannon and report of musketry in our front; the near presence of thousands of concealed foes on both flanks, made this one of the most painfully oppressive hours in the history of the campaign.

At one moment there was a wide-felt apprehension. When the enemy discovered that we had retired from our intrenchments and outposts, they sprang on the track of the army with all the fury of wild beasts seeking their prey; and their screams were calculated to carry terror to the stoutest hearts. Our army halted, and threw itself into the line of battle. A section of artillery was sent back by General Keyes, with a detachment of infantry and the 3d Pennsylvania cavalry, under General Averill. The enemy advanced boldly to take the battery, not seeing the horsemen who were concealed in the forest. General Averill charged on them, and in a few moments their entire force was in full retreat. They were driven back three miles, and thus our rear regiments were relieved from the annoyance and galling fire of our pursuers.

Before night the army passed White Oak Swamp, and placed that barrier between us and the enemy;

and after dark courier after courier arrived at the head-quarters of General McClellan, with the welcome tidings that General Sumner was holding his own, and the victory of the night was complete; and very soon another came in announcing the glad intelligence that Generals Porter and Keyes had reached the James River, and established communication with our men-of-war.

It was now thought, as the enemy had not met us in front, that it was very improbable they would attempt to pursue us over the swamp.

General Kearney crossed the swamp one mile higher up than the usual road, at Brackett's Ford, and about sundown had secured all his trains and artillery; and after advancing in security a short distance his scouts fell upon the enemy's pickets, and there commenced a very brisk firing in the woods in front. The reconnoissance made it certain that the Confederate forces were near us, and that an attempt to advance along that road would be hotly contested, and might bring on a general engagement. General Kearney drew up his men in the order of battle until after night, and then in the darkness sought to join the other divisions of the army. I have often heard the men and officers of the army speak of that night's march in the gloomy forest, where nothing could be seen but the flash of the fire-fly. The uncertainty of the way, the near presence of the enemy, the thunder of the battle not far from them, made this a night long to be remembered; and the most thoughtless were oppressed with sad anticipations of to-morrow. Many have told me

that they abandoned all hope of escape, but determined to sell their lives as dearly as possible.

Monday arose on the army with no enemy in sight.
General Sumner crossed the swamp about 9 A. M.,
bringing all his guns with him (and in all this campaign he never lost a gun or a color), and in less than
an hour Jackson, Longstreet, and Hill, with their
forces, could be seen on the hills to the north and
west of the swamp, and were preparing to cross in
force.

Here there was a brisk cannonading which lasted
for several hours, until our artillery was withdrawn
from the position and concentrated on the roads from
which we had every reason to fear a flank movement.

To guard against the success of such a demonstration, strong bodies of our troops were massed at important points on the several roads. On those leading from Richmond General Heintzleman, with the
divisions of Generals Hooker, Kearney, Sedgwick,
and McCall, were placed. Our trains and the advancing troops were to pass over the road to Turkey
Bend or Malvern Hill, called Quaker Road. This
road cuts at right angles the various highways running from Richmond east, and therefore is the great
highway to James River from Savage Station. Along
this road all the artillery troops and wagons of the
army had to pass. It was the plan of the enemy,
as soon as they discovered the course we were
taking, to cut in twain our army and to drive back
and capture such portion as could be severed from
the main body.

Franklin and Sumner held the rear, Slocum was

on the left, and Heintzleman on the right. Hooker occupied a position on the Quaker Road, to his right McCall, and again Kearney the extreme right. Those various divisions were thrown into these positions to protect our army, seeking its new base, and to repel the efforts of the enemy to break through our lines—a catastrophe which would have been fatal to all that portion thus cut off from the main trunk.

Thus, to break through our advancing troops, to capture part of our baggage trains and a portion of the army, was the purpose of Generals Lee and Magruder; and this was prevented by the valor of the men to whom the great trust of that day was committed.

To those divisions of our army thus massed on the roads, no battle on the Peninsula was so severe and the loss so great.

The country in which the struggle of Monday occurred is heavily wooded, the forests being either ragged thickets of oak saplings, vines, and thorns, or heavy, dark pine woods. The land is nearly a dead level, with only an occasional swell or break on a creek: the general aspect of the country is extremely monotonous and uninviting. Here and there a farm to the right and left of the road gave a spot of sunshine and brightness; but all around this arise, almost as clearly defined as a great dark wall, the lofty firs and hemlocks. Our troops were arranged on a line of these farms extending for three or four miles, placing, if possible, an open field in front of them; thus compelling the enemy, in the attack, to come out of his usual forest haunts.

Heavy cannonading in the rear had been heard by the infantry of our army, but the near presence of the enemy was not known until ten o'clock P. M., when an overwhelming force burst out of the forest in front of General McCall's division. This was composed of twelve Pennsylvania regiments, and they were amongst the best troops in the army, as proved in many a field before and since; but they had been in the battles of Gainesville and Mechanicsville, and had suffered most severely in both of those engagements. Of one regiment, the 12th, but few escaped.

This division was thrown across the New Market road, two regiments being on the right and the others on the left, having open fields in front of them.

At the first commencement of the attack some confusion was created by the officers and men of the "Dutch Battery" cutting the horses from the guns, and posting, pell-mell, through the lines of the troops. This had the effect to increase the confidence of the enemy and the fury of his attack.

I have seen it stated that the entire body of the Reserves, very early in the battle, were thrown into confusion, routed, and fled, a disorganized mass, through the other troops. But this cannot be the truth in regard to most of those regiments, for the number of their dead and wounded lying in these fields and subsequently found in the hospitals, was proof of the severity of the contest to them. The field, as I afterwards passed over it, was strewn with their dead, and there were all the signs to a practised eye of a long-continued and desperate conflict. It was very evident that they stood at the point of extremest danger, and that they had to endure, in the commencement of the action, the entire force of the enemy, and repelled charge after charge. I have heard officers of other divisions state that they had never seen anything more brilliant than one of the charges made by the Reserves into the open field and across it, driving the foe into the forest. And if they were broken and scattered before night, it was owing to the fact that the force thrown against them was numerically vastly superior. But it is certain that up to the shadows of the evening General McCall held his position in the edge of the wood, not twenty rods from the spot where the action commenced; and in his desperate and long-continued defence he lost more than one-third of his men. Before the going down of the sun he had twice lost and regained his batteries of sixteen guns; and as described to me by General McCall, around the last battery was enacted one of those terrible scenes which, once beheld, stand out before the mind forever.

To defend these guns an heroic band of his men had rallied. The shadows of the night were falling over the fields; before them the ground was strewed with the dead; on the left were the abandoned caissons, the dead horses, and the silent cannon. There was a lull in the fight; but again the enemy opened in front, and shell and canister crashed through the trees above them: to this the Reserves replied.

In a few moments they saw a brigade of the enemy coming out from the shadows of the forest, on the further side of the field. They came forward at a full run, and though met by a very heavy and de-

24

structive fire, they did not pause nor deliver a shot,
but trailing their guns, advanced. They were led
by a man of vast muscular strength and prowess;
cheering and shouting to his men, he ran on the
gunners; the Reserve infantry rushed forward to the
rescue, and around the cannon between them and
over the bodies of fallen horses and comrades, commenced a contest of the most furious character.
Scarcely a single shot was fired, bayonet crossed
bayonet, and frequently after a death-struggle for
two or three minutes, the foes stood breathless, with
guns locked, foot to foot and face to face, each afraid
to move, lest that would give his enemy the advantage; and in that awful moment, when the whole
being was fired by a frenzy that seemed supernatu-
ral, the countenance of each was painted on the mind
of the other forever. The shouts of command; the
yells of fury; the thrust; the parry; the spouting
blood; the death-cry; the stroke and crash of the
clubbed muskets; the battle receding into the forest,
and every tree and bush the scene of a tragedy —
and then again the pressing out around the cannon;
the officer mounted on the broken wheels, cheering
and calling his men; the pause of a moment from
exhaustion or to rally, and then the renewal of the
fight with greater fury than ever, made this a spectacle of awful grandeur.

In all this contest, the leader of the Confederates
had been successful in every struggle, and hurled to
the ground, with scornful ease, less powerful men;
everywhere a path opened before him, until a man
of equal strength sprang forward to meet him. After
they had parried each other's thrusts, for a moment

they paused, looked at each other intently, as if to determine what next to do, both feeling he had met a foe worthy of his steel; and again they rushed forward with renewed desperation, each intent upon pressing back the other, until some fall or stumble would give him the victory. But they were so equally matched that not a single foot did either recede; backwards and forwards they bent and dashed; then again foot to foot, and arm to arm they struggled; unlocking their guns, which had been twisted together, they would start back and then dash forward with the fury of gladiators. Many on both sides stopped to look on this desperate personal rencontre; around the wounded, taking purchase for blows on the bodies of the dead, they continued the struggle, until, with gun pressed against gun, they breathed into each other's faces, and while they thus stood the rush of battle bound for a second the arm of the Southern giant. His enemy was swift to improve the advantage: he darted back, lifted his clubbed gun, and brought it down with crushing force on the neck of his foe; the musket of the Rebel dropped from his hands, and throwing up his arms in the air, his whole body quivered convulsively, and he fell dead. The conqueror turned his head, looked up with a grim smile of satisfaction into the face of his general, and in a moment more disappeared in the whirl and cloud of battle.

Soon fresh reinforcements from the enemy compelled our men to fall back into the forest, and General McCall, anxious to learn the fate of the day in other parts of the field, rode up the New Market road. He was attended by a number of his staff; he had

not gone more than forty rods until he was surrounded by a considerable force of the enemy; they
started out from the forest and demanded his surrender.   Several of the officers about him turned
their horses' heads and fled.   The soldiers fired on
them.   Major Biddle, of Philadelphia, the chief of
staff, fell mortally wounded.   For his death there
was expressed universal regret, for all who knew
him regarded him as a man of the highest courage
and moral worth.

General Kearney's division was placed in an open
field, to the right oblique of General McCall's; he
had brought up a brave and noble brigade, General
Taylor's New Jersey troops, to the support of General McCall, and well did they sustain the honor of
their State.   He placed his troops and batteries to
the right of the New Market road.   On the left there
was a dark pine forest, and on the right an open
field, and about one hundred and fifty yards from
the road a small house, occupied by a negro family;
the ground gently declines towards the house, and
in a few rods beyond is the forest and then the
swamp.   Looking up the New Market road, General Kearney placed his men, and prepared for the
conflict.   I have heard many soldiers speak of the
power that was imparted to them by the general's
look and words; as they passed by him marching
into this open field, he looked on each man, and
said: "Go in, my boys, go in gayly, go in gayly;"
and during all the subsequent conflict, they heard
the voice of their general: "Gayly, gayly, my boys."

The fiercest contest raged around the negro house:
seized by the Confederates one moment and the next

driven out, and then held by our men. A color-bearer, Sergeant (now Lieutenant) Weeks, at one corner of this house held the flag of the 63d Pennsylvania, and concealed from the fire of the enemy stretched it out, waved it and shouted; at the opposite corner stood the Confederate flag-bearer, and each waved defiantly his flag in the face of the other. The great question was, "Who should be shot first?" At length the Confederates began to retire, and the flag was borne out into the open fields; and in the melee and conflict it was captured by one of the Ninth Reserves, who happened to be on a visit to our men at the commencement of the action, and being unable to reach his regiment had fallen in with us for the fight. Thus continued, with varying fortunes, the battle of the day.

I subsequently dressed the wounds of a young man, of the 4th Pennsylvania Reserves, not more than eighteen years old, who was deeply injured, and narrowly escaped death while assisting to capture this flag. He had been shot in the face, the ball entering near the nose, descending through the mouth, and coming out in the neck.

"How did you receive this injury in the face?"

"It was a musket ball," he replied. "I was bending low to escape the fire of the enemy's cannon, and when I was struck, I knew it was best to fight on. I was roused, and there was no one to help me away."

"But this bayonet wound in your back? That is rather a bad place for a soldier to be struck."

"That," said he, "I received when we were fighting for the Rebel flag. There was a furious contest

24 *

for it; for when the flag-bearer had fallen, hundreds of the Confederate soldiers hurried out of the woods to recover it. We had no time to load, but it was bayonet, clubbed musket, and pistol. While we were tossing to and fro, one of the Rebel soldiers struck me in the back. I felt the bayonet the moment it touched the skin. I bent and turned rapidly around. The bayonet was drawn off the gun, and remained in my back. The stab was not deep, but it stung me. When we had taken the flag, and they had removed me back into the woods, Jim Scott pulled the bayonet out."

"And what of the man that struck you?"

"Oh, I killed him. I had two bayonets, and he had none."

Many desperate battles were fought, and victories won. It was emphatically a fight of many fields, in which there was neither combination nor union, but resulting in the repulse of the enemy at all points.

As soon as the action had ceased from the increasing darkness, our men lay down on the field and slept after the exhaustion of many days. Such of the wounded as could walk were aided to leave the field, and in the various farm-houses found surgeons and protection. Some of our wounded, during their wanderings, fell in with Rebel soldiers, and were by them helped away.

The conduct of General Kearney in this battle was the admiration of all his corps. He was everywhere directing all movements, imparting, by his presence and clear-sightedness, the most determined courage to his men. Wherever the danger was greatest, there he pressed and carried with him a personal power

CONTEST FOR THE FLAG, AT THE BATTLE OF GLENDALE, NEAR THE NEGRO HOUSE.
Chap. XVIII.

that was equal to a reinforcement. In a pre-eminent degree he possessed that military prescience, or anticipation of what was coming, and the point of an enemy's attack, which has characterized every great man who has risen to distinction in the art of war.

To General Hooker is likewise due the highest praise for the wisdom of his plans, and for the order and impetuosity which his own brilliant enthusiasm imparted to his men. Brothers in arms, always on the best of terms, mutually admiring the strong points of each other's characters, they uniformly co-operated and stood firmly by each other in the hour of danger. Whoever commanded, they were always faithful to the army and the country.

General Heintzleman was commander of the third army corps, all the regiments of which were engaged in this battle. For him all the officers and men had the deepest respect. He was always cool, and in danger perfectly self-possessed. A man of great kindness of heart, considerate of his men, temperate, wisely discriminating and just, there was felt in him as a soldier the utmost confidence; without any of those knightly and brilliant qualities which made the names of Hooker and Kearney the synonyms of chivalry and daring, he was brave without rashness, and life-saving without imbecility, dignified in de-meanor, yet easily approached, and the friend of every soldier.

Thus ended one of the most severe battles of the Peninsula. The enemy signally failed in reaping the harvest of captures, guns and wagon trains, which he hoped to gain.

On no battle-field in the campaign was there exhibited such invincible determination to conquer or die. Our men fought as those who, hardened by an hundred conflicts, had lost the dread of every missile of destruction and the fear of death. It was a series of brilliant, sanguinary engagements, where in deep forests and open fields deeds of the highest heroism were performed on both sides.

When all fought so nobly and well, it would be invidious to distinguish. On the forethought of our generals and the invincible bravery of some of our regiments at certain moments in the battle turned the fate of that day.

General Kearney uniformly spoke of the conduct of the 63d Pennsylvania at Glendale in terms of the highest praise. He returned to the regiment his thanks for their glorious deeds on that day. It was detailed to support Thompson's Battery, the men lying on their faces in front of the guns; four several times the Confederates came out of the forests, and charged to take them. The serving of this battery was most admirable, and its sweep of grape and shell frightfully destructive. With desperate courage, in four lines of battle, one pressing on the other, the enemy came forward to take it at all hazards; they were met by a terrific storm of grape, canister, and shrapnell, and wide lines were opened in their ranks, and men fell as grass before the mower. But still the tremor was only for a moment; on they pressed, closing their broken files as they ran; another terrific burst of flame would dash scorching streams into their very faces; still on the broken fragments pressed, until almost to the muzzle of the cannon; then up sprang the protecting regiments, the firing of the artillery ceased, and musket and bayonet were left to decide the contest. The enemy could not stand the heavy stroke of the moment, but broke and fled; rallying three several times with fresh re-inforcements, they ventured out into the open ground, and each time they were repelled with even greater slaughter than before, until great heaps of their dead were lying like mounds on the field.

At length when the enemy were evidently pre-paring for a fresh charge, Captain Thompson sent a message to Colonel Hays that his ammunition was nearly exhausted, and his guns would be taken unless some device could be instantly suggested to save them. Colonel Hays immediately ordered a charge on the enemy, and before they had fully come out into the field, they saw our men dashing at them in the edge of the forest. They interpreted this bold movement as the evidence of the arrival of heavy reinforcements, and hastily retreated into the deeper woods; and before they recovered from their surprise the guns were all safely removed, and a section of De Russay's battery took their place.

The battle continued long into the night, and was here and there renewed in the forest with a frenzy not witnessed in any previous contest. I afterwards heard some of the Confederate officers speak of a false movement which they made during the night; they thought they saw indications of retreat in our army, and brought up a strong body of reserves in pursuit, and as they advanced across the open field and approached the forest, there suddenly opened upon them a long line of fire, and the deadly balls leaped from three or four thousand guns, and in an instant the ground was strewed with their slain. This was followed by the charge, and they were swept from the field with more than the fury of a tempest; and of the hundreds who had gone forth, but few returned to their companies.

There can be no doubt that in this battle the loss of the enemy was much greater than ours, for the Rebel generals threw away the lives of their men with a mad, murderous rashness which has scarcely a parallel in history.

After this night attack and defeat, nothing was seen of the enemy; and between midnight and the morning all our forces left the field of battle, taking with them all their guns, except those lost by General McCall's division, and before nine A. M. of Tuesday morning the entire army was in safety on Malvern Hill.

In this battle one of the most interesting spectacles was the arming of the long procession of the sick, who could not find their regiments, nor move so rapidly as might be demanded of those who were well. They requested to be armed and placed in positions to be of service, and rendered essential aid in the conflict that followed.

On this, as on other fields, the necessity of the hour compelled the leaving to the tender mercies of the enemy the wounded of our army, of whom I presume there were not fewer than one thousand. I shall subsequently speak of their treatment, and the condition in which I found them.

Many of our men were taken prisoners who had fought until the hour of midnight, and as soon as the battle ended fell asleep, and did not awake until the morning sun shone in their faces, and then arose to find the enemy in possession of the battle ground, and with strong guards watching every road.

CHAPTER XIX.

MALVERN HILL.

The Preparations for the Battle — The Scene — The Imposing Grandeur of the Spectacle — Commencement of the Action — Consternation and Panic of the Confederates — Scene at the Hospital.

THE distance of Malvern Hill from Glendale is about two and a half miles, and early on the morning of Tuesday, the 1st of July, our entire army was in position on this elevated plateau.

Malvern Hill, on account of being the scene of the final conflict of the Peninsular campaign, deserves more than a passing notice.

It is an elevation of possibly one hundred and fifty feet in height, and fronts on James River, which is about two miles to the south, and to the north on open fields about two-thirds of a mile in length and one-third in width. To the south and west it is quite steep and difficult of ascent, but to the north and east is a gentle slope. On the summit stands the Crew House. This was an old-fashioned but sumptuous country-seat, surrounded by innumerable out-houses and embosomed in vines and trees. On the slope and height of this hill General McClellan superintended the planting of three hundred pieces of artillery, so as to sweep the fields and forests in every direction.

As our army took their position on this hill there opened to them a magnificent prospect. They had come out of the darkness and gloom of dismal swamps and jungle scenes, and from fields trodden into barrenness. Here for miles our delighted gaze surveyed a country which had not yet been devastated. There were fields covered with tall rows of graceful corn, with their tassels dancing in the breeze. Here wide fields of almost ripe wheat, waving in long golden lines, rich with the promise of the coming harvest; while almost at our feet, winding through its green meadows, meandered the gentle James River.

After breathing the air of battle-fields and death for many days, and looking only on spectacles of misery and ghastliness, the pleasure which the delicious air, the fragrance, and the scene of beauty presented to our army is one of the things which will never fade from the mind.

Our forces were drawn up on this hill. During the previous night rifle-pits had been dug under the guns in the slope. The troops in these pits were covered with straw and fresh-reaped grain, and the glasses of the officers of the Confederate Army could not see that before they could take these batteries they would have to encounter 10,000 bayonets.

The strength of our position was increased by the presence of five gunboats, ready at a moment to open in action. The moral influence of these on our army was very manifest.

During the morning the enemy, now under the

25

command of General Magruder, assisted by Jackson, Longstreet, Hill, and Huger, advanced from different points, shelling the woods as they slowly felt their way; and at length, about noon, their skirmishers discovered our position. The field in our front was about three-fourths of a mile long and half a mile wide, and beyond it a deep, dark pine forest. On the edge of this field at different points General Magruder threw out batteries and regiments, for what purpose could not be known; and no sooner were they disclosed than they brought on them a rain of death. In a moment the regiments were swept away like chaff before a storm. The horses were killed at the guns, the carriages were tossed into a thousand fragments, the caissons were exploded, and the gunners who still lived escaped into the shelter of the woods.

About 4 o'clock P. M., General Magruder ordered an advance along the entire left wing of his line: and there were brought out into the field several divisions and batteries. Prominent amongst these were the brigades of Toombs, Cobb, Wright, and Armisted, among the finest troops in the Southern Army. They were sustained by about twenty pieces of artillery thrown out into the plain. The first column advanced with steady step towards our batteries; but long before it reached the middle of the open ground the troops were met by such an iron tempest, that the few who survived fell to the ground, and abandoning their guns commenced crawling back on their faces toward the forest.

A second column, with a courage which, on the part of their officers, was madness, but was at the moment the admiration of our army, ran out into the field and pressed towards our death-dealing cannon. These again were mowed down. They rallied, feebly shouted defiance, pressed into the cloud of smoke, and another tempest of fire lighted up the scene for a moment, and that column was gone. Here and there a straggler emerged from the smoke and ran across the field towards his friends : he was but one, while the hundreds were lying mangled and dead on the plain.

A third column was thrown out from the cover of the forest; fresh batteries were brought into play, and when the smoke had slightly lifted up from the field, the terrific conflict was renewed — again the guns of the Confederates were silenced, the horses killed, the caissons on fire, and the regiments cut down ; reforming, now prostrate, and then springing forward until their thinned and ragged lines, as they came within musket range, presented so pitiable a spectacle that our men fired with little purpose to kill.

About half-past five a powerful body of troops from General Magruder's centre were advanced into the field; their orders were to press forward over every obstacle. There is every reason to believe that these troops had been rendered insensible to fear by whisky drugged with gunpowder; and undeterred by the fate of those who had perished in previous attacks, with shouts and yells they pressed towards our men. Many pieces of our cannon opened upon them, and shell and grape swept through their lines; treading on the dead, pressing down the living who had fallen to the ground, they with unwavering step still advanced; emboldened by their example, other regiments ran out with wild cheers from the forest; on and on over the field of carnage they advanced; every discharge of our guns made great gaps in their lines, but instantly closing up, they pressed forward; another sheet of flame would spread out over the field, and the roar and thunder followed, moving the ground as if trembling in the convulsion of an earthquake. When the smoke cleared away a little, the broken columns were seen still with fiery madness pressing on. Already they had begun to ascend the slope, and had succeeded in coming so near that our artillery could no longer so damagingly sweep the ground.

With all the frenzy of maniacs they still ran towards us; the efforts of the artillery were redoubled; the men at our guns turned pale and stood aghast; another moment, and the day might be lost: — just then up sprang our concealed men in the rifle-pits, and a long stream of fire darted forth from a thousand muskets, and springing forward with fixed bayonet they met the foe, who quailed, wavered, and renewed the conflict, but it was in vain: with the insanity of men who sought death they still continued the struggle, and a long line of their dead at the base of this hill bore witness to the severity and destructiveness of the contest. The whole scene at this time was one of terror and appalling splendor.

The batteries on the heights continued to pour a constant and withering fire into the forests where the forces of the enemy were concealed, and simultaneously the thunder of a hundred great guns shook the hill, and caused the waters of the river to tremble. The firing of the gunboats added very much to the overpowering grandeur of the hour. The shells discharged from the monster guns of these vessels rushed through the air with a frightful shriek that was heard above the roar of battle; then when they entered the forests great trees were shivered into a thousand fragments, the branches were torn from others and tossed into the heavens, or thrown far into the deep shades, and when they burst it was with an explosion that shook the earth for miles. The terror inspired by these shells was such as to deprive the Rebel soldiers of all courage, and they fled into the deeper recesses of the forest.

The contest in front of the rifle-pits was but short, for, unable to bear up against the impetuous attack of our men, the enemy endeavored to remove his broken columns from the field. As they fled they were pursued three-fourths of a mile by the Union troops, and the entire Rebel army was struck with a panic; and if at this moment we could have brought ten thousand reserves into the field, we might have marched back again and retaken all we had lost, and without any difficulty reached Richmond:—this statement will be amply confirmed in subsequent chapters.

On the fleeing columns of the enemy our batteries and gunboats continued to fire until ten o'clock at night, throwing the shells into the forests; for hours not a gun replied, and not even a courier dared to show himself in the open field.

The battle was over, but the cannonading still continued, and shells and balls of every kind tore through the woods in a ceaseless whirlwind of fury.

25 *

In the meantime thousands of the Confederates fled in the wildest disorder from the scene, and hid themselves in swamps and hollows; soldiers without guns, horsemen without caps and swords, came to the hospitals in the battle-field of Glendale, and reported that their regiments and brigades were swept away, and that they alone were "escaped to tell the tale."

It is one of the strangest things in this week of disaster that General McClellan ordered a retreat to Harrison's Landing, six miles down the James River, after we had gained so decided a victory. When this order was received by the impatient and eager army, consternation and amazement overwhelmed our patriotic and ardent hosts. Some refused to obey the command. General Martindale shed tears of shame. The brave and chivalrous Kearney said in the presence of many officers: "I, Philip Kearney, an old soldier, enter my solemn protest against this order for retreat,—we ought, instead of retreating, to follow up the enemy and take Richmond. And in full view of all the responsibility of such a declaration, I say to you all, such an order can only be prompted by cowardice or treason."

And with all, hopelessness and despair succeeded the flush of triumph. In silence and gloom our victorious army commenced retiring from an enemy utterly broken, scattered, and panic stricken.

And when there was not a foe within miles of us, we left our wounded behind to perish, and any one witnessing the wild eagerness of our retreat would have supposed that we were in the greatest peril from a vigilant and triumphant enemy.

I was at the time of this battle at the hospital in Carter's house. All our intelligence from our army reached us through officers of the Confederates who came in during Monday and Tuesday, and as usual with them, every movement was a success, every battle a brilliant victory. They assured us that the battle of Glendale or Nelson's Farm on Monday was to our army a most ruinous defeat. "We had lost half our train of wagons and ambulances, and invaluable stores of every kind; that we had been driven from every field where they had attacked us; that whole divisions of our army had been swept away; that thousands of our men in small bands or alone were scattered and then hiding in forests; that we had lost six generals," and one officer assured me, on the honor of a gentleman, "that he had seen twelve of our general officers dead or prisoners; that four hundred officers were among the captives, the prisoners were numbered by thousands, and the fields for miles were covered with our dead; that thousands of our wounded, as he rode along, were crying for water and perishing of want; that General McClellan was surrounded by their troops, and the Union Army so demoralized that not a single division could be induced to fight with them; that when brought into the field whole brigades had thrown down their arms and marched over to them as prisoners; and that officers of our army were then at General Lee's head-quarters arranging the terms of surrender." Such was the gloomy picture which they painted, and with such protestations and humane regrets that we could not but fear that there might be much truth in their statements; and the dead, dying, and suffering around increased the gloom that oppressed us. For myself, I had many relatives and friends in the army whom I mourned as dead, and our surgeons and wounded officers and men were all affected in the same manner. Each one had a brother or dear friend for whom he anxiously inquired, and turned his face to the wall and wept.

We all felt deeply humiliated, and we were not anxious to outlive our shame and the ruin of our cause. I had spent much of this day (Tuesday) at Savage Station, assisting our wounded, praying with and comforting the dying, but at four o'clock P. M. returned to the hospital, of which I had especial charge. To this again had come in several Confederate officers: amongst the rest, Colonel Marshall, a son of Humphrey Marshall, of Kentucky, who, without any of the bitterness and swagger of those who had preceded him, confirmed the previous statements.

At this time we heard the roar of battle in the distance. He assured us this was the Southern Army hemming in McClellan, and compelling his surrender. The sound coming forth from the bosom of forests in the distance increased in volume, until it seemed to us that all the elements of terrific grandeur were let loose; and the mighty din, the crash, and thunder imparted such a tremor to the ground that the very earth throbbed with emotion.

All the nurses and the sick able to walk had assembled in front of the hospital, where a slight elevation enabled us to hear better. No words were spoken except prayer; each, a little apart, was absorbed by his own emotions. Was all this the work of the enemy pressing our discomfited and fleeing army? Might not hundreds of our men even at this moment be swept into the river by that tempest of fire? O horrors! what appalling scenes! what miseries would be on such a field, where rioted all the enginery of death!

Suddenly the roar of battle burst upon us in more stupendous magnitude, and the awful thunder, descending from the air, appeared to enter into the earth, and it trembled and rocked beneath our feet. With minds and senses wrought up to intense activity, we could not be mistaken. Nearer and nearer came the sounds of the battle; the shells had a wider play, and were thrown closer to us; the rattle of musketry, at first scarcely heard, was now more distinct. We looked at each other — we were slow to catch the hope. At length one exclaimed: "We are chasing the enemy back; I hear our guns." "We have defeated them; our men are coming. Hurrah! hurrah! thank God, we have a country and an army yet." We shook hands as long-parted friends, and in a moment every face was wet with tears, and the shout of triumph was blended with the song of gratitude.

It required no courier to bear to us the tidings of our victory. We were just as certain as though an angel had told us, that our army had routed the foe; and that night, after many nights of wakefulness, we slept like little children.

I subsequently learned from many of our officers that the morning of Tuesday was marked by the deepest despondency. Our men were exhausted by thirty days of constant watching, labor, and fighting: the heat withering and blasting as the air of a furnace. Many had not slept for days, and scarcely tasted food in a week; and now, weary and prostrated, they felt it would be a privilege to die.

There were likewise most ominous signs that the general officers were apprehensive of fatal disasters. The paymasters who were in the army were ordered on board the gunboats. Prince de Joinville, who had been with us from the very commencement of the campaign, and who, constantly active, had been everywhere, undeterred by danger, this morning left us, taking with him the young men his nephews, the Count de Paris and Duke de Chartres, who had acted as aids-de-camp to General McClellan.

The commander-in-chief was evidently oppressed with the deepest solicitude, for he accompanied the Prince and his nephews to the war steamer, and remained on board until late in the afternoon, communicating his orders by signals and couriers. Dr. James Rogers, brigade surgeon of Robinson's brigade, who had been ill with fever for several days, was likewise on this steamer, and afterwards related to me the events and scenes of that day as they came under his eye. He said General McClellan was evidently laboring under the deepest depression, and apprehended the worst results. But about four o'clock a despatch came from General Marcy, saying that our army was holding the enemy at bay at all points, and in all probability would drive him from the field. This message appeared to lift an immense burden off the heart of the general, and he arose and walked the deck with a buoyant step, and from this time evidently listened to the battle with new hope.

But about five o'clock P. M. the commanding general rode into the lines of our army, and remained until the action closed.

General Heintzleman had sent to him a message that the troops noticed his absence, and it was exerting a depressing influence on them, and he could not be answerable for the consequences if he longer held himself so far aloof from the scene of action and danger.

During the nights of the 1st and 2d of July we were visited by one of the heaviest of rain-storms: this continued for twenty-four hours without intermission, until the entire Peninsula was covered with water, and rivers rushed where there had been only little streams.

In this storm, on the morning of Wednesday, the army fell down to Berkeley or Harrison's Landing. This was done on account of the superiority of the landing, James River at this point being broad and deep. The position was of such a character that the army could be shielded from any force the enemy could bring against us. We could have taken many of his abandoned guns from the field, but satisfied ourselves with carrying off all our own with incredible difficulty over worse than Crimean roads.

We retired to Harrison's Landing without the enemy making any demonstration in our rear; and weary and exhausted by struggles and battles which have probably no parallel in human history, our troops found rest. And of the Grand Army of the Potomac 58,000 remained, and 60,000 were in hospitals, lying wounded on the fields, or killed in battle.

Our loss in the battle of Malvern Hill was slight

compared with that of other days. But the loss of the enemy on this single field was fully equal in killed and wounded to our losses in the seven days.

During the entire day of Wednesday, when the rain was descending in torrents, there came in the broken fragments of the Confederate Army. The Williamsburg road for miles was dark with straggling, wandering bands: without guns, shivering in the cold rain, destitute of overcoats and without food, they presented themselves at our hospitals the most pitiable objects I ever saw. They could give no intelligent account of the battle, but all spoke of the terror inspired by our gunboats. They were like the Egyptian whom King David found in the field, "who knew nothing until he had eaten and drunken." They were humble, and took upon themselves none of the airs of conquerors. Those who were from Virginia and Alabama I found most reasonable and open to truth. They were all, however, inert in mind, slow in speech, and without any of that boldness of bearing and independence of character which distinguishes the Northern soldier. The fact of their being perfectly under the control of an aristocracy was as palpable as amongst the serfs of Russia. They were thankful for shelter and food; and those from Virginia and North Carolina almost uniformly said they were forced into the army, and were now most anxious to return to their homes. Hundreds of these broken bands and gunless men came in during the day, and great numbers were seen wandering towards Richmond, occasionally cowering under the shadow of trees, and sleeping in the storm by the wayside. When met or aroused, they all eagerly inquired for their regiments or divisions, and did not know the difference between their own officers and ours. They uniformly said they had lost their regiment in the battle of Tuesday, and having escaped from the field, the rain of grape and bomb, and the explosion of the great shells thrown from the gunboats, were so terrible that human nature could not endure it. The trees were falling and shattered around them as if a hundred thunderbolts had struck upon them in a moment, and the fragments were hurled in every direction with far more power than Indian arrows; that the falling branches and the exploding bombs drove them further and further into the woods, until they were lost to the army.

The Confederate officers who appeared amongst us to-day were silent in regard to the operations of yesterday; when asked, they claimed as usual a victory, but "thought our army was safe from further attack just now." They confessed themselves greatly disappointed; they had been confident that our entire forces would be destroyed or captured.

Terrible as this storm appeared to us, and deeply as our pity was excited for our poor fellows lying out in the open fields, unable to crawl out of the water, or drag themselves to the shelter of the nearest tree, this great rain was of service to them: the battle-fields were cleansed, their wounds were washed, and their bodies cooled.

24

CHAPTER XX.

Thursday, *July 3d.*

Report of Dr. Skelton from the Battle-field — Visit to the Sick at White Oak Swamp — Visit to the Battle-field of Glendale — Condition of the Confederate Army — Nolan, the Singer — Lonely Night Ride.

On this day the heavens cleared, the sun came forth again, and although its beams were overpoweringly hot, yet with the return of a pure sky some of the gloom that oppressed us was dispersed, and we began to devise plans for the effectual relief of those near us, who had been lying wounded and sick in sheds, barns, and the deserted camps; and measures were taken to search the woods and visit every out-of-the-way house, and from these deserted dwellings and from the forests were brought in many who for days had suffered alone, and endured the agonies of desertion, thirst, and pain.

We had no definite reports of the two last battles, and knew nothing certain in regard to the fate of our army, until Dr. Skelton, of the 87th New York, came in from the Gatewood House, on the Nelson farm. He had been detailed to remain with our wounded at this house, and being destitute of medicines and food, rode across the country under guard to Savage Station for sanitary and medicinal stores. Dr. Skelton was one of the most self-denying of our surgeons — his labors were constant and humane.

He went from field to field, from cabin to cabin, looking after those who had been wounded, and left
without attendance and help. And in the hospital
at the Gatewood House he was unwearied and
sleepless in his efforts to alleviate the pains and
meet the wants of that hour. The severity of his
exertions were well nigh fatal, for he was brought
up to Richmond very ill with typhoid fever, and his
life hung for many weeks in suspense, but I was
glad to meet him again, having recruited his strength
and returned to his post of duty.

Dr. Skelton gave a vivid and heart-rending picture of the condition of our wounded, and urged
that something should be done for their relief. It
was now the fourth day since the battle of Glendale,
yet no bread or meat had been sent to the hospitals.
Eight hundred carriages, wagons, and ambulances,
accompanied by hundreds of citizens of Richmond,
had come forth from the city, carrying bread, water,
and wine to their own wounded, and had removed
them all, but passed by our sufferers unpitied, and
left them to perish. He moreover represented that
appeal after appeal had been made to Confederate
generals and commissaries, but nothing had as yet
been sent; that his medicines, bandages, and stores
had been taken by the orders of surgeons of the
Confederate army; that his surgical instruments had
been borrowed by a prominent surgeon in the Southern service and never returned, and hence he was
without the means of surgical operations, and that
death would in many cases result from that loss;
that the surgical instruments of Dr. Robinson had
been taken in the same manner, and his horse stolen;

that numbers of our men were still out on the battle-field, and he had no ambulances, stretchers, or nurses to bring them in. Such was the gloomy picture he drew of the condition of our wounded and sick.

But there was one drop of sweetness in this cup of bitterness. The doctor assured me that the enemy was driven from all points of the field on Monday night, and that, with the exception of the high ground over White Oak Swamp, occupied by our artillery, and from which the batteries had been withdrawn into the bosom of our infantry, we occupied all the battle-field on Monday night; and that the battle of Malvern Hill was a most brilliant success — the enemy, routed and trembling, had fled in every direction, and in some regiments not one-half their men could be found, and that our army was now entirely safe.

This brought to us inexpressible relief. I learned likewise from Dr. Skelton that there was a considerable number of our sick in the camp formerly occupied by General Keyes; they were men who, being unable to proceed further, had dropped behind the army in its retreat, and been borne to some tents in this camp, and there had remained. I resolved if possible to visit them, and bear such assistance and supplies as were needed. I returned to the hospital in Carter's house, and made preparations for the journey, and rode through the forests and over the fields lately the scene of carnage, and now covered with broken carriages and ambulances, which had been abandoned and fired, and with the torn garments and broken knapsacks which our men had cast away. I met on the way great numbers of Confedcrate soldiers, mostly without guns; some seeking their army, but generally inquiring for Richmond. They looked sick and exhausted; they represented themselves as being in the divisions brought into action on Tuesday, and when their men were swept from the field all were scattered. Dr. Skelton told me that he had passed a thousand such broken stragglers as he came to Savage Station. They mostly represented themselves as belonging to General Jackson's corps.

I reached the hospital tents on the hill overlooking White Oak Swamp, and found that many of our sick had been removed, as I was told, to Richmond. Those that remained had already been placed in heavy army wagons, and were lying in all possible positions: having no shelter, their sufferings in the burning sun were beyond the power of words to describe. They generally appeared to be in the last stages of typhoid fever. Several of them were so ill that I could not obtain their names. They were confused and wandering in mind. Poor fellows! I thought it was a great mercy that they were not keenly alive to the miseries of their condition. I went from wagon to wagon, distributed to each a small quantity of wine or brandy and a piece of light bread, and then went into the neighboring forests and cut some boughs from the trees, and placed them as shelters from the piercing sun in the hands of those able to hold up a little bush; and where they did not possess power to do this, I secured them in the front of the wagon, that they might be shaded for a time.

They had been placed in these wagons at two
26 *

o'clock P. M., and it was now four; still there were no orders to move. I asked the drivers of the teams why they lingered, or at least to remove the men to a place of shelter from the sun. They replied they did not dare to move an inch until "the lieutenant came." I saw then, as often afterwards, that many of the Rebel officers were dead to every emotion of humanity, and would have been glad to aid in giving a quiet passage out of the world to our sick and wounded, in order that they might be relieved from further trouble.

One of these men was so ill that it was deemed unsafe to remove him from the tent. He had been most cruelly neglected, and was evidently approaching that country where "the wicked cease from troubling and the weary are at rest." He was not, however, so far gone as to be unable to give me his name and residence. It was A. D. Leburne, of Mercer, Pennsylvania. I conversed with him, and learned from his few broken words that he trusted in Jesus and died in peace.

Some of those lying in the wagons I afterwards met in Richmond, and found to my surprise that nearly all had survived the miseries of a night journey over the worst of roads.

I returned in the evening to my hospital and made arrangements to extend the journey of to-morrow beyond White Oak Swamp, and into the battle-fields. I secured the promise of the co-operation of our guard, whom I wished to take with me to preserve me from arrest and violence.

The commandant at Savage Station was Lieutenant Lacy Stewart. I went to him and asked permis-

sion to pass within the lines of the Confederate
Army beyond the swamp, and bear supplies of medicines and food to the wounded.

In reply, he stated "that it would be impossible
for him to give me such a pass; that it would render him liable to charges and court-martial; that
if anything should happen to me, if a guerilla
should shoot me from the bushes, if some straggling
soldier should kill me for my watch or in hope of
money, he would be held responsible by his Government, and he could give me no pass without sending me under guard, and he had no men or horses;
but, if I still was determined to go, all he could
promise me was that he thought I would not be shot."

There was not much comfort in this. I then made
application for an ambulance and horses, proposing
to find the driver myself, and in this carry such supplies as were demanded and I could obtain.

He was very courteous, and assured me nothing
would give him greater pleasure than to give me a
wagon for such a purpose, but every hour he was
looking for an order to send all he had up to Richmond, and he would give offence to the authorities
there if these were not on hand.

I then concluded to load to the utmost my own
two horses and the horse of the guard, which we
borrowed from a German family under our care. I
had learned in the meantime, that at the house of
a Mr. Dudley, who had a beautiful place near us,
Mrs. Harris had stored in an outhouse all the sanitary goods she was compelled to leave behind in the
retreat. When I came to his house Mr. Dudley told
me that officers of the Confederate Government had

been there the previous evening and taken possession of the stores of Mrs. Harris, and commanded
that he should permit nothing to be removed.

The Mississippian sergeant, Howb, our guard, who
was with me, here came forward and assured Mr.
Dudley that his authority was fully equal to that of the
"Richmond overseers," as he called them; "that
they wished to eat the preserves, dried fruit, and
crackers themselves, and give the shirts, drawers,
etc. etc., to their sons and negroes, or put them into
stores and sell them; that what we wished to obtain
were for wounded men in the fields, who were without clothing and perishing with hunger."

Mr. Dudley, who was really a generous-hearted
man, listened to this appeal, took Howb's receipt,
and gave us all that we could, by any possibility,
bear away. We had the various articles we collected
placed in bed-sacks, which, being long, suspended
on the back of my baggage pony, nearly reached to
the ground. I had on my own horse two such sacks,
and Howb bore another. It was ten o'clock before
we left Savage Station and went forth into the burning roads and fields. The atmosphere appeared to
be on fire: the thermometer was 105° in the shade.
Even in the desert of Arabia I never suffered so
painfully from heat. Not a breath of air stirred the
silent woods, and the leaves of the trees were crisp-
ing in the intense glare.

We passed beyond the swamp and were soon in the
field of the battle of Glendale. The carcasses of dead
horses were lying in the roads and fields. This was
the scene of the artillery fight at the commencement
of the action. I saw but few graves. Our artillery

was merely here for the purpose of holding the
enemy's forces in check as long as possible; but
the great body of our infantry was one or two miles
in advance, holding the main roads to Richmond and
the James River.

On the heights over the swamp we came upon
strong bodies of troops of the Confederate Army.
They were of General Jackson's, General A. D. Hill's,
and General Longstreet's divisions. They were free
and familiar with us, asking many questions; and
uniformly supposing me to be a Confederate surgeon, I was never challenged. There was in their
camps none of the air of comfort and abundance
seen in ours; the men were poorly clad in the coarsest
homespun, such as I had seen formerly worn by the
slaves in the South; the greater part of them were
without tents and sheltered under booths.

They had nothing for food but the dirtiest bacon
sides and flour — salt was an unknown luxury. The
flour was moistened, rolled into a ball, and baked in
a fire on the point of a ramrod; of other bread they
had none.

They were without knapsacks and overcoats, and
many of them had no blankets, and therefore accomplished long marches with great haste and ease; but
their sufferings in storms and in the chilly nights
must have been well nigh unendurable.

Everything on which I looked was immeasurably
inferior to the equipments of our army. The horses
were poor and fed on corn only; the army wagons
were of the fashion in use on the National Road
when I was a boy, with such length of coupling that
each wagon looked like a section of a pontoon

bridge; the bed was deeply hollowed in the centre, and running back and forwards like a pair of huge horns. The harness of the horses was old and dried in the sun. In these wagons there were no commissary stores, but guns and ammunition.

The gun-carriages and caissons had evidently passed through trying scenes, and looked as if they would soon shake to pieces. The artillery horses were quite as poor as those already mentioned, and had all the appearance of neglect.

In the camp there was little of that order and military discipline which we could have seen even in the newest regiments in our service. There was none of that careful guarding of roads, that scrutiny of citizens and soldiers to which I had been accustomed, but as it appeared to me great carelessness in all these respects. But they were in a country of which they knew every path, and were familiar with every resident.

After passing through these various divisions of the Confederate Army, I was more than ever surprised at the success of their late movement.

But in one thing they had greatly the advantage of us; they were well, the air of the Peninsula did not palsy their strength, and the heat did not interfere with marching and action in the field. In another respect their condition was better than that of our soldiers — they were not burdened with sixty pounds weight of impediments, and therefore were not exhausted by a few miles of marching or by a run of two miles at double-quick.

I now came to the Brackett House, about one mile and a half beyond the swamp. This was one of the old Virginia plantations; the land had the exhausted appearance of a region which had been in cultivation for ages. The house stands a few rods to the right of the road, and far in the rear stretches the innumerable outhouses of a slave estate. Between these huts and pens were sweltering masses of barn, kitchen, and stable offal.

In the fields were encampments of General A. D. Hill's troops; some of his regiments were on parade, and presented lines of men in all conceivable costumes — some dressed in grey, others in the blue cloths of our troops, others in brown; many were ragged, some sleeveless, and a multitude I thought were shirtless.

When I came to the front of this house the spectacle was at once novel and distressing. Within twenty feet of it stands a large poplar tree: under the shadow of this was lying and reclining a great number of our wounded and sick soldiers. Some of them were almost naked, having cast away the coats, pantaloons, and shirts which were saturated and stiffened with blood. Some were screened under a few bushes; others had boards so placed as to shelter them from the sun; some were hobbling around on rude crutches; others were lying passive and dying on the bare ground. Mingled with them were many Confederate soldiers: some of these were sick, but the great majority were there for conversation and from curiosity.

I first found the surgeons in charge, Dr. Osburne, of the 42d New York, Dr. Kittinger, of the 100th New York, Dr. Underwood, of Cambridge, Massachusetts, and to them made known the fact that I had brought

supplies of food, clothing, and medicines from Savage
Station. A portion of the last I placed in their hands,
and requested permission to distribute the others at
pleasure through the various tents, houses, and stables where our sick and wounded were lying.

This was kindly granted: I then went through the
mansion house; all the furniture had been removed
from the rooms. Our wounded men were lying side
by side on the bare floor; they were strewn along
the passages and porticoes; and wherever there was
a foot of room there reclined or couched a poor
sufferer. I stopped and talked with each one, asking
him of his condition, of his pains and wants, and
giving to all, if they found it possible to eat, a piece
of soft bread or cracker. Many of them had no
hope of life: they knew their wounds were of such
a character that death was certain.

I often asked them if they regretted that they
had made the greatest sacrifice that man can ever
make for his country. I do not now remember one
solitary instance in which was expressed any regret,
but they generally said, "No, we felt we were right,
and that this rebellion was a great crime against
God and man, and we took up arms for the defence
of our country and her laws, and if we have to die
in such a cause, why should we murmur?—we give
our lives to our country and our names to our
children." When this last word was repeated there
was always a tremor of the voice, and the eyes filled
with tears. And very frequently they would say, "the
bitterness of death would be passed if we could but
see our parents, or wives and children before we die,
but that cannot be." I spoke to many of them of the

consolations of religion, and that our Lord knew what it was to be wounded and to die, and He was very pitiful and of tender mercy; and if they looked to Him in this hour He would grant them such a sense of His gracious presence and forgiving love as would soften their beds and prepare them to die in peace. In many cases they assured me that they had found it so already; and as they were lying alone on the fields, and through long painful nights, with no companions but the stars, they had lifted their hearts to God in prayer, and confessed their sins and sought mercy, and they hoped they were heard, for the fear of death was now gone; they had placed themselves like little children in the bosom of the Redeemer.

Many of the men most severely wounded were cheerful and happy. One of these noble fellows I shall have occasion to mention again; his name was Nolan, of Blair County, Pennsylvania. He was very badly wounded; his left limb was taken off above the knee, but he uttered not a word of complaint, sung hymns, his soul was full of joy, and his lips of praise. The goodness of God and the love of Jesus were his constant themes; his face was radiant with peace, and if we had not seen the bleeding stump we would have thought he was in perfect health.

When I spoke to him he knew me, and immediately burst out in most touching language, in acknowledgment of the mercy of God to him; his pains had not been worth mention, while his joy had been ecstatic and full, and when he was lying in the fields it was as if the angels had been sent to minister to him, his God was a covert from the tempest.

27

He never knew until now how wide the ocean and how unfathomable the depth of God's love.

Such were some of the men who deserve to have their names recorded as amongst the martyrs of Jesus. He had a magnificent voice, clear, rich, and sweet, a little more tremulous and warbling from the pain and exhaustion of the last few days, but one of the finest I ever heard; and as he would sing,

"Jesus, my God, I know His name;
His name is all my trust;
Nor will He put my soul to shame,
Nor let my hope be lost,"

many a poor groaner would suspend his moans; the words of faith and hope fell upon all as gentle dew, and it was a gleam of sunshine in the darkness of their prison-house. This man deserved the gratitude of many, for he brought to them the cup of salvation, and taught them to bear their pains with patience, and by his words of comfort and songs in the night lightened their miseries.

Lying alongside of Mr. Nolan was a young man from the mountains of Pennsylvania, of the Reserves, who had been struck by a six-pound cannon-ball. It had passed between the large bones of the thigh and abdomen and lodged in the muscle of the hip. The ball was cut out after he had been brought in; the physicians placed it in my hands and made it a present to me, but the difficulty of carrying such a ponderous thing, under the circumstances, compelled me to leave it behind, much to my regret now.

He bore his sufferings heroically; he was a man of splendid physical proportions—his muscles were iron and his bones brass. No one could see from his face that he had suffered such a prodigious shock. The physicians spoke in astonishment of his surviving the blow half an hour, and had not now the slightest hope of his living from day to day. Yet that young man survived, being borne up to Richmond, fourteen miles, in an army wagon, and lived eighteen days, and then died, not so much from his wound as from breathing the pestilential air of the Libby Prison.

In front of this house was lying on the ground a soldier from Franklin, Pennsylvania, David Courson; his left thigh was broken by a musket-ball, and he was then awaiting amputation. He told me that he had remained on the battle-field from the night of the 30th until the 3d, when he was brought in. He said that the Confederate soldiers had been very kind to him, stopping as often as passing by. One of them cut branches from a tree and made a booth to shelter him; they brought him water, and they would come from their camp and sit by him for hours, to cheer him and to enable him to better endure his sufferings.

I saw him again on Saturday after the amputation; he had borne it well, and I hoped he could live: he continued to improve in the open air, but when removed to the dungeons of Richmond, he as well as others soon perished. He was a brave man. In one of my morning rounds in the prison I came to the place where I had left Courson on the previous night, suffering from heat and nervous exhaustion, but not complaining nor apparently near his end. But the next morning his place was vacant.

"Where is Courson?" I said to a wounded soldier.

"Gone up, gone up," said he.—Thus suddenly did many drop out of life.

During my walks through the rooms of the house a young officer came to me and invited me to come upstairs and see some officers who were lying in one of the chambers. I record the name of this young man,* because though wounded he was nursing all his brother officers—bringing to them water, superintending the preparation of such food as he could obtain, and I have rarely seen a young man in whose face shone out such force of benevolence. And I was deeply grieved to learn afterwards that he had been sent to Richmond and compelled to walk fourteen miles in the hot sun, and reached there exhausted and feverish, and died in two days of lockjaw, another victim of the heartless cruelty of the Confederate officers and Government.

In this room were lying Lieutenant-colonel Mc-Intire, 1st Reserves, Pa.; Lieutenant-colonel Woodworth, 3d Reserves, Pa.; Captain W. W. White, 7th Reserves, Pa.; Captain McCleary, 5th Reserves, Pa.; Captain J. Culvertson, 9th Reserves, Pa.; Captain P. J. Smith, 2d Reserves, Pa.; Captain E. B. Gates, 4th Reserves, Pa.; Lieutenant I. Lehman, 3d Reserves, Pa.; Adjutant W. W. Stewart, 1st Reserves, Pa.; Lieutenant J. G. McCauley, 7th Reserves, Pa.; and Lieutenant August Muller, 20th Massachusetts.

It was the fourth of July, and though most of these officers were severely wounded, yet they found heart to sing the "Star-spangled Banner" and the "Red, White, and Blue." They likewise hung out

---

* Sergeant Ross, from Lockhaven, Pennsylvania.

of the window two small American flags. The songs and waving flags deeply angered some Confederate officers, and they threatened to have a volley fired into the window; but at length satisfied themselves by shouting, "You can never take Richmond, for you will have to cross a very wide (*Lee*) lea, and the biggest kind of a Stonewall, and then toil up two very high (*Hills*) hills, and fight your way every step through a (*Longstreet*) long street, and after all have (*Huger*) huger difficulties to surmount." And then the whole affair ended in a mutual laugh and shout.

There were lying around this house on the open ground and in the outhouses 450 men. And I fear there was good reason to believe that some of the complaints of the officers and men, in regard to their surgeons, were not without foundation. It certainly betrayed extreme heartlessness in a surgeon who, when told of the miserable condition of many of our wounded men in the wet, muddy fields, and urged to go to their relief, to most positively refuse to go out from the house, " for he did not wish to soil his white canvas shoes!"

Dr. Osburne, whom I subsequently saw in Richmond, was unwell, and bore with him for many months the seeds of disease contracted on the Peninsula. All spoke in praise of Dr. Kittinger, who faithfully attended to the patients of his division; also of Dr. Underwood, who most assiduously day and night sought to relieve all. The severity of his labors, the heavy pressure on his nervous energies, brought him down nearly to the gates of death; but I hope that long before this, in the bosom of his home, one whose

27 *

ear was ever open to the cry of suffering, and who,
though he staggered and fainted, still persevered in
his work of mercy, has regained the health which in
the service of his country he lost.

After going from group to group, ministering to
them as my means would permit, uniformly stopping
for a few moments with the severely wounded and
praying with the dying, in order to reach other hospitals I was compelled to leave Brackett's house.
Proceeding along the New Market road, I came to
the Nelson house, a short distance to the left. At
this hospital there were lying about 200 patients.
The surgeons were Dr. Skelton and Dr. Robinson.
Many of the patients were very badly wounded:
they were amongst the worst cases gathered in from
the field. They were generally from New York regiments in General Hooker's division, and had been
warmly engaged in the contest of Monday afternoon.
At this hospital were lying Captain Bagley, of Pittsburg; Lieutenant-colonel Woodand, of Philadelphia;
Captain Reed and his son, of the 20th Indiana, and
many others. I left with the surgeons here the remainder of my supplies, and went with Dr. Skelton
over the ground of the battle of Glendale. One
mile and a half to the left, in the direction of the
Chickahominy, we came to the Gatewood house.
In this were lying some of the wounded of Slocum's
division; the injuries they had endured were from
shells and grape. Amongst these were Captain D.
A. Moore, Captain Demming, and Captain W. H.
Spencer, 61st New York. All three were severely
wounded, but bore their sufferings with Christian
fortitude; and I was much rejoiced to find that they,

were sustained by faith in God. If these officers, in
their culture, manners, and gentlemanly bearing, represented their regiments, they were associated with
very superior men. Captain Moore was, I learned,
a professor in some college; Captain Demming, a
successful and popular lawyer. There was no surgeon with the forty or fifty wounded lying in this
house. Dr. Skelton visited them twice a day. They
had but little food, and only three nurses. There is
scarcely anything in the world more trying than
under circumstances like these to bid such noble men
farewell, and leave them alone in their sufferings. I
could see but few graves in this portion of the battle-field; here and there we came on a heap of fresh
earth, which covered some soldier in the place where
he fell; and on the edge of the forest we saw the
spots to which the wounded had been borne from
the sun for shelter, and here had breathed their last,
and the hand of some fellow-soldier had cut the name
and regiment on the bark of the nearest tree.

From here we rode across the fields to the other
extreme of the battle-ground, passing over the ground
occupied by Sumner, Hooker, McCall, and Kearney.
After riding about a mile to the west of the Nelson
house, we came on the ground where General Mc-
Call's division had been posted at the commencement of the action. This field over its entire extent
was covered with the mounds which marked the
spots where our brave men had fallen. Extended
over a portion of the field was the breastwork of
rails they had hastily constructed, and along this
there were many dead. I saw no one unburied. In
this field was a farm-house surrounded by apple and

peach trees; under these had been buried a considerable number of our soldiers. Dr. Donnelly was
in charge of the wounded lying in the house. I did
not remain long at this hospital on my first visit, for
I wished to ascertain their wants, and return with
supplies on the morrow.

We then rode to the scene of the severest fighting, on the edge of the forest, near to the New Market road. In the space of a few yards we counted
forty dead horses, and the carcasses of many more
were lying where the batteries had stood during the
action, and the forest in the rear bore witness to the
destructive power of the enginery which had been
at work here. This was the scene of that twilight
struggle which I have described in a previous
chapter.

We now crossed the New Market road and entered the field which had been occupied by Kearney's men during the action. This field gradually
declines from the road to the forest on the right, and
after proceeding two or three hundred feet in the
woods there is a swamp: our lines extended across
this field to the slough. In the field, about one hundred yards from the road, stands a house occupied
by a negro family. In this house and the outhouses
around it were many of our wounded men, under
the care of Dr. Collins. The garden was inclosed
with a picket fence, nearly every strip of which bore
witness to the severity of the battle. Balls of all
descriptions had torn through the house. It was a
point of great importance during the conflict, and
therefore so perseveringly sought on the one side,
and defended with such determination on the other.

The members of the family had returned, and had been unceasingly kind to our wounded men. These were all, I believe, of General Kearney's division. They were entirely destitute of food, and had been sustained for several days on corn-meal gruel. The negro man described to me the battle, as he had witnessed it. He was an intelligent and sober-minded man. When he saw our troops march up the road and take position across his field, he had no thought that a place so quiet was to be the scene of a battle; he had heard nothing of the Confederates coming down from Richmond.

He and his family had gone out to look on the brilliant spectacle, but did not know what it meant; the banners were flying, the batteries were wheeling into position, and troops of cavalry were drawn up on the edge of the woods. While they were admiring the gay pageant, and contrasting the fine appearance. of our troops with the Confederate soldiers they had seen, and full of wonder asking each other what all this could mean, an officer, he supposed General Kearney, rode over the field and told him to remove his family instantly, for in less than ten minutes there would be a battle, and his house be in the centre of it.

His wife and children ran in, seized each one some garment, and started across the field in the direction of the Quaker Road; they had reached the forest, and were skirting along the woods, "when there was a dreadful crash, as if the sky had fallen and all the thunders I ever heard had been rolled into one." At first they all screamed, fell to the ground and called on the Lord for mercy, and hid their faces in the leaves; but as the branches of the trees around and above them were cut and falling, he called on his family to follow him, and running a few steps he had to return and carry in his arms one of his children, that appeared to be struck with a palsy of fear. They all escaped: a sister-in-law had refused to leave, and when the first shell struck the house fled to the cellar, but, said the man, "her hair turned grey." From the neighborhood of this house the Confederates had removed all their dead.

In one of these outhouses was lying a young man from Pittsburg, William Davis, the son of James Davis, Esq., deceased. In the course of two days he was brought to Savage Station, thence taken to Richmond, then returned to the Station, and with the other prisoners removed to James River, and thence to Baltimore, where he lingered and finally died in January, 1863. He was an excellent soldier, a good Christian, and most affectionate son. His stricken mother has been twice honored in the privilege of giving two sons to her country.

The shadows of evening were falling over the fields when I turned my horse towards Savage Station. I had about ten miles to ride, and most of the way through the encampments of the Confederates.

From the Brackett house I was entirely alone. I had to ride very slowly, for my poor horse was very tired, and had been all day without food. I can never forget that night's ride through the fields of battle. Until I came to the White Oak Swamp I had frequent greetings from the officers and soldiers whose camps I was passing, and was often asked to stop and spend the night. I thanked them, but told them I must go that night to Savage Station for medicines and supplies.

No sentinel challenged me. When I passed the swamp I was alone. The dark woods were silent as a cemetery; by the side of the road every few rods was the body of some poor soldier, who, wounded, had fallen by the way and died alone, and with no other covering than his overcoat and blanket he slept as sweetly as if buried in the sepulchre of his fathers, and certainly with more honor.

The road was covered and in many places nearly obstructed by broken wagons, ambulances, and dead horses and shattered trees. The moon, nearly at its full, threw over the dark forests and lonely fields a robe of silver, and her rays stole down through the pines, and here and there threw her quiet light on the way, and it was not difficult to fill up the scene with spirits clothed in white flitting from spot to spot.

The great owl hooting amongst the trees, and the whippoorwill singing on a grave, were the only living creatures to speak to me and keep me company. When I passed through one of those dismal forests and entered a field equally tenantless, the deserted house, surrounded with the mounds of the dead, was quite as oppressive. I had seen all those ruins and wrecks of war in the glare of the sun, but now, as viewed in the tremulous light of the moon, they wore another aspect, and strange and spectre-like were a thousand objects which started up before me.

The trees standing in the deserted fields looked

as if clothed in flowers, and the wild rose blooming on the roadside shed its fragrance over the dead. Not the sound of the foot of an animal, not a single ray flickering from the window of a house, not a human being or voice, relieved the gloom of that valley of death. Here and there were deserted garments hanging from the branches of the trees, looking so much like men suspended between heaven and earth that I approached them with a shudder.

For miles I was entirely alone, and passing through the former encampments of General Keyes and General Kearney, I reached the forests on the Chickahominy. I resolved to find my way to Meadow Station and Carter house hospital through the woods along a dim path which I had travelled before. I succeeded in threading my way through the labyrinth of bush and vine, and in one of the darkest portions of the path, on a sudden turn, two powerful negro men stood before me. Fortunately they were more frightened than I was; they sprang into the bushes, and I heard the click of cocking pistols: I said, " Good night, boys, don't be afraid of me—am I near to the mill on Meadow Creek ?" With a wise caution they still stood on their guard, but replied, " Yes, massa, you come to him soon." I thanked them, gave my horse the spurs, and quickened him into a gallop, and did not feel altogether comfortable until beyond shot. I then supposed that these were refugee contrabands of the neighborhood, who had stolen out from their hiding-place for forage, or to find their way to a safer retreat.

At length I reached the mill on the creek; there was a large, deep mill-race to be crossed on a bridge.

I spurred my horse on to this, but when he had gone one or two steps, no urging nor spurring could induce him to advance an inch. I felt assured there must be some unusual cause for this stubborn rigidity of the animal. I thought of Balaam and his ass, and alighted to reconnoitre. To my surprise I found all the bridge but the first few logs gone, and a single step more would have carried horse and rider into almost certain death. I patted the horse by way of making an apology for scolding and spurring him. I then rode back to the mill; I saw a light shining through its cracks, and shouted aloud, but no one answered; I called again, but still no reply. They supposed I was a Confederate officer looking after stragglers. I called again: "Can you tell me how to cross the mill-dam?" Instantly the voice of a Southern soldier answered and gave me the proper direction. I followed his advice, and about one o'clock in the morning reached the hospital, and found, to my relief, that no one had died during the day.

28

CHAPTER XXI.

Sabbath, *July 6th.*

Return to the Hospitals in the Battle-fields — Captain Reed and
his son William —Visit from the Rev. Mr. Moore, of Richmond
— The Dead Soldiers — The Hospital in the Willis Church —
Dr. Marsh — Visit to the Hospital of Dr. Donnelly — Adjutant
O. H. Gaither—Conversation with an Irish officer.

The morning brought up from the east one of
those suns whose very first rays are spears of fire,
and at the very moment of his rising the whole
world, enveloped in a robe of flame, is melting in
his heat. Very early I assembled all the nurses of
the hospital, and the sick who were able to come
out, to a morning service. Read the Scriptures,
spoke of the lessons suggested by the morning and
our circumstances. We sang a hymn, and I prayed
with them. I then prescribed for the sick, and told
them of my purpose to be absent for two days, but
I would request Dr. Swinburne to visit them during
this time. I then went to see the patients at Meadow
Station, made the best arrangements for them possible, and provided for supplies of food and medicines.

I resolved to take with me our hospital steward,
Mr. Luke, of the 105th Pennsylvania, whom I had
found to be very skilful in dressing wounds, and
willing to do the utmost for the relief of the suffer-

ing. We obtained supplies from Mr. Brunot and
Mr. Reed. It may not be uninteresting to record
the articles which were borne out to the hospitals : —
I make the extract from my diary, for some of those
articles may suggest to those whose charity dropped
upon us as the dew of blessing, what use was made
of their gifts.

"Left Savage Station, both horses heavily laden,
about ten A. M., bearing for the use of hospitals in the
field, turpentine, whisky, wine, chloroform, quinine,
opium, laudanum, morphia, Sellers's pills, dried
apples, desiccated potatoes, crackers, toasted bread,
dried meat, prunes, coffee, tea, cocoa, corn-starch,
soap, drawers, bed-sacks, shirts, napkins, pepper,
salt, mustard, bandages, lint, paper, and ink."

The heat on this day was even more oppressive
than on previous days; and as in former excursions,
we met a great throng of Jackson's men retiring
towards Richmond. They had the appearance of
being in the last stage of exhaustion, and I have no
doubt that a multitude of them died from this cause
alone. But at the same time we passed several
regiments of Alabamians going towards James River.
It was evident there was then some not fully matured
plan for attacking us in our new position.

We reached the Brackett house hospital, and remained there for an hour. I held a short religious
service in the open grounds under the shadow of
the great tree, and there were gathered around me
the wounded and the sick of our army, and many
Confederate soldiers, and all listened with evident
satisfaction to the words of life.

I found that many of our men were approaching

their end, and the nurses in charge of such came
to me and entreated that I would delay long enough
to talk with and pray for them before they died. A
father besought that I would go and see his son, and
tell him what he felt unable to say. A brother came
to me and told me with tears that his dear brother
was fast sinking, and if I would only speak to him,
probably when he knew that a minister talked to
him he would arouse to answer, and leave some
word of comfort. With such and many similar re-
quests I endeavored to comply, and stood and knelt
beside them. The work to be done here by a
chaplain was so great and blessed that I felt the
deepest regret when I had to leave them. I was
sorry to find to-day that my friend, Dr. Underwood,
was so unwell as to be much of the time confined
to his room and bed.

The first articles of food which the wounded had
received from the Confederate authorities was on
the previous day, and then only a little flour and
side bacon. This they had in various ways prepared
to prevent starvation. And many of our wounded
were actually dying for the want of food; for, as
the consequence of the absence of suitable nourishment, the sloughing of their wounds was greatly
increased, and the tendencies to fever and gangrene
could not be arrested.

Amongst the officers lying here was Captain A.
Reed, of the 20th Indiana. He was wounded through
both shoulders. His company had been detailed as
skirmishers, and were so near to the enemy's line of
battle in the slashings and heavy thickets before he
became aware of their presence, that escape was im-

possible, and for six hours the company remained crouched on their faces, exposed to the direct and cross fire of both lines. As the cloud of smoke increased their position became safer, and though nearly all wounded they were able to fire with deadly precision on the foe. Seven color-bearers of the enemy fell by one hand.

Captain Reed was accompanied by a noble, beautiful boy of sixteen years of age, who had been taken from college at his own importunate entreaties, to follow his father; and though commissary-sergeant, he could not be prevented from attending the captain to the field of action. Soon after the battle had commenced he heard his son exclaim: "Father, I am shot, I am badly hurt." The captain ran to him and lifted him up, saying, "My poor boy!"

He found that he was struck through the bowels, and concluded in a moment that the wound was mortal. For an instant he was unmanned. William rallied soon, smiled, and said: "Father, leave me; take care of the men." The captain placed a few leaves and a coat under his head and returned to his post. Soon the father was struck twice and lay disabled, but still directing the fire of the few men by his side. When the battle closed after night they found themselves within thirty feet of the enemy's lines. One of the wounded men went forward and made known that ten or more of our wounded were lying in the clump of bushes near them. Some of the Confederate soldiers came forward and helped them to rise. The captain surrendered his sword to Colonel Gorman, of the 14th South Carolina. This the colonel generously returned, and with his

28 *

own hand replaced it in the sash of the captain. After remaining for five days in a negro hut, the father and son were taken to Nelson's house and placed under the care of Dr. Skelton.

While lying without food or any medical attendance in this hut, they were visited by a party of gentlemen from Richmond. Amongst these was the Rev. Mr. Moore, pastor of the most influential Presbyterian church in that place. When Mr. Moore saw William lying with the sufferers, he exclaimed: "I declare, here is a fine blue-eyed boy amongst the wounded Yankees. Why did you come from your father and mother and school to murder us, burn our houses, and destroy our cities?"

"Stop, sir," said the captain, "that is my son; I brought him; the fault is mine if any one's, and mine must be the punishment. I think it cruel in you to come and insult us, and instead of bringing us relief adding to the misery of our condition. You know we are in no state to answer you."

"Sir," said Mr. Moore, "I beg your pardon;" and left the cabin.

The Rev. Mr. Moore is a Pennsylvanian, born near Huntingdon, and was educated by a ladies' educational society; and after finishing his preparation for the ministry was invited to Richmond. Here he distinguished himself by the most bitter denunciations of the North and her free institutions, and literally forgot his people and his father's house. Some of his relatives were amongst our wounded men in Richmond; but I never heard of his visiting one of the hospitals where were lying many of the sons

"THE SWEETEST TEARS THAT HEAVEN SHEDS ARE THE DEWS THAT FALL ON THE DEAD SOLDIER'S FACE."—*Page 326.*

and grandsons of those ladies who were his benefactors.

William Reed bore his sufferings with the greatest
patience: he was far more anxious for his father than
for himself. They were lying together in an upper
room in one of the houses at Nelson's place. On the
Sabbath when I saw them there was reason to hope
that both might survive their injuries. William was
in excellent spirits, and was trying to comfort his
father by pictures of home, and their joy when his
mother would dress and bandage their wounds.

During the night several dead men had been borne
to the green plot west of the house, and on the following morning there were ten or more lying side
by side. The dew had fallen heavily on their faces,
and in the light of the rising sun glittered on their
brows like gems. William, seated at the window,
looked down upon them and said: "Father, the
sweetest tears that heaven sheds are the dews that
fall on a dead soldier's face." With a nature so rich
and gifted, what a blessing might this noble young
man have been to his parents and country! but after
living fourteen days, he died in the Libby Prison. I
reached the room in which he lay just in season to
commend his spirit to God—one of the most precious
offerings laid on the altar of our country.

I next rode to Nelson's house, and found the place
surrounded with troops of the Confederacy.

There were very few complaints amongst our men
of any insult, offence, or wrong done to them by
these men; on the other hand, they mentioned with
gratitude many acts of kindness. There was a troop
of cavalry in the field near at hand. It was com-

posed of Texans : they were savage-looking men, with long uncombed hair, nearly as dark as Indians, and the face covered with enormous beards; they certainly looked more like Bashi-Bazouks than Anglo-Americans.

There was a great deal of thieving around this hospital. The horses of the surgeons had been stolen, also their saddles and bridles; their tents were entered, and everything, even to castor oil, was mysteriously filched away. Much of this we have reason to fear was done by our own soldiers, and the things sold to Confederate officers. On the previous day Lieutenant Lowell, of Massachusetts, had died : he was known to have had in his possession one hundred and fifty dollars, a gold watch, and other valuable articles, which all disappeared; and though a rigid examination was instituted, the veil was not lifted. His servant had the reputation of a "fool," but certainly was one of the shrewdest blockheads I ever saw : he had tears of grief over the death of the lieutenant, the photographs of his mother and sisters, which he bore in his breast, protestations of indignant innocence, letters of character, scratches of briers or bullets received in the service of his master, an empty purse, a shoeless foot, all to parade as the proof that he could not commit such a crime. I do not believe that even a New York criminal lawyer could have wrung the story out of the fellow.

I cannot now distinctly enumerate the interesting conversations I held at this time with officers and soldiers from various States. For many I had letters to write, assuring their friends of their life. In other cases, memoranda in regard to property were committed to me. Some of these letters were most touching and instructive. The letters of husbands to their wives, describing the scenes, dangers, and struggles of the battles, the nature of their wounds, the hopes of return, etc.; of sons to their mothers, full of affectionate remembrances and thanks for the years of faithful, patient, loving care.

There were several cases of the deepest interest: one man confessing a sin which now hung like a dark veil on his soul, that as often as he besought forgiveness a cloud arose between him and God. Poor fellow! often did I go to him, and with closed eyes, unconscious of my presence, he was confessing his sin and praying for mercy. Amongst the wounded here was Captain Adams, of Sharon, Pa., whose case was almost miraculous. He had been struck by a ball about one inch above the heart, which passed through the body, and yet in a few days he was able to walk around, and was free from pain.

During this day I visited the hospital under the care of Dr. Marsh, of Honesdale, Pa., then the surgeon of the 4th Pennsylvania Cavalry. This was about three-fourths of a mile from the Nelson house, in the forest. The hospital was in Willis's Church, on the Quaker road. There were about one hundred wounded men lying in and around it: until I came, there had been brought to them no supplies of any kind. For four days they were without bread, and though the doctor made known their distressing condition to General Lee, General Jackson, and other officers of the Confederate Army, nothing was sent them until the evening of the fourth day, when came two hundred crackers and one hundred and fifty pounds of fat bacon sides. With this the doctor and the nurses created such food as was possible. On the following day they received two barrels of flour, but they were without cooking utensils of any kind, and had to roll the flour into small cakes and roast them in the fire on the end of a stick. This was the food on which the wounded were living when I first came to the hospital.

Dr. Marsh, like a true patriot and generous-hearted man as he is, shed tears as he described to me the sufferings of these miserable days. He said nothing so much distressed him as the ceaseless cry for bread, coming from those who were evidently dying from exhaustion and hunger; and that in several instances, those who might have recovered perished for want of nourishment. The demands of the first day exhausted all the medical stores he possessed, and from that time all he could do was to wash and bandage wounds, and break and distribute to twenty mouths the solitary cracker found in the haversack of a dead soldier. The wounded men of this hospital were mostly New York troops, of General Sumner's corps. Near to the pulpit was lying on the floor a dead officer: he had just departed. Under his hand was a pocket Bible; I gently lifted up the hand and removed the book, that if possible I might find his name. On the front leaf was written: "Sergeant Joel Chester, 3d Pa. Reserves."

"Sir," spoke to me a soldier lying by the side of the dead man, "be so good as to leave the book, for the print is plainer than in my Testament, and I can sometimes read a few words."

"I had no intention of taking it, my friend; I only

wished to learn the name of our dead brother. I am glad you wish to have the book; I know its words and promises can give you the most precious balm in this hour."

"Yes, sir," he replied; "I know it to be true; the man who is lying by me read the Bible aloud as long as he was able, and when he could no longer hold it up nor see the words, then I read. We prayed together, and during the long nights we encouraged and comforted each other by repeating hymns and passages of the blessed book. The sergeant was a good man, and died in perfect peace; he entered into rest only a few hours before me. Come, Lord Jesus; come quickly."

I then asked him if the hope he had as a Christian was long standing or recent.

"Six years ago," said he, "I first confessed my Lord, and since then I have tried to serve Him, but now I find He is far more precious to me than ever; before, I had to go to Him, but now He comes to me and places my head on His bosom. I shall soon see Him, for I know that my Redeemer liveth."

I found on inquiry that his name was John A. Price, Sergeant 3d Pennsylvania Reserves. He was evidently near his end, and I afterwards learned from the doctor he died the evening of that day. Standing by, I commended him in prayer to the care of the blessed Redeemer, and felt more deeply than ever in the past how precious was that Gospel "which robs death of its sting and the grave of its victory." When I bade him farewell the open Bible of his friend was lying on his bosom.

I next visited the hospital under the care of Dr.

Donnelly; this was in a farm-house, near to the New Market road; in the open fields about it was fought the severest part of the battle of Glendale; hundreds of graves or mounds of the dead were scattered over these fields. The fruit-trees were shattered and the branches torn and twisted as by a tornado; each of the houses which formed the cluster had been the scene of a conflict.

The house was surrounded by many Confederate soldiers, who were talking with our wounded men. The first person I saw was Adjutant O. H. Gaither, of Bedford, Pennsylvania, son of John A. Gaither, of Somerset, Pennsylvania. He was lying on a small cot-bedstead, wounded in the right breast, the ball passing out near the spine. He breathed with considerable difficulty. I was greatly impressed with the remarkable beauty and nobleness of his face; his eye had the piercing light which I have often seen in the look of the wounded. By his side sat a Confederate officer fanning him. The room was full of wounded men, several of them cases of amputation.

"What do you think," said he, "doctor, of my case? Is it possible for me to recover?"

"You may; but your position is very critical, and the heat, the absence of all comforts, and want of suitable food, increase the danger. You are in the hands of God; He only can heal and save from death."

"Sir," said he, looking intently into my face, "are you a clergyman?" I assured him I was. "Then," said he, "you are not one of our men; you don't belong to the Union Army."

I told him I was a chaplain of a Pennsylvania

regiment. Instantly his eyes filled with tears, and he said:

"This is the answer of my prayer; I entreated God to send to us some minister to talk with us and pray for us, and now you have come as by a miracle. How did you get here?"

I told him, from Savage Station; that I had remained and been taken prisoner, in order that I might be able to do this very work. He grasped my hand and had a seat brought for me and said:

"Now I want you to tell me of the blessed Jesus. We want to hear of the sinner's friend."

The poor sufferers around ceased their groaning; those who were able arose on their elbows and listened, while I spoke of the acts, words, and promises of the Redeemer. These blessed truths fell like balm upon many hearts, and even the Confederate officers shed tears. We sang together one of our hymns, and we prayed with each other. It was a most affecting scene.

The adjutant then told me that for years he had been a professed follower of Christ, but that lately he had been very much occupied with his military duties, and had not those opportunities for retirement and prayer essential for spiritual strength. But he had never departed from his God, and now as a sinner he clung as his only hope to the promises of the Gospel; and that during all the time he had been lying here the words of the Saviour had been to him more precious than water in the desert; and he wished to bear testimony to the goodness of God to himself. He never felt so fully assured before of the divinity and absolute truth of revelation. In his

29

darkness and suffering the Saviour had visited him
and said: "Son, be of good comfort; I will never
leave thee nor forsake thee." He wished me, if I
never saw him again, to convey to his father and
mother his dying blessing: he thanked them for all
the patience of their parental love, for all the lessons
they had taught him, for all the prayers they had
poured forth for him, and asked their forgiveness for
whatsoever sorrow he might have occasioned them
by thoughtlessness, or neglect of their desires and
counsels; that he never felt for them such deep
affection as now, and he would wait for them at the
gate of heaven. And to his brothers he sent his
dying love, and would urge them to make early
choice of the Gospel, and live by faith in the Son of
God.

All listened with the deepest interest and emotion
to these words of the young officer. I had rarely
seen one more gifted in face and speech, and my
desire was strong that his life might be saved.

The Confederate officer, to relieve the solemnity
of the scene somewhat, remarked "that the adjutant and himself would meet in better times; that
he would have the privilege of entertaining Lieutenant Gaither and myself at his table in New Orleans,
and showing us that he was a Christian and a gentleman, though a tiger." His language betrayed
that he was not a native American, but an Irishman. In a few moments he alluded to the land of
his birth, and said that we might think strange that
he, an Irishman, should be fighting against us. He
then told us that his father had left Rathmelton,
Donegal County, Ireland, many years since, and set-

tled in New Orleans; that his grandmother was still
alive in the old country; that he remembered Loch
Swilley and the hills around the old village, and the
graveyard where his ancestors were asleep. He
talked with all the freedom and eloquence of an
Irishman, and, amongst other things, said that he
did not regret the taking up arms against the North;
and when the independence of the Southern Confederacy was acknowledged, as he had no doubt it
soon would be, should the war be rekindled his
sword would be always at her service. In this struggle she had appealed to arms in order to defend her
rights, and the people of the South would rather die
than endure the indignities and wrongs inflicted on
them during the last few months.

I said: "Will you be so good as to tell us what
rights of yours we have invaded? what wrongs have
we inflicted on you? We have given you a country,
and, by your own account, prosperity. And what
have we done to justify your drawing your sword
and leaguing yourself with those who are now endeavoring to overthrow the Government of the
land?"

"Well," said he, "I read the Declaration of Independence in my own country, and thought it a noble
instrument, and still think the same. But every
principle which the Revolutionary fathers there as-
serted as justifying an appeal to arms, we gather into
our declaration, and all the oppressions the fathers
complained of are ours; and if they were right, we
are. My father and myself are slaveholders; much
of the property we have accumulated since we came
to this country is in slaves. You wish to rob us of

our servants, and set them all free to cut our throats. Ought not a man to defend his property, and shoot down the robber that comes to despoil his home and take from his children their inheritance?"

"Did you ever lose one of your slaves? did the United States Government ever seize one of them and pronounce him free? did a Northern officer ever go to you with an Act of Congress in his hands, seize your negroes, and scornfully set aside your claim? did a white man from the North help away one of your slaves?"

"Well," said he, in reply, "I must confess that we never lost any of our blacks. But that is neither here nor there; others did, and our slaves ran away from us, and you sheltered and protected them. You permitted the organization of societies for the very purpose of aiding the escape of our negroes; you permitted meetings to be held in all your towns and cities, in which we were abused, and slaveholders classed with thieves and murderers; you passed your personal liberty bills, and when we caught our negroes in the North you sprang on us writs of habeas corpus, flung us from the magistrate to court; excited mobs, who hooted us in the street, stoned us, created tumults, and in the *mêlée* assisted our slaves to escape. After all these evidences of hostility to us and our interests, you ask me what are our wrongs!"

"Yes, my friend," I replied, "I must ask the question again. Nothing short of the greatest oppressions and the most grievous and long-continued injuries can justify a people taking up arms against the Government under which they were born. 'The powers that be are ordained of God.' The laws and institutions of government are essential for the happiness, civilization, and protection of mankind. No slight wrong, no transient oppression, will excuse the appeal to the last resort. The man who takes up arms against a good government crucifies the most sacred of human interests. By your own statement you had suffered no grinding despotism; everything went along pretty much as you desired. All the wheels of the Government were under your control; the army marched and ships sailed as you ordered. Treaties were made, compromises annulled, compacts broken at your bidding. The entire policy of the Government was changed every five or ten years, at most, to please you.

"But when we dared to elect a President who was not a Southern man, nor came into office pledged to sustain your platform — on the very night that his election is announced you commence scraping lint in Charleston, and the next day you organize militia by companies in New Orleans; take measures to seize the forts and the arsenals, the ships of war, and to rob the United States mint and custom-houses, and you rush to arms, and openly in the court of the world denounce the North as having violated the Constitution of the United States, because once in fifty years we dared to elect a President who had some sympathy with freedom. *That last act* of oppression utterly exhausted a patience which has no parallel for long suffering and sublime endurance, except in the history of the martyrs. *That last act* was so great a wrong that your manhood, your sense of justice, your love of liberty, all impelled you to

29 *

rend in pieces a government which protected and blessed all who bore the American name, and constrained you to stop the industrial pursuits of millions, crimson all your rivers with blood, stain a thousand fields with human gore, and consign half a million of your countrymen to the graves of battle. As for the injury done you by the "personal liberty bills," have you no laws against kidnappers? are there no such scoundrels in the South? Occasionally such a villain finds his way North, and hatches up a claim against some poor negro who was born free or emancipated by his owner, and obtains the aid or connivance of Federal officers in hurrying to bondage a man entitled to freedom. To protect such persons and to prevent the perpetration of such crimes, the personal liberty bills were passed. And as for our permitting meetings to be held in which you were denounced, it is utterly impossible to prevent assemblies where the people shall have perfect freedom of speech on all great questions of morals and government. If we attempted to strangle liberty of speech, we would create the worst despotism the world has ever seen.

"But I have been in the habit of thinking that everything which is just and right welcomes discussion and investigation, and only things which are evil seek the darkness. It strikes me that a people so free of speech as you are, so unmeasured in your denunciations of all you deem mean, are guilty of an amazing inconsistency when you demand of us that we should create dungeons in the North to be the grave of liberty. Our fathers fought for freedom of speech, legislation, and action. You have taken

up arms, according to your own confession, in the
first place, to perpetuate in perfect security the bondage of your fellow-men whom you hold as slaves.
In the second place, to imprison and banish from our
country all who dare to hint that slavery is not a
'Divine institution,' and may have connected with
it abuses and oppressions. In the third place, to
compel us to expunge from the statute books of our
States every law which would secure justice to a
negro.

"Do you not see that our fathers struggled for freedom, but you for slavery? They did so because they
believed that all men had certain inalienable rights,
'the pursuit of life, liberty, and happiness;' you
for power and the rights of property in man. They
took up arms to destroy Bastiles and dungeons; you
to create them. They to defend the rights and aid
the oppressed; you to extinguish forever the inalienable rights of millions. They fought to secure for
themselves and their children the blessings of a free
government; you to extend the dominion of slavery,
and to destroy in all our States freedom of speech
and legislation. Is it not a great outrage on language to call yourselves the 'soldiers of freedom,'
and your dead the 'martyrs of liberty?'"

But as our excited and earnest conversation might
disturb and injure the wounded men in the room, I
proposed that we should continue our discussion in
the open air.

"Before you go," said Adjutant Gaither, "let me
say to our friend that we in the North did not take
up arms to subjugate the South, but to defend the
Constitution and to vindicate our insulted laws. We

did not wish to deprive the people of the South of
one right which they had under the Constitution,
but we felt bound, by every principle of duty and
honor, to sustain our Government in her efforts to
maintain her rightful authority. For my own part,
I do not know that I shall ever rise from this cot;
but if I die, I have no regrets or misgivings. I
left my profession and entered the army as a private soldier, because I felt that when my country
needed me I could not remain at home without disgrace. I know that we had no desire to trample
upon the South, or to inflict any injury upon her
people, but we were compelled, by the strongest sense
of duty to God and man, to defend the most sacred
of trusts, and our cause never appeared to me more
worthy the sacrifice of my life than now."

I was rejoiced to hear this testimony from the lips
of the adjutant, speaking as he did with great difficulty, often panting for breath: his words were most
impressive, and listened to as the last utterances of
one who had given his life for the cause he was defending. The Confederate officer and myself went
out and stood under the shade of a large apple tree,
which cast a cooling shadow over the space between the
main house and the kitchen. Around us, within ten
feet of the door, were many mounds, the last rest-
ing-places of our dead. Several of our wounded had
dragged themselves to the shadow of this tree, and
to others near at hand, and were sitting and lying in
every conceivable posture around the trees. Many
Confederate soldiers, mostly of the "Louisiana Tigers," were seated among our men smoking and
talking. Nearly all these men belonged to the class

known at the South as the "poor whites." When
we had advanced within their circle the Confederate
officer again addressed me, saying:

"Doctor, you do not understand us: we had come
to the conclusion that the government of this country
was to be administered for the benefit of the North,
and moreover we were sick and tired to death of the
perpetual noise you were making over slavery. We
could not go North without being insulted, and hearing ourselves abused in your churches, and seeing
the most infamous things said of us in your papers.
These annoyances, insults, and wrongs drove us to
such a state that we no longer wished to live under the
same Government with you. And surely, when such
was the state of feeling in the South, it was best for
us to go off and set up for ourselves, and separate as
Abraham from Lot: we did not want to go to war,
but we did want to be let alone. And all we demand
now is for you to permit us to work out our own
future, make our own laws, and do as we please with
our own property. What can you hope to gain by
this war? If you conquer us, you can never be secure everywhere in the Confederacy until you have
killed the last white man, and turned the land into
a desert. Even after you have wasted and destroyed
us, what have you gained? Nothing to compensate
for a long war, a great public debt, and the death ·
of half a million of your sons and brothers."

To this I replied: "There were undoubtedly many
citizens of the North perfectly willing that you
should be permitted to separate yourselves from the
United States, and start a Confederacy of your own.
We were so fully convinced of the essential barbarism

of the South, that we had lost all desire to continue a union with such a people. We saw plainly, too, that there was such an irreconcilable hostility between your institutions and our own, that we could not live together in peace, and we were prepared to listen to any proposition for a peaceful division of the Union. But instead of this you seized the forts, arsenals, ships, and arms of the United States Government. You tore down the time-honored flag of the country, and drove out of the South all loyal officers and patriots. Like the assassin, you rushed upon us with drawn knife, giving no option but to fight or die; you fired upon Fort Sumter, held by a small garrison of our troops; and on the night of its fall, in a congratulatory address by your Secretary of War, your President and Congress being present, it was announced that, in less than a month, your troops would be in possession of Washington, and that you would dictate terms of peace in Philadelphia or New York. Your leaders plotted the assassination of President Lincoln in Baltimore, and fully intended that he should never be permitted to take the oath of office. We have the proof that you intended to subvert the entire Government and take possession of Northern cities, and 'call the roll of your slaves at the foot of Bunker Hill.' After all this, when the President summoned 75,000 men to defend the capital, you sprang upon them unarmed, and murdered them in the streets. Everywhere, throughout the entire South, you rushed to arms, and did everything you could, by insults, pillage, the murder of Union men, and deeds of violence, to hasten and make inevitable a conflict. We have the evidence that

in more than one Southern city you had bands of
assassins who had sworn to murder President Lincoln and the members of his Cabinet, and then seize
the reins of Government.   One such infamous band
we know existed in Richmond, who were bound by
the most horrible oath to proceed to Washington
for the murder of the President; and part of that
conclave of murderers actually made their appearance in the capital, and were only prevented from
the accomplishment of their infamous design (April
5th) by the timely exposure to the Government of
their presence and plot.   How perfectly preposterous
to talk of peace and an amicable separation, when
such was your spirit and revolutionary plans!   No,
while we were saying, 'Let there be no war—let us
compromise — let us meet in a peace convention,
and adjust in the spirit of Christ and catholic patriot-.
ism all matters in dispute,' you were rejecting every
such overture, and steadily and earnestly preparing
for war, capturing troops in Texas, seizing all the
property of the General Government and of Northern
citizens, leaving us no alternative but dishonor or
war: we had no escape but to fight, or yield to you
as our masters and the future rulers of the country.
We know that you were not satisfied with merely
withdrawing the Southern States from the Union,
but you had organized in many of our Northern
States associations and clubs of men to co-operate
with you in overturning all the institutions of the
country, and endeavoring everywhere to introduce
a reign of terror.   You never intended to go off
peacefully; you grasped at the reins of Government,
and aimed at the utter subversion of all the princi-

ples of constitutional liberty. You drew the sword,
and placing it at our breasts, demanded that we
should yield or die. I will do you the justice to
say that you had no idea of the consequences of
your rebellion. You thought we would be terrified,
and submit without a struggle; that you could dis-
mantle the Ship of State, cut down her masts, and
cast her unmanned into the sea, without a hand being
lifted to avenge the insult. But, as usual with the
proud and arrogant, you had no correct estimate of
the character of the people you despised; you let
loose upon the country all the horrors which follow
in the train of civil war, and now you must take the
consequences. It is too late now to talk of peaceful
separation; that was not in your thoughts when you
plotted to seize the capital and humble all the
Free States. We must fight for our homes and
our children; and if your cities are burnt, your country wasted, your property confiscated, and your
slaves set free — when more than half your men fall
in battle, and the remainder are compelled to flee
the country as traitors, it will be but a righteous
retribution. On you rests the responsibility of all
the calamities of the time. And you will appear in
the presence of God stained with the guilt of innumerable murders. From every grave in this field
there goes up a cry to heaven against you.

"And an Irishman, I feel, is especially without
excuse,—you that have filled all Europe and the civilized world with your eloquent denunciations of
tyrants, and come to this country as a refuge from
the oppression of Great Britain; and yet you are
here the defender of an oppression such as Europe

"I WILL ASK YOUR GRANDMOTHER TO BLOT YOUR NAME OUT OF THE FAMILY BIBLE."—*Chap. XXI.*

has not seen for a thousand years. For Southern men, born slaveholders, and who have been from their cradles reared to the exercise of absolute power, I have some respect — I appreciate their position. But for you I feel naught but contempt: the last man on earth I can excuse as the defender of slavery is an Irishman. The heroic endurance of your martyred ancestors, their solemn leagues and covenants signed with their blood, your oft-repeated and most eloquent pleadings for freedom, pledge an Irishman, more than any other man, to be true to liberty in whatever land his lot may be cast. You, like the masons of Como in the Middle Ages, who went forth over all Europe to rear those noble Gothic temples which to-day are the greatest monuments of art and genius in the world; you leave Ireland, solemnly pledged to all nations to be everywhere the defenders of the oppressed, and to rear in all lands the temples of human liberty. Nearly all your countrymen are faithful — more than three-fourths of the dead of our army lying over this field are the sons of Irishmen — the principles they had been taught by their fathers impelled them to arms when liberty was attacked. They were true to the pledges of their ancestors, and showed themselves worthy of such fathers. But what of you? I have been in the town where you were born; I have preached in the old church where your fathers worshipped: I expect to go back again to Ireland, and amongst the first things I will do will be to find your grandmother, tell her your story, and get her to blot your name out of the family Bible as false to the vows of your baptism, and unworthy the name of an Irishman."

30

The man quailed, stammered out some excuse, and tried to say that the force of circumstances had made him against his will a slaveholder. I found on looking around on the throng of Rebel soldiers, that the language I had used to the officer excited no anger, but rather pleased them. It was probably that he was arrogant and severe, and they were gratified in seeing his evident mortification: and as often before and afterward I took occasion to assure them that we had no controversy with them; that if they only knew it, we were fighting their battles as well as our own; that this was a war of the aristocracy against the principles of republicanism and freedom.

They dared to say but little in reply, but it was plain that, dull and ignorant as they were, they felt that there was some truth in my words. I discovered in them none of that bitterness of language and malignity of scowl so often heard in the speech and exhibited in the looks of distinguished citizens and officers. Indeed, the soldiers of the Confederate Army were, when the wounded fell into their hands, generally kind and often most humane; but, with a few honorable exceptions, the wealthy citizens of Virginia and the officers of the army were without pity, and influenced by a hate so intense that the most violent language failed to express it. After spending three or four hours in this place I bade the wounded and dying farewell, never expecting to see Lieutenant Gaither again on earth.

After stopping at various small houses, where were lying from twenty to forty of our wounded, I started on my return to Savage Station. I was glad to learn

at these various small hospitals that Dr. Swinburne
had visited them, assisted in difficult amputations,
and brought their condition before the Confederate
authorities. Many of these poor fellows were left
in a state of the greatest misery and want. Officers
from General Lee's army would frequently ride up
to our large hospitals, such as Brackett's house and
Nelson's house, and upbraid our surgeons for permitting many of our men to remain in those remote
cabins without food, nurses, or medical attendance.
But all the medical stores of our surgeons had been
taken from them or exhausted; of food they had
none, and they were physically unable to attend to
those brought to their tents. It was most palpable
that the Rebel Army was but poorly supplied with
those sanitary and medical stores which with us were
deemed so essential. And what they had were dispensed without method.

CHAPTER XXII.

Removal of Mr. Brunot and Volunteer Nurses to Richmond — Funeral at Carter's House — Soldier's Conversation with Stonewall Jackson.

WHEN I reached Savage Station I learned that Mr. Brunot, the volunteer nurses who had come from Pittsburg, and the Rev. Mr. Reed, were ordered up to Richmond. They were already on the cars for departure. I had only time to receive from Mr. Brunot instructions to take his tent, and dispense his stores of medicines and sanitary goods among the wounded and destitute. From this time (July 8th) until our removal to Richmond, I spent the day at Savage Station, returning each evening to the hospital at Carter's house.

No one can give the history of those wretched days. We were in the midst of the field of battle. The air for miles became intolerably offensive. If the warm, stagnant atmosphere was stirred for a moment by a wind, there was borne to us not a breath of sweetness, but an odor so foul that we turned sick and shuddered as in a palsy.

To the hundreds of wounded and suffering men who were in all the conditions of human misery, we daily and hourly ministered as we could. But in consequence of the removal to the Richmond prisons of Mr. Brunot and the corps of volunteer nurses, the labor that devolved upon the surgeons and nurses who remained was severe and exhausting beyond endurance. Several were prostrated with sickness, and in a few days one-half of the surgeons were unable to attend to any duty whatever. In the meantime our distresses were increased by the taking from Savage Station and removal to Richmond of all the stores which had been saved in the general conflagration. This was done on the pretence that all our wounded men were to be immediately removed and paroled. Our men were thus robbed of the articles essential for their recovery, and were left without bread, fresh meat, crackers, prepared soups, dried fruits, and all those delicacies which had been sent to us for such a time. Fortunately I had secured, in the retreat of our army, some beeves and sheep, which were guarded with the greatest care; and these gave food and soup to the men of three hospitals for some days.

To this Dr. Swinburne alluded in his report to Governor Morgan, of New York. He says: "Up to this time we had been enabled to furnish ourselves with some fresh meat and soups, from some beeves which remained in the charge of Rev. Dr. Marks, U. S. A., who had charge of a small fever hospital about one mile from Savage Station, of about one hundred patients, the management of which requires some notice; and though I have not any statistical report, I think it the best-managed and disciplined hospital in Virginia. But now the remnants of our stock, including instruments, medicines, ice, bandages, lint, etc., having been taken by the Confederate

30 *

Medical Director, under the alleged impression that we were to be removed to Richmond and paroled.

"But all was gone and our removal delayed, we were obliged to depend on the material furnished by requisition upon the Confederate government, or by purchase with our own funds. Up to this time the officers had furnished the principal part of their own subsistence by purchase. The rations furnished by the Confederates were only flour and poor bacon, while food for the sick was very expensive and difficult to obtain. The inhabitants were unwilling to sell except for gold, and were also instructed from Richmond not to sell to the 'Yankees.' It was therefore difficult to obtain anything, even at the most exorbitant prices.

"In this dilemma, I wrote to Dr. Guild, M. D. C. S. A., our condition and wants, who answered by sending next morning Dr. Winfield, Medical Inspector of Hospital Camps, and accompanying him was Colonel ——, of General Lee's staff, and sent by him. In answer to these gentlemen as to what we were feeding our patients, I stated that flour and bacon were our only food and medicine, and the meat was not only limited in supply, but absolutely maggoty. This statement was confirmed by Lieutenant Lacy Stewart, commanding post. I referred them to the war-worn and exhausted countenances of the patients. What little choice stores we had were removed on the 15th instant."

In this statement the doctor speaks of purchasing articles of food from the inhabitants of the country. I knew of but one farm on which anything could be purchased, and this was the place of Mrs. Couch,

which General McClellan had encircled with guards
for its protection.   The corn, sheep, and cows that
remained were sold to our sick and officers at fabulous prices.   Strawberries one dollar a pint, milk
one dollar a quart, a lamb ten dollars, a pint of
blackberries fifty cents, and twenty-five cents for an
egg, and even at these rates there were but few who
could obtain anything.   In order to meet these demands on them for food, the officers and surgeons
sold their watches and clothing.   I was obliged to
sell my own watch, which I valued principally on
account of its having accompanied me in journeyings
in other lands, for fifteen dollars in Confederate money, but I had the satisfaction of knowing that it
purchased many a loaf of bread for those who were
hungry and destitute of means.

During those days when the pressure of want was
constantly increasing, the sufferers were no longer
in trouble that their wounds should be washed and
bandaged; but when we entered their tents, one
hundred hungry faces were turned towards the surgeons, and the cry was "bread! bread!"

Dr. Swinburne did everything in his power to
obtain supplies of medicine and food, and made renewed appeals, stating that the wounded were dying
of want; and amongst the surgeons and nurses,
nearly all were ill with fevers from exhaustion and
want of proper nourishment; that our medicines
were entirely expended, and all were in danger of
perishing; that the bacon which was sent us would
be considered anywhere else the most miserable
offal.

In reply was received:—Camphor, 1 lb.; cerate,

1 lb.; adhesive plaster, 5 yards; iodine, 1 oz.; opium, ¼ lb.; tincture of iron, ½ lb.; whiskey, 5 galls.; bandages, 6 doz.; lint, 1 lb. These articles were sent as the supply, for more than a fortnight, of fifteen hundred sick and wounded men. This was but to mock our misery, but may have indicated as much their poverty as their inhumanity. But we could not evade the conclusion that the Confederates had no desire for the restoration to health of those whom the fortune of war had thrown into their hands.

In the midst of these distresses our indignation was greatly increased against the Rebel government by the bringing into Savage Station of one hundred wounded men, who had been left on the battle-field of Gaines's Mill, on Friday, the 27th of June, and from that day until the 16th of July had nothing but flour and water. The flour was prepared by the surgeons and nurses in every way that they could devise to nourish and eke out life. But without salt, no effort could make palatable the tasteless porridge and half-baked cake. And thus for twenty days, within eight miles of Richmond, and their condition fully known to the officers of the Confederate army, these wounded and disabled soldiers were left to perish of want.

The sufferings of these men, as described to me by Dr. Churchill, of the 4th New York Volunteers, who remained with them during all these dismal days, were most painful. Many died of hunger and exhaustion, and some of them, when brought to Savage Station, lived but a few hours. Dr. Smith, now of the convalescent camp near Washington, was at this time one of the most active and humane of the surgeons. After those brave and skeleton-like men had been brought in and laid down on the grounds near the station, he approached a group of them; they begged for bread; he took out of his haversack four or five hard crackers, which he had gathered up to preserve himself from starving; these he gave to them, telling them, with tears, that they were the last, and he was very sorry that he had nothing more to give. He left them, but their wan and haggard faces haunted him. He begged a few drops of liquor from a brother surgeon and returned and administered it to them.

Dr. Smith subsequently met two of these soldiers at Fortress Monroe, who spoke to him and reminded him of the scene when he gave his last cracker to the wounded soldier at Savage Station, and told him that they felt sure that cracker and ounce of whisky had saved their lives, for from that hour the pulses of life began to return to them, and they would never forget him. "The bread cast upon the waters returned before many days."

All this time, while our sufferers were perishing for food, around Carter's house the fields were covered with ripe blackberries, and the woods were filled with whortleberries, which would have been at once food and medicine. But there was no one to gather them; the nurses were already exhausted with their labors and hunger combined; not one could summon strength or courage to go into the open field and run the risk of meeting bands of Confederate soldiers who might fire upon him. However, the time came when this coveted fruit seemed within their reach.

I had left Savage Station, to attend the funeral of

a Mr. Coates, of the 57th Pennsylvania, of Tioga
County, Pennsylvania, who died of typhoid fever.
We carried the body into the orchard, our custom-
ary place of interment. All that were able to leave
the house attended the funeral service, and after
singing an appropriate hymn we laid the dead soldier
alongside of many of his departed comrades. When
they were assembling it was a most touching sight;
some hobbling along, others carried in the arms of
companions scarcely stronger than themselves, all
coming to show their respect for one who had so
faithfully nursed them. I took occasion to impress
upon them that the two great duties of the hour
were, first, patience, the uncomplaining endurance
of their sufferings; second, charity, making the effort
to do all that was possible for others in a worse condition, and that rarely in the life of man was there
such an opportunity to display heroic endurance on
the one hand and heavenly charity on the other;
that we gathered from the sacred Scriptures that
nothing was more pleasing to God than deeds of
charity; that, though they were wounded and staggering, and had scarce strength even to care for
themselves, yet they ought to be deeply affected by
the sufferings of those that had more to endure than
themselves, and by words and deeds show that they
were prompted by the spirit of the Gospel, and remembered Him who pleased not Himself. I then reminded them of how greatly they had been benefited
lately by the use of the wild fruit which grew so
abundantly about us, and that the diseases of many
weeks, which had defied all the usual medical reme-

dies, had disappeared under their influence, and they
had found these better than balms or elixirs.

At this very hour, at Savage Station, within a mile
of us, were lying two thousand of our fellow-sol-
diers, prostrated by wounds and fevers, unable to
obtain a single one of those luscious berries which
grew in such profusion under their eyes. They, in
their feverish longing for that beyond their reach,
no doubt prayed the blessed God to send down His
angels to bear to them the fruit which they deemed
would be almost a life-restorer. Could they not be
those angels? Would they not be stronger in consequence of the endeavor to be benefactors? I left
this appeal with their own hearts, reminding them
that in all probability such another opportunity would
never come to them, and begging them to remember
that in the day of God's judgment we should find
mercy as we had shown mercy. In a few moments
after the service was concluded, I was delighted to
see every man who could stagger moving over the
fields gathering the fruit, not for themselves but for
others. Every face was lighted with greater satisfaction, because engaged in unselfish labors. At
sundown, when their cups were emptied, more than
a bushel of berries had been gathered by men who
were scarcely able to drag themselves from their
beds. On the following morning this labor of love
was renewed. Before nine.o'clock, Corporal Robert
Speer and Sergeant Temple, of the 105th Pennsylvania, brought to my tent at Savage Station more
than three bushels of berries, which had been gathered by the sick at Carter's house.

The persons who had brought up these berries

carried them round to the various tents. Many were the expressions of gratitude and many the tears. When they entered the tents, the inmates hailed them with, "Come here, mister, I'll buy from you!" "Where did you get them?" "What's the price?" And when they were told that they had been gathered by sick men for those who were in a worse condition than themselves, their astonishment was unbounded; they wondered that any one had chanced to think of giving them such a treat. Some entreated the donors to take money; others kissed their hands, with every expression of gratitude. To some it seemed a painful pleasure, it so forcibly brought to mind home and distant friends. One poor fellow, as the fruit was handed to him, shed tears, and exclaimed, "One year ago I was in the mountains gathering berries with my wife and children: shall I ever be able to do so again?" Speer and Temple returned to my tent and told me of this affecting scene, and thanked me that I had assisted to teach that it was more blessed to give than to receive. And from this time until our removal to Richmond, all the sick and wounded who were able to crawl into the fields at Carter's house daily found recreation and delight in gathering fruit for the wounded sufferers at Savage Station.

During the days that intervened between our captivity and removal to Richmond, we had frequent visits from some of the most distinguished Confederate officers. In their excursions from their camps to Richmond they would often gratify their curiosity by stopping an hour at our hospitals. Amongst the most noted of these visitors was Stone-

SCENE AMONGST THE WOUNDED AT SAVAGE STATION, IN THE REAR OF THE HOUSE.

wall Jackson. I had heard of him as alighting at several hospitals near the James river. On one of these occasions, when the general had ridden into the grounds in front of the hospital, one of our wounded soldiers, a man who would stand unabashed in the presence of Queen Victoria, and speak with as much freedom to the Grand Sultan as to the captain of his company, approached and spoke to him:

"How are you, general?"

"Well, I thank you; how are you, soldier?" Are you badly hurt?"

"Not very dangerously, general; war is a terrible thing, is it not, general? There ought to be some very good reason for tearing poor men to pieces, as you see these have been; do you not think so, general?"

"Yes, certainly, soldier, war is a dreadful curse; there is a great sin somewhere. Are many of your men dying, soldier?"

"Yes, eight or ten every day, and if we do not receive food, we will all perish. General," continued the soldier, "how many men did you bring down from the valley?"

"I cannot tell you, certainly; how many do you think?"

"I suppose," said the soldier, "seventy thousand."

"You are not far wrong," said the general; "who is your general?"

"Kearney, as brave a man as ever drew a sword; do you know him, general?"

"Oh, yes, well; you are led by a good officer. Good-bye, soldier."

31

"Just one word more: general, you believe in prayer, and that God is on your side, do you not?" said the soldier, turning up his bandaged face, and looking with his one well eye at the general, and at the same time toying with his bridle rein.

"I believe in prayer, and that God is on the side of right."

"Exactly, general, so I believe; but because you think you are right and I am wrong, you command your soldiers to shoot me; and because I think our cause right and yours wrong, I try to shoot you; we cannot both be right—one of us must be a great sinner, and who is to decide? I should like to tell you, general, the talk I had with my wife and children before I enlisted, and how my prayers were answered."

. "That would be very interesting, soldier, but not to-day; I have far to ride and much to do. Good-bye."

General Jackson had more personal power and popularity than any officer in the Confederate Army. He was easily approached; never severe nor stern; unwilling to inflict military punishment, except where every other expedient had failed. He never indulged himself in any luxury, but partook of the simple and frugal fare of the common soldiers. He had but little of the manner of a slaveholder, but was patient, considerate, and unselfish. The love of order was one of the most striking and remarkable things in his character. If he was in the tent of a brother officer, he invarialy left it at nine P. M., and retired to his own. If any persons were in his tent after nine o'clock they were expected to unite

with him in his evening devotions, and not linger a
moment after the prayer was ended. He was by no
means a broad-minded man, but ardent, intense,
honest. Deeply conscientious, and always true to
his religious convictions. Into the tumult and wickedness of an army he bore all the devout habits, rigid
temperance, and austere piety of his home. His
great force of character moulded all who came around
him, or were under his command, and soon they followed him as invincible, because uniting as they
thought to the highest military genius the sanctity
of a prophet. He impressed his own religious views
upon all the officers and men of his portion of the
Confederate Army. Rarely did an oath pass the
lips of one of his men, and in the side pocket of each
I saw invariably a New Testament. In appearance,
General Jackson was rather a commanding man;
the expression of his face was grave and sad; his
words were few, and did not flow with freedom; but
his whole manner was that of one who felt that he
was equal to any emergency; with him to deliberate was to act, and to plan was to do. His success
as a commander was due in part to the enthusiasm
of his troops, but in a great measure to the fiery impetuosity with which he rushed his soldiers against
some weak point of our lines, and if at first defeated,
he brought up another column, and if again these
were compelled to fall back, another, and it mattered
not how many of his men fell, he persevered, breaking the line by the force of repeated blows and compelled a retreat on our part, or a readjustment of
our forces. My impression from all that I could
learn was, that he had entered into the war with

hesitation, for he was well acquainted with Northern people, and up to the commencement of hostilities had been a Union man. But when Virginia threw herself into the Southern Confederacy, he offered his services, and whatever conscientious scruples he may have entertained at the commencement of the contest were lost in his enthusiasm for action. And he soon began to entertain the idea that he too was a "soldier of destiny," and raised up to demonstrate that it was possible to make some most important improvements in the science of war. The devotion of his followers, his military genius and energy, his unfeigned piety, would have done much to prolong the present contest, for his presence was equal to half an army.

It is remarkable that amongst his dying words there are none which speak hopefully of the future of the Southern Confederacy, or give the assurance that he was convinced of the righteousness of that cause for which he had given his life. But from whatever side we look at him, he was one of the most remarkable men whom this war has brought forth from the bosom of obscurity.

CHAPTER XXIII.

Removal of the Sick at Carter's house and Meadow Station to
  Richmond — The Confederate Commissary's Criticisms on our
  Generals — The Removal of seven hundred and fifty of our
  Wounded to Richmond on the 13th July — Scenes in the Streets
  — Libby Prison.

On Saturday, the 12th of July, there came from
Richmond several wagons and omnibuses to remove
the sick at Carter's house and Meadow Station, and
about dark the long train from these places started
on its way. The nurses and men who were able to
walk part of the way were placed in line and sent in
advance. I rode with the sick for two miles. They
were all full of hope, for this was a step out of the
wilderness of sorrow and was bearing nearer the gate
of deliverance. There were three of the sick whom
I never expected to see again. The Confederate
officer who had command of the train was from Baltimore, and was one of those free, easy and swelling
characters, who under the greatest freedom and loose-
ness of speech conceal the deepest cunning. We
rode together through the forest, and he imparted
to me freely his views of the Confederacy and of their
generals. I asked what were his hopes of their ulti-
mate success. He assured me that they would certainly be conquerors; that they were united, while

31 *

we were divided; that they had made up their minds to sacrifice everything rather than yield; that no offer we could make to them would be listened to for a moment; they wished to be independent and establish the grand Model Republic of this continent.

"Yes, sir," said he, lifting himself in his stirrups and stretching wide his arms as if with one hand grasping the shore of the Atlantic, and with the other touching the waters of the Pacific, "we will do it. Everything favors us; the star of promise beckons us on,—and we follow it. Providence says to us, arise and conquer. We have generals equal to Moses and Joshua, and greater than Cæsar."

"Colonel," said I, "do you think we lost as many men in the recent battles as you did? You know the battle of Malvern Hill was very fatal to your men."

"Think," said he; "sir, I know and assure you, on the honor of a gentleman, that you lost three to our one."

"Do you judge, colonel, from the appearance of the dead upon the field, or from other sources of knowledge? For if your conclusion has been reached by riding over the fields of battle my judgment may be as good as yours, for I have been there and must confess that some things struck me with amazement. In some fields where great numbers of your men fell there is not one of your dead, but all have been removed, even the horses which fell at your batteries are buried, and the graves of our dead are made as prominent as possible; for each one there is a mound of earth, while in places where your dead were so numerous that you could not remove them you in-

terred three, four, and even ten, in the same pit,
thus concealing your dead and taking every measure
to display ours to the full; and at the head of every
grave of a Union soldier you were certain to leave
out his cap or a fragment of his blue coat, or a shred
of his pantaloons, as a sign that a Yankee had fallen
there; and I have every reason to believe that you
scattered these mementoes of our troops amongst
the graves of your own men. I have been enough
among you to know what you hoped to gain by all
this. Have I not seen riding over those same fields
great numbers of gentlemen from Richmond, and
even ladies, and have heard here and there a hundred times the remarks: 'Look at those graves, but
the caps, blue clothes, and even shoes, show who lie
here; our men must have killed more than a hundred to one of the Yankees.' 'Look at those horses;
that is where we took their batteries.' And in those
portions of the fields where even you confess you
suffered terribly, none of your dead are found, and
around that negro house in the battle-field of Glendale, where, at the lowest calculation, you left five
hundred dead men, not one grave of yours is seen,
and after you had removed nearly all your slain and
buried them in out of the way places and scattered
these fragments of the clothing of the Union soldiers
about every grave, then you invited all Richmond to
ride over the fields of your glorious exploits; and if
all these were disconsolate on account of their dead,
they were sent back to your capital with the delightful assurance that, for every one you had lost, there
had been ten Yankees killed.

"Yes, colonel, what I witnessed there more fully

convinced me that your Confederacy is a sham, as is
the case in every sinking concern, you keep yourselves in courage by whistlings, swaggerings, and
concealments. The Confederacy is like an old wind-
shaken, sun-dried, unoiled wagon, which, as it comes
rattling down a hillside, makes more noise than a
whole army-train."

He burst into a loud laugh. "Now," said he,
"have you lived to your time of life and not yet discovered that the world is governed by shams? What
was all that talk of your Government, your generals,
and your papers, about strategy but the emptiest of
all shams? The fact is, Doctor, sham is the horse
that wins the race in these days, and truth is blown
out and distanced in less than a mile. I am far from
agreeing with you in regard to the policy of our
generals in disposing of our dead. I call that a piece
of brilliant strategy; it kept our people in heart and
made them think that if Richmond was full of
wounded and dying, we had broken and destroyed
your army. Doctor, you may as well give up this
contest. God is not on your side, or else he would
have given you generals with some brains. Why,
we planned all this campaign for you in Richmond,
and had our friends in Washington to secure its
adoption. It worked better than we anticipated.
You took the very course we had chalked out for
you, except that you dug the graves of many thousand more men at Yorktown than we had dared to
hope for. There will be many astounding things
brought to light when this war is over."

"You know," I said to him, "that General Mc-
Clellan alone is responsible for this campaign, and

I have heard you express very great respect for his ability, and you said this was the sentiment of the officers of your army."

"That is true," he replied, "General McClellan deserves credit for being one of the greatest engineers of the age. He has thrown up here and before Yorktown monuments of his genius, but he needs some man of ability and common sense to tell him where to construct them ; they are just about as valuable as the first five miles of a railroad to the moon. General McClellan digs his entrenchments, throws up his redoubts, and if we would only accommodate him by standing still, or by not advancing upon him till he was fully ready, he would certainly whip us. But when he looks for us in front, we are turning his rear, and when he expects us to attempt to carry his works by storm, we determine to change his base of operations. But here we part; when you come to Richmond let me know of it, and I will take you over the city, and aid you in every way in my power."

Sunday, July 13th.—Very early on the morning of this day there came down from Richmond a long train of dirt and box cars, for the removal of all the wounded who could be carried on them. There was great uncertainty in regard to the design of this change. The orders were indefinite, the officers who brought them had no authority, and thought we were not to stop in Richmond, but to be taken to James River, and placed on our transports ; others supposed we were to be sent to Lynchburg and Salisbury.

Soon every spot was crowded with men eager to escape from the confinement and misery of a place

where so much suffering had been endured. We
had little food to give to the seven hundred and fifty
men who crowded the cars, and many of them, in
the charity of hope, gave all the crackers in their
haversacks to those whom they were leaving. Two
or three surgeons and myself were detailed to go
with them. Before the hour for starting, I visited
the tents where were lying the persons most dangerously wounded. Amongst this number I came
to a young man, whom I saw at a glance was rapidly
nearing the veil which separated the present from
the mystery of the future. His right limb had been
amputated. I had seen and talked with him before,
but now, feeling that the last words were to be spoken,
I lingered for many minutes by his side. He told
me his name was Randolph Spear; that his father's
family were living in Elizabeth, Pennsylvania; that he
was of the 8th Reserve Corps; and, as in many cases
of death from wounds, he possessed to the full all his
faculties, and could speak with ease. In the course
of conversation I found that he had no hope of life,
but felt certain that he had not many hours to live.
I asked him of his hopes beyond the grave; if he
had made any preparation for meeting his Maker.
He was like most soldiers, free and frank in speech.
He said that he had intended to become a pious man,
but had deferred from time to time, until he now
felt he must die, and it was too late, and did not
know that it was worth while for him to pray or give
himself any trouble about his fate. I urged the duty
of confessing his sins, and like the prodigal son, returning to the Father whom he had offended; that the
greatness of Christ's love was beyond all our thoughts;

that He delighted to lift us up out of the depths of our sinfulness and misery; that even now he could look up to the Lamb of God and live. He asked me to pray for him before I left. I clasped together his cold and now palsied hands, and lifting them up in my own commended the dying soldier to Him who endured for us the sufferings of death. When the prayer ceased his face was wet with tears. I saw that the rock was smitten.

" That prayer," said he, " reminds me of my mother. I knelt at her knee when I was a child, and she prayed for me, and now all her holy words come back to me. Oh, my mother! shall I see her in the kingdom of God? her Saviour will be mine!"

I bade him farewell. On the following Wednesday a soldier met me at the depot in Richmond and said, "The soldier that you talked with and prayed for in Tent No. 5 died the night after you left, but prayed until the last; and, after you had gone, said many things that deeply moved us all." May we not hope that the prayers of a pious, sainted mother were answered, and the angels sang, "The lost is found, and the dead is alive again!"

About noon I took my place in the cars, bearing with me one or two blankets for bedding, and two trunks full of such medicines and sanitary stores as I had saved. I had preserved nearly a hundred dollars' worth of quinine, some surgical instruments, bandages, some papers of cocoa, and a pot of butter; all which had been left by Mr. Brunot. When I had taken my place in the midst of the wounded, I was surprised to find that there were none of the surgeons who had been detailed to go with us

but Dr. Fox, a volunteer surgeon from Philadelphia. We bade farewell to the surgeons and
nurses, expecting them to follow the next day, and
slowly the cars moved away from Savage Station.
We stopped at Fair Oaks and Orchard Stations,
taking on board parties of gentlemen from Richmond. I found myself seated alongside of two well
dressed and very communicative gentlemen from
the city. They soon told me that they were the
moving spirits of a benevolent society in Richmond,
the special mission of which was to look after their
wounded, collect such property of their dead as could
be found, and to visit the battle-fields for these purposes. In the prosecution of this most charitable
work, these gentlemen had laid in a large supply,
not of bread and wine, but of Confederate money,
which they were most industriously exchanging with
our men for *greenbacks*, " because they pitied these
poor hungry, fainting wretches, and they could obtain nothing in Richmond for Federal money." And
though they assured us it was at a loss, they ex-
changed dollar for dollar. For the time I thought
that some little of the milk of human kindness was
left in the Rebel capital, and looked on these grave
and hard-faced Southerners as men who truly pitied
us, and who, at some loss and peril, would benefit
even their enemies. I talked with them with more
freedom, and pardoned the bitterness and rage
with which they spoke of our invasion of the sacred
fields of Virginia, because, though they gave us no
bread, nor even looks of pity, they took our unne-
gotiable money, and gave us in return that which
would buy us food; but, alas, the quality of their

mercy was to confer the largest blessing on themselves. When we reached Richmond I found that
our money was selling at seventy and eighty per
cent. premium, and these affable representatives of
a benevolent society were making, in the exercise of
a most self-denying pity, two dollars for one. They
were likewise loaded down with revolvers, which
were worth in their market forty and fifty dollars,
which they had kindly relieved our men of at the
rate of two or three dollars a piece. They had likewise, with the aid of four or five negro servants, collected a large number of our overcoats and shawls.
They were "looking after the interests of their brave,
heroic men," but everything was so managed as to
contribute to the well-being of their own houses —
wisdom walked by the side of charity. These gentlemen were so kind as to point out to me the strength
of the defences of Richmond, and to likewise inform
me of the number of guns in the several fortifications crowning the heights. Every half mile the old,
crazy locomotive attempted a whistle, and stopped
on the track; this would summon to the road a brigade of wild, savage-looking Confederate soldiers,
who crowded around the cars, and with evident delight looked in on the "wounded Yankees."

My friends of the benevolent society considerately
made me acquainted with the names of various regiments and their commanders; and I was further indebted to them for glowing details of the brilliant
feats of those "Southern heroes." "They had never
been whipped and never could." "Two regiments
of them had defeated an entire corps of McClellan's
army," etc., etc. Again the wheezy, consumptive

32

engine would attempt a move ahead, and if there was an ascending grade, frequently half an hour was expended in pulling and dislocating jerks, and after the progress of another mile, we again stopped and summoned another crowd of Rebel soldiers. Of these, my friends of the Confederate money had even more astounding deeds of valor to relate. " These were the heroes of an hundred battles—from every field they had returned conquerors," which I suppose accounted for the fact that they were nearly all dirty and ragged.

When we reached the depôt, my friends of the charitable fraternity bade me farewell, and were so kind as to assure me that it would afford them the greatest pleasure to call upon me if I remained in Richmond. Possibly I might need a little Confederate money. As an expression of regard, they should esteem it a pleasure to exchange for "greenbacks." I thanked them. I had no need of money at present. We separated, they assuring me that they would call to-morrow; but, I am sorry to say, I was forgotten. Their benevolent labors were so unintermitted and absorbing that they never had time to honor me with any remembrance. When we entered Richmond there were many evidences of former wealth and prosperity. There were many fine suburban residences on the hills, and lofty, commanding warerooms and storehouses stood behind the wharves and depôts. But these were now empty; the streets were gloomy and silent; the grass was growing in the great thoroughfares at the depôts; the boats in the canal were sunk and rotting; not a vessel was lying at the wharves. When we entered the York River depôts we were surprised to find no one there to receive us. . Here and there a guard walked on his beat, but it was evident our coming was an event unheralded. In a few moments the arrival of the "wounded Yankees" attracted a crowd of citizens, officers, soldiers, children, and negro servants.

An hour and more passed away, and it began to be highly probable that we would have to remain in the cars all night. In the meantime the crowd increased; and, with the exception of the German women and children, I looked in vain for one human face that lighted in sympathy, or softened in pity for our miseries. The negroes stood at a distance, with the appearance of those who beheld a spectacle that startled and overwhelmed them. But well-dressed officers and gentlemen walked near the cars, and looked in on pale, bleeding, and maimed sufferers with complacent satisfaction. And even ladies came near, and gazed in on spectacles of the most touching distress, without one expression of compassion. But one uttered the wish of many: "It is a great pity that all of them were not killed."

As I stood on the platform I was addressed by an officer of a Georgia regiment; he was a major in rank, and a fine-looking, powerful man.

"In Richmond, doctor?" said he, with a sneer, supposing, as a matter of course, that I was a surgeon.

"Yes, sir, I presume so."

"Somewhat sooner than you expected?" he said, with a sneer.

"Oh no, sir; I expected to be in Richmond more

than a month ago, when we whipped you at the battle of Fair Oaks."

"And why did you not come then ?" rejoined he.

"Because our right wing could not come to our aid, and we did not know soon enough how complete was your defeat."

"Well," said he, "you have found this a hard road to travel, and no holiday work to meet the chivalry of the South. I suppose that you are tired and sick of the business, and all you wish is to get out of this war with some show of honor?"

"No, sir, you were never more mistaken; we can lose ten armies and not exhaust our resources. We have entered upon this contest because you attempted to destroy the government which we love; not because we wish to conquer you, or gain one foot of your lands; we have enough — we covet nothing that is yours, not even your 'institutions;' but we cannot consent to see the country drift into anarchy to please you. We must uphold the laws and institutions we esteem sacred. You have forced this war upon us. We have taken up arms most reluctantly, and we cannot lay them down until we see you peacefully dwelling under our flag again."

"Then," said he, "you have a war for the next century upon your hands. We never can go back to the old government. Our dead would rise from their graves and curse us, if we consented to such dishonor. No, sir, never! You may burn our cities, ruin our estates, steal our negroes, and cover our fields with the bones of our slain — but go back into the Union with the hated Yankees, never!"

An hundred voices most emphatically exclaimed,

"never," and all these dark-browed children of passion scowled in anger.

"We," continued the major, "can carry on this war as long as you can. The South was never more prepared than now, and our negroes never so loyal; the faithful creatures cannot be induced to forsake us in our hour of need. Any hopes you may have of assistance from them are utterly futile."

It required but a glance at the excited throng which surrounded me to see that a single word would produce the wildest storm of rage, in which more than one unarmed prisoner might fall a victim to their vindictive anger. Here, and on many subsequent occasions, I learned to place a low estimate on the honor and magnanimity of Southern chivalry. Who ever saw, in any of our cities, a prisoner from the Confederacy surrounded by an excited mob, waiting for one indiscreet word as the signal to tear him to pieces?

In the midst of this conversation, Captain Turner, who was in command of all the prisons and their guards, came to the depôt. The captain was a young man, about twenty-five years of age, evidently possessed of ability and energy. The expression of his face was that of one who had been in a passion ever since he was born. He trod the ground with a short, fiery stamp, and looked at us with an expression, which said: "Expect tears from stones, but no pity from me." His indignation against somebody was unbounded. His grey eyes flashed fire.

"Who sent you here? We have not a spot for these miserable wretches; I wish the whole concern
32 *

was in ——." And waiting for no reply, he hissed
out innumerable oaths and maledictions.

What I saw at this time throws additional light
upon a part of Dr. Swinburne's report, "In reference to the removal from Savage Station and other
hospitals to Richmond." (Page 6.)

Captain Turner left us with the hint that he might
send us back to Savage Station; but in a few
moments Lieutenant Taylor appeared and ordered
all the men able to walk to come out of the cars,
and arrange themselves in line in the street. In a
short time five hundred sick and wounded soldiers
formed themselves into a broken, ragged column.
Some of the men were fainting from exhaustion,
but the dread of being abandoned, or lost from their
companions, stimulated them to move and follow.
Very soon these fell down, and had to be carried
from one halting place to another.

It was now the middle of July. The heat of the
day was such as to make the thinnest garment
oppressive to a feverish body. Many had cast away
their shirts and coats, and others their pants and
shoes, which, saturated with blood, and consequently loathsome, had become exceedingly uncom-
fortable. The spectacle was most distressing — so
many wounded men in the streets of the Rebel
capital, pale, bleeding, and, above all, nearly naked.
Fortunately, Mr. Brunot and Mr. Reed had left
more than one hundred shirts, and I had in my
stores, received from the Sanitary Commission,
more than one hundred pairs of drawers. With
these we were able to cover many partially, who
otherwise would have reached Richmond in a state

bordering on nakedness.   Certainly the appearance
of this wounded throng, starting on their march
for the prison on Corey street, was calculated to
have excited pity in the hardest heart.   Many
were hopping on rude crutches; others, with amputated arms and shattered shoulders, moved as far as
possible from their staggering companions, and were
constantly pressed back into the mass by the bayonets
of the brutal guards.   Several entirely blind men
were guided by the arms of the wounded, who leaned
on them for support.   Others, confused and uncertain
about every step, groped and staggered like the
palsied.   Here one wounded in the leg had thrown
away his torn and bloody pantaloons, and was limp-
ing along with nothing on his limbs but the crimsoned bandages.   Another, wounded in the chest
and arm, had thrown off his stiffened shirt, and with
all the upper portion of his body bare moved along
in the crowd leaning upon a less injured companion.
There two compassionate nurses were bearing in
their arms one to whom suffering and loss of blood
gave the ghastliness of a corpse.

Such was the procession which left the depôt,
and slowly moving round the canal, approached the
prison — No. 2, on Corey street.   Here we stopped
and waited for orders, but none came.   In the
meantime the sidewalks were lined with citizens.
But few pitied the sufferers: I thought they did not
dare to, for spies and informers were everywhere in
the crowd.   Now and then a kind German woman
thrust out her hands, and gave to one who excited
her especial pity a little cake, and when commanded
by the guards to stand back and give nothing,

answered with a charming naiveté, "Ich verstehe kein Englisch."

While we were halting before this prison the shades of evening began to fall over the city, and here and there a dim gaslight attempted to illumine the wretched capital. In the meantime many of the sick had fallen down on the sidewalks and in the streets from sheer exhaustion, and dropping asleep, were for a time unconscious of pain and misery. While we waited, a German of fine appearance and good manners approached me, and drawing me into the shadow of the prison, whispered in my ear that "he was a friend, and was anxious to do something for the relief of our sufferers; that all he had was at our disposal." He said he had plenty of money, and offered me his pocket book, saying that we would need bread. He said when he looked upon our wounded men he shed tears, and resolved that he would risk his life for our relief. No words can express how much I was affected by the kind words and the generosity of this noble German. It was the sunbeam suddenly lighting up the dark prison-house. I thanked him, refused to take his money, and begged him to be careful and to show no such sympathy as would attract attention. In reply, he cursed the confederacy, and hoped the whole concern might soon be in ——. Certainly, I never before, nor since, heard swearing that sounded so appropriate; and the tears of gratitude, I hope, blotted out the sin. He then intimated to me the secret of the fact that the Germans were the only persons who dared to show us any sympathy. The most important and valuable workmen in their armories, arsenals, and ordnance foundries, were Germans, and these women were their wives and daughters. These Germans had been engaged in manufacturing in the South before the rebellion, and at no time had there been an opportunity for removing their families, and necessity compelled their working in their present employment. But they were all most eagerly hoping for our success, and looking for our army. "And will Mr. McClellan never come?" I could not answer hopefully, but told him that the time would most certainly come when Richmond would be ours. He then told me that the confederacy had suffered beyond our estimate in the recent battles; that every house, hotel, and ware-room, was a hospital; that the city was in the deepest gloom over their dead — some one gone from every house; that a few more such victories would sweep away all the aristocracy; that they were without any of the luxuries, and almost the necessities, of life; that the inhabitants of the city were under a reign of terror; that General Winder, the Provost Marshal, and Colonel Baxter, the Judge Advocate, were the most cold-blooded and heartless of men; and that, after having enriched themselves under the old government, they now took a malignant satisfaction in ruining every man who was suspected of any lingering regard for the Union. The judgment he passed upon these worthies was confirmed to me by subsequent events.

After remaining more than an hour before Prison No. 2, we were ordered to remove to Prison No. 4, on Main street. Toward this we marched as fast as the nature of the case admitted, attended by an immense throng of curious citizens. When we reached this prison we were halted in the street, and again more than half the men laid down in the dust and fell asleep. In the office, or reception room, of the prison, were three or four officers, who appeared to have been selected for their non-acquaintance with either mercy or charity. Prominent among these was a captain of commissary, named Tuthill: he was a short, stout man of thirty-five years of age, with black hair, round face, and a voice like a lion's growl. He made his appearance in the office, swearing like a Flemish trooper, and in a towering rage, with the air of one feeling that language was too poor to express his mighty emotions, he strode to and fro, looking for objects upon which to vent his fury. He soon, however, began to work off his passion by kicking in the sides of several empty cracker boxes, hurling the fragments against the sides of the room, as though he expected the walls to totter. He next kicked over all the old chairs in the room with an evidently damaging effect upon their few remaining legs. He now moved up to an old rusty stove, which stood near the centre of the room, looking as if he would pitch this into the street, or hurl it through the ceiling; but, after a moment, satisfied himself with covering it with indignant tobacco juice. This was the more amusing, as it was evident that much of it was merely good acting.

Tuthill was really not a bad-hearted man, nor unpitying, but he was obeying instructions, or imitating the meanness of his superior officers. Richmond was then full of prisoners, and many of them might be able to handle a gun in a few days, and their guards were few, and it was thought essential for safety that the prisoners should be impressed with a salutary dread of the ferocious qualities of the Confederate officers. If they could succeed in making us think they were not to be touched by any sentiment of humanity, it would deliver them from a thousand annoyances. Who would dare, after this display, to approach Tuthill and tell him that in four days he had had but one loaf of bread, and an ounce of meat in a week?

In a few moments I was ordered to bring in the men, four at a time. An officer stood at an old dilapidated desk, and, with the tragic air of a martyr, rolled up his coat-sleeves, and took up a pen. Another stood by his side, holding a broken tin lantern, in which glimmered the feeble rays of a tallow candle; another candle was stuck in the top of the stove, and, softened by the heat of the room, leaned for support against the stove-pipe. Thus illuminated, the officer announced the duties of the evening.

First was brought before them a shirtless Union soldier, with an amputated arm. In a stern, angry manner, the officers asked his name, his regiment, his corps, demanding if he had any Confederate money, any fire-arms; when satisfied that he had none of these, his knapsack was opened, and all his little souvenirs of home, wife or children, which the soldier had carried with him in many battles, and borne through weary marches, were thrown upon the floor, with letters, papers, Testament, and hymn-book. The knapsack was taken from him and thrown aside, and he commenced to remove the coat, blanket, daguerreotypes, etc., etc., which were lying at his feet. The look of the poor fellow was that of the utmost amazement. What was he to do with those things, and how could he carry them with one arm? His knapsack was of no use. Would not they give it to him? "No," with a bitter oath; "take away your miserable rags." And the poor fellow was compelled to stoop down and gather up, with my assistance, the articles strewn on the floor. Some were bound up in a torn handkerchief, some in the pockets of his pants, and such as he could, he carried under his only remaining arm.

The next one brought forward was a soldier with a wound in his head, from the effects of which he was confused in utterance, and had lost all remembrance of his home or his regiment; the fury and swearing of the officers served only to confuse him the more, and drive away his few remaining ideas, and he began to think that he was before a criminal court, charged with some great crime, and his face and body became convulsed, as if in perfect despair.

One after another were brought forward and examined, their knapsacks opened, and all the soldiers' valuables dashed out upon the floor. There were many most painful scenes during the collection of these articles, and more than one poor sufferer fell fainting on the floor during the effort.

The prison was one of the large tobacco warehouses, and was three stories in height. The rooms were large halls, poorly ventilated, and disgustingly filthy. The dust and tobacco-juice of years had accumulated in ridges and hillocks on the floor. From the same cause every step of the stairs was as uneven as if covered with pebbles. The odor of

RIFLING THE KNAPSACKS OF OUR WOUNDED—MAIN STREET PRISON, RICHMOND.

Chap. XXIII.

these apartments was indescribably foul; they had
been filled with prisoners, who had been removed
but a few hours, and had left behind them all the
offal of mortal maladies, weaknesses, and wounds.
There had been no sweeping, nor cleansing. Into
these dismal rooms our poor men were pushed, and
compelled to drink in an air, the first breath of
which caused me to shudder. Many of the sick and
wounded were without blankets, and were obliged
to lie on the bare floor, as nothing was provided
them by the Confederate Government.

We had received no food since breakfast, and to
my request for bread for the fainting men, the reply
was, "that they had none; that if McClellan had
not burnt hundreds of barrels of flour, and thousands
of boxes of crackers, they might have had something to give us, but now they had not enough for
their own men."

During the time occupied in taking down the
names and regiments of the prisoners, I asked permission of Captain Tuthill to go down to the depôt
and look after the men we had left in the cars unable to walk. He answered me kindly, and obtained
a pass. I went out into the street to find my way,
in the darkness of the night, to the depôt. But
after I had gone a few steps, I was joined by my
German friend, who had been lingering in the
shadow of a building near the prison. He insisted
upon going with me, telling me the guard would
certainly shoot me otherwise, and leading me around
by his house, took especial pains to impress its locality upon me, saying, " If you ever want a breakfast or dinner come here. If you want money, or

33

need bread, so long as I have a cent or a crumb you shall have it." He then accompanied me to the depôt, and was of the greatest assistance in placing the remaining wounded in the ambulances which had been sent, driven by negro drivers. When this was done, he walked with me until near the Main Street Prison, and then left me, again offering his pocket-book, and urging me to come to him the next day. I never compromised this generous man by calling at his house, for I felt assured he was already under surveillance, and any open act of kindness to us would have led to his imprisonment; but I have marked the locality of his house, and daguerreo-typed on my mind his features, and I hope I may yet have an opportunity of thanking him, in Richmond, for his generous sympathy and fearless proffer of aid, when we were poor prisoners. Upon my return to the prison, after aiding those who were yet to be examined, I secured a candle, and went from room to room. The despondency and misery of the men had now reached their acme. Many of them said that they wished to die, and prayed that their sorrows might end with that night. Stretched upon the naked floor, or leaning against a brick wall, without food and medical assistance, their suf-ferings were extreme, and rendered them spiritless and hopeless. But to all such I endeavored to speak words of cheer and encouragement, remind-ing them of the many to whom their lives were most precious, and encouraging them, for their sakes, to make a great effort to live. Doctor Fox had, during the evening and night, been occupied with dressing and bandaging the wounds of those whom he found the greatest sufferers.

About midnight we were informed that our quarters were to be in "Libby Prison," and the doctor and myself were marched under guard to that place. When we reached it we were taken into the office, and our trunks and baggage examined. Captain Tuthill, and a young man named Ross, were appointed to search us, and confiscate any contraband articles which might be found in our possession. I had brought with me a supply of medicines, and some sanitary stores. I had eight bottles of quinine, and these were taken from me, together with all the bandages I still retained; but they left all my personal property, except papers, which they took for examination. I had with me several packages of the "Christian Banner," published by the American Tract Society, Boston. These they examined, and told me they were familiar with the paper, for several copies had been brought into Richmond, which had been given to their officers and men in different places. They expressed themselves as greatly pleased with it, and told me I might give away as many as I pleased; that such papers could do no harm, but good. And such tracts and books as I had with me (obtained from the Rev. Mr. Alvord for the sick in the hospitals) I was permitted to distribute without restraint. These officers were very obliging with me, and Captain Tuthill took occasion to say to me, that much of the violence I had seen on his part was assumed; that he had to obey orders; but he assured me that anything he could do for me would afford him the greatest pleasure. Subsequently, I found

Captain Tuthill to be the most humane Confederate officer with whom I came in contact in Richmond.

While in this office, my friend Doctor Fox was placed under arrest. He had by his side a canteen of whisky, which he carried with him for the benefit of patients. This canteen was demanded, when the doctor walked to the door, took out the stopper, and commenced emptying the whisky into the street. He was immediately arrested for "contempt," and threatened with the bayonets of the guard. For a few moments there was a scene of the greatest excitement, which ended in restoring to the doctor his empty canteen, and permitting him to remove his blanket, for his night's rest, to another room of the building.

We were at length conducted to what is called the "East Room." This was dimly lighted, and here and there was the flickering candle of a nurse over some pale, suffering face. Libby Prison covers an entire square. It fronts, I think, three hundred and seventy feet on Caress street, and is one hundred and twenty feet deep. It is four stories high. The basement rooms were used for a dead-house, kitchens, bake, and wash-rooms. The rooms occupied by the prisoners were great halls, ninety feet wide, and extending the depth of the building. It was possible to ventilate, to some extent, the rooms with side windows looking to the east and the west; but the central halls could not receive a breath of air, except through the north and south windows, and therefore were hot and foul to a degree entirely incomprehensible to one who has not been so unfortunate as to have been an inmate of that loathsome dungeon. I

think it one of the things beyond the region of possibility, that Southern prisoners in our hands should
be consigned, even for a day, to quarters so incon-
ceivably vile. In the lower rooms, the dead were
carried, remaining uncoffined for days; and from
thence ascended, through all the rooms, the pestilential breath of a charnel-house. In every crack and
crevice millions of vermin crawled and swarmed.
The floors and walls had not been cleansed for years.
To consign prisoners to these rooms was to sign
their death-warrant — crowded together, every inch
of the floors covered, every breath they inhaled
loaded with the poison of fever and the exhalation
of wounds, how could they live? In the centre
of these rooms all the men were gasping and crying
out, "I shall die, unless I have a little fresh air."
And yet, with all their boasted civilization and humanity, the Confederate Government continues to
immerse thousands of men in living tombs.

It should not, therefore, be a matter of wonder
that one-third of the men consigned to those chambers of death never came forth but to be coffined —
a bane with them for years, the consequences of
breathing an air so pestilential. The treatment
which our prisoners here received at the hands of
the Rebel Government displays, more than anything
else, how completely it has thrown itself out of the
pale of Christian civilization.

Was there no lumber in Richmond, out of which
buildings might have been made, as was done in
Washington, Baltimore, Philadelphia, etc., etc., for
the accommodation of the sick and the wounded?
Were there no more houses that could be thrown

33 *

open for such purposes? Were there no trees in the forest that might have been cut and split, and houses erected on open grounds, where the panting and suffering prisoners, if they were denied food, might at least enjoy the air of heaven?

If, after the first battles, they were forced to consign hundreds to those dungeons, for want of suitable places for their confinement, was there any necessity for continuing a cruelty absolutely infernal and Satanic? Possibly the Confederate Government thought, in this manner, to make unendurable to us the continuance of a war, so fatal to the men who fell into their hands. But there never was a policy more ill-advised; for every man who has passed through the tribulations of the Richmond prisons, and beheld his companions perish from want and confinement, bears ever in his heart a thirst for revenge, which seeks gratification in the destruction of the city where he suffered such indignities and miseries.

CHAPTER XXIV.

Night Scene and Conversation in Libby Prison — Nolan and his Song — Scene at the Depot, July 16th — Feeding the Hungry — German Charity.

VERY soon after entering the officers' room, I was addressed by many familiar voices, and had the gratification of meeting some whom I feared I should never see again. Amongst this number was Lieutenant-colonel McIntire, Captain Bagaler, Captain Demirey, Captain Reed, Lieutenant Smith, of the 3d Michigan, Captain Adams, etc. All these had rather improved since I left them in the hospitals on the battle-fields. Of these I made inquiries for other wounded officers and soldiers, and learned that many of them were dead.

"And Adjutant Gaither?"

"Oh, he still lives, and lies on that cot."

I was surprised, and with glad eagerness advanced to his bed: he was awake.

"Yes, my friend," said he, "I am still here, and, thank God, better. I breathe with more ease, and if I cannot live, I am grateful for this relief."

He spoke with ease; his cheeks were slightly tinged with hectic fever, and his face was beautifully placid and radiant. He told me he had suffered much in his removal, but had been most kindly nursed by

a New England soldier, who was then standing on
the other side of the cot fanning him.   He said this
man had watched him, and in every possible way
ministered to his relief, with more than the self-
denial and love of a brother.   He said he was glad
to tell me that all the fear of death was gone, and
all the conflict of the first days of suffering was
ended; and now, like a little child, he was resting on
the bosom of his Saviour, and felt assured that whatever fate awaited him, "it was well."   While I was
yet talking with him, a nurse approached me and
said a soldier in one of the other rooms, who was
thought to be dying, wished to see me.   I followed
his light, but stopped a moment by the side of the
cot where William Reed, son of Captain Reed, was
breathing his last; and then passing on by the cots
where were lying Lieutenant-colonel Woodward,
Dr. Donnelly, Dr. Skelton, and Colonel Dodge, I
stopped a moment to speak with each, and following
the candle of the nurse ascended the stairs, when
we stood in the second story hall.   The dim lights
burning here and there revealed a scene never to be
forgotten — there were no cots nor beds, but the
bare and naked floor was covered with a ghastly
multitude lying, leaning against the posts and walls,
standing, reclining on one arm, and in all possible
positions that could be assumed by sufferers.   We
ascended the second stairway, and stood in a similar
room, and looked over a throng, where the features
of misery were only a little varied.   Through a door
which had been cut in the brick wall we passed into
a similar hall, likewise covered with a great company of groaning and suffering men; through another

such, and again another, we passed until we came to
the third story room of the western halls.   Here we
stepped over one after another, and carefully avoided
the amputated limb, from which the imploring ges-
tures of the sleepless sufferer warned us.   We stopped
for a moment to speak with a young man whose
face, pale as marble, and his eye bright as a star, told
us that "many of his nights were wakeful, and in
this place all his life came back to him; and it was
strange, he knew it must be mere illusion, but he
heard at times the church-bells of his native village,
and sometimes heard the congregation sing, at other
times the tones of the organ, and stranger than all
he several times heard his father and mother call
him as when he was a child."   Poor fellow, that
bright eye was soon dim, and that throbbing brain
quiet forever.   We at length came to the place
where two or three benevolent nurses were holding
up in their arms the dying soldier that had sent for
me.   He had seen me at some of the hospitals on
the field, and wished me to assure him that Jesus
Christ would receive a sinner such as he felt himself
to be; he wished to tell me of some sins that were
now lying very heavily on his heart, and to know if
even these could be forgiven, and to pray for him
before he died.   While I talked with him, many of
the wounded lying near dragged themselves closer
that they might hear — many of those, whose every
breath was a moan, listened in quiet to the words of
mercy.   While talking and praying with this man,
I heard, coming up from a remote corner of the
great room, the voice of one who was pouring forth,
in the richest and tenderest tones, the words of hope

and peace. I felt certain I had heard that voice before, and anxious to see one who, at the midnight hour, was filling the prison with his song of praise, I threaded my way through the throng, and came to his side. It was Nolan, the wounded soldier whom I had first seen lying on the floor of the Brackett House.

"Why, my friend," said he, "you come to us as strangely here as you did at Glendale; some of us whom you saw there have gone up, others are still here, and like the angels returning to the gates of heaven, we try to send our voices before us, for I am not the only singer here; at times many join. I find, too, that after our first sleep all are restless and miserable for a time, and nothing quiets us like one of the hymns we sing in our churches at home; and many a time these songs have been like a spring in the desert. Often, during the day and night, Warburton, Mecum, Coursan, Jeffries, or some other of the poor fellows who lie around, will be so pained that they will think they must die, and will ask me to sing, and one after another will join, and then away off in other parts of the room one and another will take it up, until sometimes a hundred or more will try to murmur the words of a dear old hymn; and, doctor, it fills the room with light, and many of us are lifted up into the bosom of our Lord, and all feel better. Oh, it is a great thing to be able to say, 'I know that my Redeemer liveth!'"

True to himself and his religion, this noble soldier was forgetful of himself, singing and talking to relieve and comfort those around him who were greater sufferers. His whole nature was joyous and cheer-

ful, and no one would have known, by his looks or
words, that he was one who had endured a tremendous shock. His countenance was peaceful, and
I could see by the light of his eye, the compression
of his lips, and the throbbing about his temples,
that he suffered acute pain; but he had resolved to
bear all uncomplainingly, and to sustain those who
were despondent and dying. Though he could
not move from one to another, and with gentle
hands and words relieve those who were suff'ering,
his voice could reach many of them, and the words
of his song might drop on them like blessed balm
from heaven. Such was the influence, that many
an one wept as he was reminded of other days
and the dear voices of his own fireside; many a
darkened heart was enlightened, and the tempest-
tossed and fearful were aided to trust and hope.
Noble man! have not many appeared in heaven to
thank him for the light he shed over the darkest
nights, and the relief he imparted in their days of
misery? Near to Nolan was lying the young man
wounded with the six-pound cannon-ball: he was
cheerful, and had hopes of recovery. In this portion of the room were many of the worst cases of
amputation in the prison: they told me, that in the
open houses, barns, and sheds, where they had been
for many days before removal, they had improved,
but during the week that followed nearly all these
died. If they had not been compelled to breathe
an air so loaded with foul exhalations many of them
might have recovered.

On the following morning I was permitted to visit
the Main Street Prison. This led me, to some extent,

through other streets.   There was little or no business transacted in the city; almost every large house
was a hospital, and few of the stores and shops were
open.   There did not appear to be as many goods
in Richmond as would be required, in ordinary circumstances, for a village of one thousand inhabitants.
The prices to be paid for all articles of food were
fabulous, and making the condition of the poor de-
plorable.   Beef was 50 cents per pound, ham 75
cents, sugar 80 cents, salt 25 cents per pint, coffee
$2.50, and tea $10 to $12 per pound.   All articles
of clothing were on a scale equally extravagant; a
pair of ladies' shoes were $10 to $12, a pair of gents'
boots $50 to $75, a wool hat $30 to $40.   At this
time gold was at $3.00 premium, but since those
days the value of gold has tripled, and consequently
the price of everything in the market, and all the
necessities of life, have steadily advanced, thus inflicting on all classes the sufferings of want and
poverty.   The citizens whom I met in the streets
were morose and gloomy; there appeared to be little
of that hopefulness I had seen in their army; here
all were careworn, haggard, and desponding.   During
the morning of July 14th, about three hundred and
fifty of the five hundred prisoners in the Main Street
Prison were ordered to prepare for a removal to
Belle Island, in James River; the distance was about
three miles.

The wounded had been now without food for
twenty-four hours; many, when they came forth
into the streets, fell down from exhaustion and the
weakness caused by hunger.   I went to Tuthill, and
begged bread for those men; but he told me that

an order had come in early that morning from some newly-arrived regiments for bread, and this, together with the demand for their own hospitals, had exhausted the supply to the last loaf; that the government had no bakeries, but the daily supply was obtained by requisition upon the bakers of the city; and that nothing could be obtained from these for several hours.

Again the kind German women came to our relief, and passing along the line with baskets, they here and there slipped a cake. There were positive orders against such charity. But, as before, they were fearless of the bayonets of the guard, and to their commands, "Stand back!" "Stand back!" replied, "Ich verstehe kein Englisch." After remaining in the burning sun in the open streets for hours, at length the command came to march, and the people of Richmond were again gratified by the spectacle of a weary and staggering, crippled and fainting throng of "wounded Yankees." Many of them fell down before they reached the Island, and were unable to move another step; others fainted, and remained insensible for hours. No assistance was tendered to these in the more aristocratic streets. The German women did not dare to follow here, and not even a cup of cold water was offered; few, indeed, spoke words of insult, but all passed them by unpitied. When they reached the Island their condition was much better than when in the prison, for they had some liberty of action; and though always poorly and capriciously supplied with food, they had the open air, and the shade trees.

On Wednesday, the 16th of July, about ten o'clock,
34

A. M., a Confederate officer, whose name I never
knew, sent for me into Libby Prison, and wished to
speak to me for a moment. When I came out into
the street to see him, he told me that there were
lying at the York River depôt four hundred wounded
soldiers, who had been brought up from Savage Station on the previous day, and were without food,
medicines, and nurses; that he had come to me because, though he pitied them, he was powerless to
help, for no appeal from him would be listened to.
I thanked him, and told him we would never forget
his kindness and donation, and that he would yet
reap a reward for going out of his way to be-
friend us.

I then went to Captain Turner, and told him of
the condition of the Union soldiers lying at the depôt, and that they had not tasted bread for many
hours, and were in the greatest distress. He said
he had no bread, nor could he obtain any. I must
look to Captain Tuthill. I asked him, if I should obtain the order from Captain Tuthill for bread, would
he sign it? Certainly, he said. I then sought Tuthill, and found him in the basement rooms, superintending the cutting up of the soup-meat for the
prisoners. The meat was strewed about on a floor
covered with every kind of nastiness; a few feet beyond, in the same room, were lying several dead
bodies; there were some on the floor and others on
stretchers; a short distance further, were four or
more men preparing rude coffins, those of the officers being painted brown. In one part of this room
was a large furnace, and in this a number of iron
vessels or kettles; in these were boiling the bloody,

GERMAN WOMEN GIVING NOURISHMENT TO OUR WOUNDED AT THE DEPOT, RICHMOND.

Chap. XII.

saturated cloths, which had been removed from wounds, and were in demand for re-dressing. In this room were fifteen most savage-looking wretches, who were the cooks for Libby Prison. While here the cloths were taken out of the vessels, the dirty water drawn off, and fresh poured in, and without any more ceremony the meat was thrown in for the soup for dinner.

In a few moments Tuthill was disengaged, and I immediately approached, and told him of the four hundred prisoners lying at the depôt, and their wants. He drew me away some distance from the crowd of servants and loungers, and said, "go to Turner and get an order from him for bread, and I will fill it." I went back to Captain Turner's office, and after some delay and rebuffs obtained the ear of the captain for a moment, and requested an order from him for bread, "regretting much that the necessity of the case compelled me to trouble him." He stormed and swore, stamped on the floor, but very gently for him, and asked me "if Tuthill had sent me back?" I replied that the commissary felt sure that an order from Captain Turner was all that was necessary for securing the bread. He growled something about skulking out of responsibility, and wrote off the order. This, without a moment's delay, I placed in the hands of Tuthill. There were about him a large number of hungry Confederate soldiers; some ragged officers of regiments; all on half rations. When he glanced his eye over it, he assumed the manner of the utmost astonishment and indignation. "Had he not enough to do to find food for their own hospitals? Could loaves be rained from heaven? He would like to know where this bread was to come from? People that were such fools as to burn up their own flour and crackers should be left to starve? Wounded and sick men should not be as hungry as wolves?" Holding the paper between his forefinger and thumb, looking as if the mere touching it gave him all the sensations one would be supposed to have in carrying a dead snake; he strode up to the desk, and dashed off orders on several bakers for bread. The Confederates around looked at one another and winked. Some evidently pitied me, and hinted that the commissary was too rough; one swore that "he did not believe in robbing Peter to pay Paul, especially if Paul was a great rascal." But Tuthill I perfectly understood, and his fine acting was stagely and amusing. In a few moments, two hundred and fifty loaves were brought in and thrown down in the dead-room. I had brought down from the prison, and became responsible for their return, five or six nurses, who were to convey the bread to the depôt. One of these, Sergeant Temple, bore the pot of butter, which had been left in the store of Mr. Brunot. This I had brought up to Richmond, to be dispensed at the right hour. Robert Spear and Steward Juke bore some cans of preserves and fruits. We carried the bread in sheets, which I had borrowed from the store-room.

When we came to the depôt, I stepped on the platform into the midst of the throng. The cry was raised, "bread!" "bread!" and many rushed toward me with all the eagerness of maniacs. There was a wild tumult for a moment. But this was soon stilled by my assuring them that if they were patient, we would give each one-half a loaf and a little good butter on each piece. We then divided the loaves, and all those who were able to walk came forward and were supplied; but there was a multitude to whom we had to bear it.

The wounded and sick were lying under open sheds, on the wet ground, for it was near the canal; many were on the platform, some in the street, and others in secluded places under the shadow of walls and boards. The heat of the atmosphere was intense and withering beyond all that I have felt in Missouri and Illinois, or even in Africa; the thermometer was standing at 103° in the shade. Many of these poor sufferers had endured until the nerve of sensation was palsied, and sank into that dreamy, languid repose that is the harbinger of death. There were striking illustrations of how much men can bear and live.

I found with these men a surgeon, Dr. Churchill, who had the appearance of one in the last stage of exhaustion. He had suffered intensely from fever, weariness, and the presence of a wretchedness he could not relieve. He told me he had applied in vain for bread, and that no one would listen to him, and that he had returned to this scene of want and misery, exclaiming: "Let me die; it is better that I should die than live."

In my passing from one group to another, I came to a wounded soldier seated on the platform, and leaning with his back against the cars. When I came close to him, and asked him if he could take anything, he said he could not, for he was very ill,

34 *

but asked me "to examine his wound, and tell if it was possible for him to live." The ball had passed through the right lung, and gone out near the spine. He was breathing with great rapidity, but spoke with ease. I felt his pulse, and discovered that life was nearly gone. I said: "I am afraid you cannot live. Are you ready to die? have you made any preparation?"

"Oh!" said he, "I have been praying to God to send some one to talk with me and pray for me; and now you, good sir, tell me what I must believe, what I ought to say to God, and what I must do to die safely."

With an interest I had rarely experienced in my life — for I felt certain that this man would be soon standing before the Infinite — I sat down by him, and spoke of the character and promises of the blessed Redeemer, and that the greatest of sufferers would most surely pity and help a dying soldier; that, for just such as he was, God had made the provision of the Gospel; that his sins could be forgiven for the sake of Him who tasted death for us all. While I spoke to him many gathered around, and some wounded men dragged themselves closer, or were helped forward, that they might hear. The dying man then told me that he had some years before became connected with a church in or near Philadelphia; that he had never forgotten the vows then made, and during his soldier life had endeavored to act as a Christian; but now, when he came so near to death, he wished to know, with absolute assurance, that our Lord would remember him. He felt he was a sinner, and needed the help of One mighty to save.

"Now," said he, "I feel what a great thing it is to die; one can never come back to try and do better, but I must meet again all the past and be judged; I must see God and stand before him, and the holy angels about me. Oh, I need some great friend in heaven!"

I had never seen one so near to death talk with such ease and emotion. I repeated the first words of the 23d Psalm, and he joined with me, changing it, however, into the Scotch version:

"The Lord's my shepherd; I'll not want.
He makes me down to lie.
In pastures green He leadeth me,
The quiet waters by.
Yea, though I walk in death's dark vale,
Yet will I fear none ill;
For Thou art with me; and Thy rod
And staff me comfort still."

The words of the Psalm lifted the vail off sacred memories, and with a face wet with tears, and a voice tremulous with emotion, he told me of his mother; that she was a widow, and he her only child; that he was greatly indebted to her, for she had been a faithful, good mother, and had taught him to pray and love his Bible; that he feared his death would be a sore blow to her, for he was her earthly hope and staff; that all the time he was in the army he had thought of the great pleasure of returning home, and living again with his mother. And there was another friend that was very dear to him and very good, but all that was gone now. They would find him in heaven.

"My poor mother! this will be a very heavy blow to her, for I was her only bairn. She had a great

struggle before she could consent to give me up. I
had told her many times that I would never go to
the war without her consent, but felt it my duty to
help my country, and could look no man in the face
if I stayed at home. To my many and earnest
pleadings she at length yielded; and now I am
afraid she never will forgive herself for allowing me
to come. But God has ordered it all; I had come
to my time. It is all right. But will you, good sir,
write to my mother — she is a member of a church
in Philadelphia — and I will die happier if you tell
me what you will write to her, and let her know
that I thought of her and loved her to the last." I
assured him that I would write to his mother. He
then gave me her name: — "Mrs. Isabella Virtue,
No. 1635 Moravian Street, Philadelphia."

I prayed with him, and endeavored to lift him
up and place him in the bosom of Him who bore
our sicknesses and carried our sorrows. No sooner
was the prayer ended than many spoke to me, and
urged me to come with them and see sufferers that
were in great pain, or near to death. To many, and
indeed all of these, I went, and in the course of an
hour returned, and the soldier was dead; he was
still lying on the platform, and his face was as peaceful as that of a little child. Those near him told me
that he gently fell asleep. There was no terror inspired by the presence of the dead; but many sat
near him, and hands touched him, without a shudder. I wrote to his mother, and subsequently saw
her, and met one who is truly a daughter of grief,
but to whom it gave unspeakable comfort, that she
knew where her son had died, and that he had re-

membered her, and fell so calmly to sleep.* How great
is the debt of gratitude we owe such a mother! She
gave her all, and now sits a lonely, desolate weeper;
her sun has gone down while it is yet noon-day.

Alongside of Thomas Virtue was lying a New
England soldier, very badly wounded; he was in
great pain; he called me to him. "Sir," said he,
"I perceive that you are a clergyman; I am very
glad you have found us; I have no words to tell you
what I have suffered, but my anxiety of mind has
greatly increased my misery; I was afraid that I
should die, and no one would be able to tell my wife
and family where." He then told me that he was
from Bedford, Massachusetts; that he had, at the
commencement of the war, been settled as a farmer
in his native town, and was doing well, and Providence smiled on him in everything; that his wife
was one of the best of women; and God had
given him three children, and they were dearer to
him than life; his home was all that he could have
desired, and more than he ever expected to find on
earth. The strength of the ties that bound him to
his family caused him to hesitate many days before
he could seriously consider his duty; but at length
he began to feel that the interests at stake were more
valuable than his life, and he resolved that, with the
consent of his wife, he would enlist. After much
hesitation, and many tears, she at length yielded to
the conviction that it was their duty to their country
and children to make the sacrifice. The sorrow and

---

* Mrs. Virtue is a member of the church of the Rev. Dr. J.
Dales, of Philadelphia, one of the most comforting and commis-
serate of Christian ministers.

anguish he felt in leaving never could be told, but he had borne it because he knew he was doing right. During all the weary months of absence, the hope of return sustained him, and he counted the days until he should be again at home. But when he was wounded in the battle of Glendale, and gave up for many days the hope of living, the sorrow he felt at the thought of leaving forever those whom he loved, was a greater suffering than his wounds. But during those long, painful, and wretched days, God had mercifully upheld him; and it added much to his distress, that he could find no one whom he knew, and would listen with sympathy to his story. It had been his great anxiety to find some one who would promise him that his wife should be made acquainted with the facts in the history of his last days. I assured him that I would consider it a sacred duty to write to his wife, and whatever his fate, I would do so. But I had hope that he might live; his arm was, indeed, very badly wounded and broken, but his constitution was good, and I thought he might live, and believed he would. With many tears he thanked me for the words of comfort, and said that, since I had promised to write to his family, he felt relieved, and if he never should meet me on earth, that in heaven he would thank me. I soon found Dr. Churchill, and interested him in the case. He examined the arm, washed it, removed the thousand larvæ, and applied wet bandages; and in the course of a few moments we had the satisfaction of seeing a faint smile of hope gleam on the face of the soldier, and when I bade him farewell in the evening he was tranquil, resigned, and even hopeful. I never saw Mr. Cotton again ; that evening he, with all lying at the depôt, were taken back to Savage Station.

At the battle of Bull Run I lost all the papers and memoranda I had brought from Richmond, and was not able to recall the name of the town and regiment of my friend, but subsequently, when I recovered my lost portfolio, I immediately wrote to Mrs. Cotton, fearing that she was a widow, and that I would be the first to make known to her the certainty of her great misfortune; but rarely have I met with anything in my life that gave me greater satisfaction than the receipt of the following letter :

"Boston, *February,* 1863.

"Dear Sir :—It is with pleasure that I attempt to answer your kind letter, which reached us a few days ago. I have thought of you many times, and wondered if you were in the land of the living. I was happy to learn you was released as a prisoner, and are again with your regiment. God has seen fit, in His great goodness, to spare my life, and I am now enjoying a good degree of health. Could I see you, I would like to tell you all I passed through after I saw you ; but time will not permit. After I saw you at Richmond I was taken to our boats on the James River. The next Saturday, I think, when I got to Fortress Monroe, I was taken to a hospital there ; I then telegraphed to my wife, and she came to me there; we were then sent to New York, where my left arm was amputated ; I then remained there until I received my discharge from the service, which was received the 14th of November. I was very weak, and the doctors thought, for a long time, my case was a very doubtful one; but the great Physician of the soul and body healed me. Thanks be to His name. What could I have done, had I not had that Anchor to cling to.

"After I saw and talked with you I felt a great relief, for I thought my dear friends would then know something about me, if I should die. Had I died there, your letter would have been the first intelligence received concerning me. I thank you for your kindness, and hope and pray that you may be shielded from every danger, and see a rich reward for your labors. I am now a messenger in the State House, in this city. I live in Charlestown, Cottage street, No. 14. Should you ever visit the city, I would be very happy to have you call. My wife wishes to express her thanks to you for the great kindness done her. Hoping you may long live to be useful, and that I may meet you on the right hand of our blessed Lord,

"I remain your affectionate friend,
"ALVAH COTTON,
"(Formerly of the 22d Regiment Mass. Volunteers,
"Company F, Captain Thompson.)

"The REV. DR. MARKS,
"Chaplain 63d Reg't Pa. Vols."

In a few moments after we reached the depôt, an officer arrived with the order that all the wounded men lying in the house should be taken out, and the building locked. There were no goods in it, not even empty boxes and barrels. Into the rooms of this structure had been borne many of the worst cases of amputation and sickness. In the house, though lying on the hard floor, they were protected from the burning sun, the rain-storms, and the damp ground. To order them out then was an act of malignant cruelty, for not an inch of the building was demanded for the purposes of trade. It was in vain that Dr. Churchill and myself remonstrated; the order was positive. "The company wished the building vacated." We had to lift and bear down stairs, at the cost of untold suffering, the men to whom the least jar gave a pang of agony, and some poor fellows were carried out in their last moments to the open street to die.

In passing from one to another, I found lying alongside of a train of box-cars a soldier, over whose face was gathered his overcoat. He was so motionless that I stooped down and lifted the covering, supposing the man was dead; but he was alive, and one whom I had often seen and ministered to at Savage Station. I spoke to him.

"Is it possible this is you, Sergeant Bracken, and still alive?"

"Yes," said he, "and I cannot express my gratitude to God that you have found me. Oh, how sweet, in a place like this, is the voice of a friend!"

This young man I had first seen in a tent at Savage Station. He was very badly wounded in the face, the shoulder, and thigh; the last was the most painful, being a compound fracture, but no one would have known, from his voice, that he was fatally injured. But he spoke with the manly clearness and force of a soldier on duty. At my first interview he gave me a very intelligent and graphic

35

account of the battle of Mechanicsville, and spoke in very high terms of the courage and military pre-science of General Meade, and predicted for him a bright future. He then said to me that he had no expectation of recovery; that he knew his injuries were of a character to forbid hope; but he was not afraid to die; for years he believed his peace had been made with God, and now he knew in whom he had trusted. That, as he spent many hours entirely alone, he reviewed the past and looked into the future; that, in the review, he had many things for which to be very thankful. God had given him the best of parents; he had been brought up by them to revere God, and to trust in the Redeemer, and their affection had thrown over his life a happiness greater than many.

There had been given him, moreover, the most affectionate of brothers and sisters; and he wished, if I ever saw them, to say to them that the memory of their affection was always a well spring; and that, during his absence in the army, he had looked forward with the greatest desire to the time when he should return to them again, never to be parted; that there was no society in which he had such pleasure as their's. And now, as that hope was gone, he wished me to tell them that in death he remembered them all with a deeper love than he had ever known before; and he felt that one of the greatest enjoyments of heaven would be in meeting them and communing with them forever. If I ever saw his father and mother, to assure them that he had never, for a moment, forgotten their prayers and instructions, and their God had not forsaken him;

that he felt certain the Saviour would comfort them, and wipe away their tears, and they would see it was all right.

And never did Christian martyr more calmly speak of his end, or more patiently bear his pains. He gave me the address of his father; it was: "Rev. W. Bracken, Armagh, Indiana County, Pennsylvania."

As I now found him, he was suffering greatly, and had been praying that he might die. His wounds had not been dressed for several days; he had been a long time without food; the annoyance from insects, flies, and millions of larvæ was unceasing. When he told me of all he had suffered, and I comprehended the hopelessness of the future, I took his hand in mine, sat down by his side, and wept. But he had no tears; his manliness and faith did not forsake him for a moment. He said he had no regrets; these sufferings were but for a moment, while the joy of eternal freedom from sorrow and pain would be thereby greatly enhanced. He again enjoined on me to let his father know where I had seen him, and that, to the last, he clung to his Redeemer; and to say to his brothers and sisters that he loved them to the end, and that only a little before them he was entering into rest.

While I was listening to him there came two or three German women near to us with some warm rye coffee and herb tea. They had with them several small boys, their sons. They passed through the crowd, stopping with one and another, and giving a cup of beverage and a small cake. The guards stormed and ordered them away, but they still were happily ignorant of English; "nicht ferstehe," answered every command, and where they could not dare to go for them, the little boys were sent. One of these came near to us; I begged a cup of coffee for the sergeant, and with the assistance of Mr. Wrightman, of Pittsburg, lifted his head and gave it all to him. I brought to him some wine from my own stores. While I still sat by him, there came near to us Dr. Wells, of the 61st New York. I invited him to look at the sergeant; we unbandaged his wounds; I returned to the prison and brought down chloroform and turpentine, and with these the doctor thoroughly cleared away and destroyed the tormentors. The doctor remained with the sergeant three-fourths of an hour; washed and placed fresh lint and bandages on each wound, and in the progress of his most self-denying labors became deeply interested in his patient. His fortitude, patience, and gratitude all convinced the doctor that Mr. Bracken was no ordinary man.

I have not met Dr. Wells since those memorable days, and know not where he may now be, but I rejoice to say that he is one of the most humane and self-sacrificing of surgeons. His ear was open to every moan of pain, and when exhausted and fainting, he would rouse himself to relieve another sufferer.

About three o'clock P. M., I returned to where the sergeant was lying. He was greatly relieved, and said that he thought with proper care he might recover. I commended him to God, and bade him farewell, promising to come down in the morning.

During the night all those wounded men were placed in the cars and taken back to Savage Station.

I made inquiry of many soldiers whom I subsequently met in regard to Sergeant Bracken, and gathered from all that he died at Savage Station, three or four days after his return.

After the recovery of my memoranda, I wrote to Mr. Bracken, at Armagh, and received the following reply, which I subjoin, because it will give additional interest to the memorial I desire to erect in honor of one of the best of son's and noblest of soldiers:

"ARMAGH, *October 4th*, 1862.

"REV. AND DEAR SIR:—We received yours of the 8th of September this afternoon, and I now gladly reply. You say you saw our dear son, Watson R. Bracken. That is the first we have heard of him since the memorable battle of the 30th of June. One of his company, a messmate, fought in the same regiment, though not their own, that day, but they were separated in the fight, and that is the last we could hear from him. His captain, A. J. Bolar, sent us several letters before that fight, always speaking in high commendation of Watson, as one in whom he could confide, and he with others of his company, in their letters of condolence, gave the most satisfactory accounts of his conduct as a Christian and a soldier, so that you are borne out in the opinion you kindly express "that he was a man." Oh, he was a faithful, dutiful son, a kind-hearted and affectionate brother, and devoted to the cause of God and his country, and beloved by all who knew him. We are glad, indeed, that you became acquainted with him, and thank you kindly that you ministered to

35 *

him in his sufferings, and that you have made us acquainted with his condition when you saw him. May heaven bless those women who pitied him. We thought he was likely to be killed on the battle-field, and rather desired that his sufferings might not be protracted; but still it gives us satisfaction to know that he still maintained his integrity, and clung to the Saviour. Oh, it is worth more than every-thing else to have the favor of Him who is touched with a feeling of our infirmities, and can administer to our wants when earthly helps and friends fail. It almost rends our hearts to know that our dear Watson had to suffer so much for want of attention, but we submit, believing that He who holds the reins of government in his hands is wise and good.

"Our son belonged to Company H, Captain A. J. Bolar, 12th Regiment Pennsylvania Reserve Volunteer Corps.

"And now, dear brother, I subscribe myself, though a stranger to you,

"Your affectionate brother in Christ,

"WILLIAM BRACKEN.

"The Rev. Dr. Marks,
"Chaplain 63d Reg't. Pa. Vols."

There were lying on the platform many other cases of great interest, and a volume of most touch-ing conversation and incident might have been col-lected on that day. I find a note made in my memoranda of conversations more than usually im-pressive with Charles Volence, of 1st Reserve Corps, Pennsylvania Volunteers; E. S. Perkins, of the 57th Pennsylvania; and James M. Shepherd, of the 11th

Pennsylvania Reserve Corps.   The last named was wounded in the chest, and I suppose did not live more than two days.   In each of these cases, and in their words, there was much worthy of perpetual record — each one was bearing patiently his suffering, and sustained by faith in Him who trod every path of human sorrow and pain, in order that we might be led to look to Him as our Saviour, and lean upon Him as our God.

CHAPTER XXV.

Suffering in Prison — Captain Demming — Death of Adjutant
Gaither — Heroism of Warburton — Haversack of the Dead
Soldier — Deathless Love — Sergeant Abbey.

THURSDAY, 17*th July*. — This was a day memorable for the most oppressive heat; the atmosphere
appeared to be filled with flame, and many of our
wounded who had been through exposure for days
in the open fields, and endured the pain of removal
from place to place, began to sink, and the mortality
of the last days of this week was frightfully great.
The heat of confined rooms — the poisoned air —
induced fever, gangrene, tetanus, madness, and death.
The surgeons were destitute of nearly everything
essential for the relief of our wounded. We had no
lint, and cotton had to be used; this imbedded itself
in the broken flesh, and in its removal tore off the
thread binding the arteries, thus endangering life;
for bandages, we had nothing but the coarsest bag-
ging; of stimulants, we had none; food was dispensed most capriciously, and in such small quantities as only to mock our wants; all the stores of
medicines and sanitary goods were exhausted. But
the sufferings from want did not compare with those
endured from lying in rooms crowded to suffocation,
from breathing an air so exhausted, that profuse
streams of sweat burst from every pore, and the

healthiest panted as if in the last stages of fever,—and in dungeons, loathsome beyond description, where every breath brought an air more foul and poisonous. In some of those chambers all died to whom death was possible; the others lived in defiance of every natural law.

I have mentioned before Captain Demming, of the 61st New York, as a very superior and accomplished man, and as having been wounded on Monday, the 30th of June. When removed to Richmond his case was hopeful; when I met him, after the separation of ten days, there had been such an improvement that I was confident his buoyant spirits and fine physique would secure his recovery; but, after being two days in the prison, he began to fail, and soon became partially insane, and in his madness there was the method of a refined, cultivated, and noble nature. Often he would grasp my hand in his, trembling, and say, "I wish you to stay by me, my friend, for I am greatly troubled; pray for me that I may do nothing wrong." Then, again: "Do not detain me now; I see my wife across the street, she stands at the door and beckons me; excuse me, I must go to her." Thus he was again with one for whom he so fondly yearned, and of whose virtues and Christian excellence he had spoken to me in terms of the warmest affection. Rarely have I seen a stranger for whom I felt a deeper interest, and when he died there passed from us one of the most accomplished men I met in the army.

On this day, John C. Warburton, of the 5th Pennsylvania Reserves, likewise died. I love to recall the name and image of this young man. Captain

McCleary, his commander, who was at the same time lying badly wounded in the prison, assured me that Warburton was one of the best of soldiers and faithful of Christians. I had first seen him on the battlefield of Glendale; his left leg was off; and such was his cheerfulness and the appearance of the stump, that there was every reason to hope in his case. But on this day was developed the terrible tetanus, or lockjaw; with the first spasm he was aware of his doom, and sent for me. He then recounted his private, family, and spiritual history; wrote his will; gave most minute directions for the distribution of his property; dictated with unbroken calmness his last instructions to his widowed mother and blessed her, and, with words of affection and faith, sought to comfort her. He then prayed that God would give him strength and patience to endure the fierce pains and anguish of the day, and not permit one improper word to fall from his lips. In the moments of spasm not a groan escaped him, but compressing his lips, and clasping the cover of the cot, his entire frame would tremble for a moment, and then he was as calm as before. I had never seen such heroic endurance, which not only made him deserving of the glory of a martyr, but ennobled human nature. He then, in words of unshaken trust, committed himself to the Saviour, as one receiving the baptism for the dead, and said, "now all is done: I have nothing to do but to die." I often returned to him during the day and found that the spasms were increasing in frequency and violence; but still his peace was unbroken, not a cry or moan was heard, and except from the convulsive heaving of his frame, no one near him would have known that the soldier was dying in the greatest agony. Late at night I came to him for the last time, and in his moments of ease he assured me there was not a cloud nor a fear, but the "crucified One" was with him. Early on the following morning I came again, but the cot and sufferer were gone.

"Where is Warburton?" I said to Nolan, who was lying near.

"Gone up! gone up!"

"How did he die?"

"Peaceful to the end: thanking God that his road to heaven was so short."

On one of my visits to his room, Dr. Marsh brought to me the haversack of a soldier, who had this morning breathed his last. There were in it several daguerreotypes, a New Testament, and a diary. This last was a record of camp-scenes and battles, and a description of places and officers, of marches, and stirring adventure, and showed the writer to be a man of excellent sense and education. The record was continued to the morning of the fatal day of Mechanicsville. And there was written on an open leaf:

"Libby Prison, July —:—As you would receive the blessing of a dying soldier send this to my brother in Canonsburgh, Pennsylvania."

I went with the doctor to look on the face of the departed; and as we stood by the dead, talked of many great truths in regard to human nature that we were witnessing in these scenes; and that the affections of the heart were the last things in man to die. We had seen men who had lost even the memory of their own names, but everything came back to them when we asked of mother, wife, or child. We had seen those who had become entirely insensible to the presence of those around them; but with all the strength and more than the tenderness of heart, they talked for hours, with a depth of feeling and pathos that moved us to tears, to their beloved ones, whom they imagined about them. Those who, in the greatest distress and pain, had no tears for themselves, but wept abundantly at the thought of the distress and anguish that would fall on their homes; that we had seen many so far gone, that no question or sound could arouse them until they were asked if they had no message for wife or mother, and in a moment the eye brightened, the lips moved, and the dead was alive again. There was one name the dying soldier never heard without being moved. That as we had stooped to listen to the last whisper from the lips it was, "Oh, that you could say to my father and mother that I revered and loved them to the last;" or, "Oh, that my wife knew that I thought of her, and loved her to the end;" or, "My precious children." That we had often found, when the wounded had lost everything, and were without shoes, coat, shirt, or pants, they bore with them the picture of wife and children. That we had often found the letters of wives and mothers lying on the bosoms and their daguerreotypes upon the faces of dead soldiers. That long absence of home and domestic scenes developed affections, which, in the quiet of their previous life, had been hidden or unknown. I took charge of the haversack, and bore it with me to the West, and sent it to the living brother.

Close to Libby Prison there was a large Confederate hospital, called the College; into this we had seen many ladies enter, bearing with them those thousand delicacies and tempting viands for the sick, which only the hand of woman can prepare. But not one of these ever spoke to us, or cast even a look of compassion toward us. But one lady visited our prison; this was the sister of Major Clitz, who was amongst the wounded. His sister, a kindly and beautiful woman, was the wife of a General Anderson, in the Confederate Army; and attended by her husband came in nearly every day. But even she did not dare to look beyond her brother, or show that she felt the slightest pity but for one sufferer. Of the clergy of Richmond we never saw one; neither did they visit any of our hospitals. Indeed, I am convinced that such was the reign of terror in Richmond, and so narrowly was every man watched by the thousand Government spies, that they did not dare, without bringing on themselves censure and suspicion, show to the Union soldiers the slightest pity.

On this day Adjutant Gaither died. He began to sink very soon after entering the prison, and was often revived by the faithful watching of his nurse: but, as the day drew to its close, it became evident that the sufferer was soon to be at rest. His intellect continued unclouded, and his peace was unbroken. Often, as I went to his cot, he would say: "I have no dread of death, it is but the fate of life. I have delightful views of the heavenly world, and my Saviour

36

appears unspeakably lovely." And then he would say: "Remember to write to my father and mother, and tell them all. Say to them that I entreat them not to grieve for me. I am at rest, and we will soon be together forever." About ten o'clock at night it became very plain that the dying lamp was in its last flicker. He said to me: "I am dying now, lift my hands in yours, clasp them together as you have done before, and commend my departing soul to the Lord Jesus." I did as he directed me, and endeavored to lift him up and lay him in the bosom of the great Master. I repeated the words of the 23d Psalm; he followed me, and repeated a second time with emphasis and raised finger: "Yea, though I walk through the valley of the shadow of death, yet will I fear no evil: for *Thou* art with me," etc.

Just before he departed he repeated the words: "'I have fought a good fight; I have finished my course; I have kept the faith; henceforth there is laid up for me a crown of righteousness, which the Lord, the righteous Judge, shall give me at that day.' And tell my father and mother that I thank and bless them, and that I will look and wait for them in the kingdom of God;" and while he was whispering such words, the bright eye became glassy, and over the finely moulded and beautiful face settled the solemn grandeur of death; and he who had been a moment before with us was a companion of angels and a son of God.

In the same room of Libby was lying a most interesting young man, Sergeant Abbey, of the 20th Indiana. He was most tenderly nursed by a young man of the same regiment, "John Tappan." The

sergeant had been wounded in the battle of Glendale, and lingered until July 20th, and died in great
peace. He did not suffer much pain, and therefore
could give more attention to preparation for death.
He exhibited the deepest religious earnestness, and
the most fervent desire to know the truth and trust
in it. He manifested a strong wish to partake of
the communion, and thus, on this side of the grave,
acknowledge the Redeemer as "his Lord and his
God." And in this I intended to gratify him, but I
was sent away from Richmond in the midst of my
labors, and at an unexpected moment. He died
peacefully and safely.

.

CHAPTER XXVI.

FRIDAY, *July* 17*th*.— Early on the morning of this day a great number of ambulances and wagons were assembled in front of Libby Prison, for the purpose of removing as many of our wounded as it was possible to James River, and thence to our flag-of-truce steamers. About six hundred were placed in the various vehicles: sixteen of our surgeons went with their patients. Most of the officers were removed at this time, and it gave to those of us who remained the greatest pleasure to see many hundreds of wan faces lighted with hope and the anticipation of home; and this made them bear, without a groan, the pains of removal. I visited, during the day, the prisons on Corey street and Main street, of which there were three on Corey and one on Main. I found that the removal of some of their companions in tribulation had given hope to all, and they were enduring hunger and pain with great patience.

On this day one of our surgeons came up from

Savage Station, and described the suffering there as most harrowing and constantly increasing. He said that all their stores of every kind were removed, and their requisitions on the Confederate Government received no notice, except the promise of speedy parolement; that the wounded were perishing in great numbers from the want of suitable food; that they had nothing but flour and maggoty bacon; that all the surgeons were sick, one-half of them unable to rise from their beds, and the others incapable, from prostration, to attend to even a few patients.* Such was the gloomy picture of the misery of those we had left behind; and as the death of one after another was mentioned, we shed scarcely a tear, but rather rejoiced that they at least had escaped from the miseries which pressed so heavily on the living.

Amongst the cases of deepest interest in the prison was Sergeant Whitfield, of the 63d Pennsylvania. He had been wounded in the battle of Fair Oaks, but so far recovered as to return to duty, and bore up with the greatest courage until a few days before the retreat, when he was prostrated by fever, and had to be borne to the hospital. On the approach of the enemy, he arose and staggered after our army

---

* The surgeons at Savage Station were: Dr. John Swinburne; A. Churchill, 14th New York; P. Middleton, U. S. A.; H. H. Page, Volunteer Surgeon, U. S. A.; A. Palmer, Assistant Surgeon 2d Maine; O. Munson, Assistant Surgeon New York Volunteers; E. J. Marsh, Assistant Surgeon, U. S. A.; H. J. Schell; W. A. Smith; A. P. Clark, 87th New York; G. F. Perkins, 22d Massachusetts; Will Falkner, 83d Pennsylvania; —— Fox, Volunteer Surgeon; N. Milnor, of Philadelphia, who died of hunger and exhaustion; —— Sutton, who died of fever.

for several miles, and then was compelled to yield
to faintness, lie down, and become a prisoner.
When the Confederate Army had passed he dragged
himself back to Savage Station, and found himself
again amongst friends.   He was now far gone from
protracted suffering and want, but in the course of
a few days very much revived, and everything promised a speedy recovery.   I had him removed from
Savage Station to Carter's house, in order that he
might be constantly under my own care.   He slowly
improved until sent up to Richmond.   After being
placed in Libby Prison, the worst symptoms returned, and on Friday, the 18th, it became plain
that but a few hours remained to him here.   He
continued, however, vigorous in mind and wakeful.
When it became manifest that his end was approaching, I came to him, and as gently as possible
broke our fears.   He aroused as one from a trance,
and said :

"Doctor, do you think I am in great danger ? I
had not dreamed of this ; I knew that I was very
ill, but did not fear a fatal termination."

After further conversation, he calmly said he placed
himself in the hands of Jesus ; he knew in whom he
had believed.   He then took from under his head
all the mementos of affection which he had borne
with him : letters, daguerreotypes, etc., etc.   He gave
me his watch, and told me what directions to give
Mr. Appleton, his brother-in-law, in regard to his
property.   He then placed in my hands one article
after another ; looked for the last time on the face
of his betrothed ; for a moment his voice trembled
with emotion, and then said, "that tie is broken ; I

have nothing now but my Saviour. But while I am able to speak, let me say to you, doctor, that there is no man on earth to whom I owe so much as to you; you taught me, prayed for me, and led me to Jesus, and ever since I was baptized in Camp Johnson, my peace has been unbroken; and now, in my dying hour, I am cheered by the faith you taught me to exercise. I thank you here, and I will thank you again in heaven." He then requested me to fold his hands, and commit his soul unto God. He then stretched out his hand, and bade farewell to several companions in suffering, "until we should meet in the kingdom of God."

From this time he fell into a gentle slumber, which continued unbroken until the following morning, when he went up from the darkness and misery of the prison-house to the glorious palace of the Eternal King.

In the afternoon of this day, my friend Dr. Marsh came to me, and said:

"Do you know that Nolan will have to die? Secondary hemorrhage has commenced, and the ends of the arteries have sloughed off; it will be impossible to save him."

I hastened to the hall where he was lying, and as I approached, heard him singing the beautiful hymn:

"The place of my conversion."

When I came to his side I said: "Mr. Nolan, how are you?"

"Never better," said he, "the doctor thinks I am going to die, but he is mistaken. I may never recover, but I am not to die in Richmond."

"But you are perfectly willing, Mr. Nolan, to die here, if God wills it?"

"Oh, yes," said he; "that matter was settled long ago. I have no doubts nor fears; I am my Lord's, and He is mine. Why should I doubt His mercy? He has answered me too often to permit me to call His love in question. No, doctor, I am not to die here; I am to live through this scene and sing God's praises on our side. You pray with me, and commit me to the Heavenly Keeper, and I am safe."

I did so, and as I left his side, the Christian soldier's voice rose clear and sweet in a song of praise.

In the evening I again approached his cot, and found that the bleeding had ceased; he had rallied.

"Doctor," said he, "I shall live to go out of this place. God has heard my prayer, and will not permit me to die here."

And as I bade him farewell for the night, and stopped by the couch of another sufferer, Nolan filled the room with the beautiful melody of the hymn:

"The Christian's home in glory."

I never saw him again. That night I was ordered away from Richmond, and supposed that Nolan was buried in the aceldema of the Rebel capital. But at Centreville, on the Sabbath after the second battle of Bull Run, a soldier spoke to me in a hospital, and said:

"Sir, I saw you in Richmond, and have a message for you; you remember Nolan, the singer, and good Christian?"

"Yes; well, what of him?"

"He lived to be taken away from Richmond; we were in the same hospital at Fortress Monroe; he was still joyful, and singing his hymns to comfort the wounded men and dying. He told me to tell you, if I ever saw you, that he had lived to be taken from the Libby Prison, and continued to rejoice in God, his Saviour."

Seldom has anything occurred in my life that gave me greater gratification, in that wretched scene of confusion, anarchy, and death; it was a beautiful flower in the barren desert.

I subsequently learned from another friend, that Mr. Nolan lived to be removed to Washington, and died in one of the hospitals of that city.

May we not hope that many learned from him the value of that faith which lifted above all human weakness, and gave him peace and triumph in suffering and death?

I was in one of the upper rooms of the prison, after night of this day, when I heard some one call aloud from the head of the stairs:

"Chaplain Marks! Chaplain Marks!"

I answered, and appeared before the Confederate officer.

"Sir," said he, "you are ordered to be ready to leave Richmond to-morrow morning, at four o'clock."

"Where am I to be sent, sir?"

"That I cannot tell, but I suppose to James River, to your flag-of-truce steamer."

"I have not requested to be sent away: I came voluntarily with these wounded men, and I wish to remain with them until they are released, or die. I have sent no petition to General Winder to be released. Our physicians and nurses are but few now, and some of these are sick; I think I can be of service to these sufferers, and should prefer remaining a few days longer."

"Doctor," said the officer, "I know nothing about the intention of General Winder in ordering you off, but this I will say for your good, what he commands you to do, obey instantly; send no petition to him, ask no favor of him; and let me tell you, if you are not off to-morrow morning, it will be a long time before you will have another opportunity; there will be something hatched up against you, and you will be treated as a dangerous man, or a spy. You had better go; take my advice."

I thanked him, went into Captain Turner's office, and found that orders had been received to remove me from the prison, and place me under guard for Petersburg.

On Saturday morning, at three o'clock, I was up and dressed, and ready to start, and by a mere accident was able to save most of my baggage. When I reached the depôt, the light of the morning enabled me to see distinctly the faces of hundreds of wounded men — mothers, fathers, officers, and servants. There was a great multitude of broken, haggard-looking sufferers helped along by the crowd of friends, or borne by on stretchers, and with groans, tears, cries, and shrieks were lifted and placed in the cars. It required a heart of adamant to be indifferent to the misery of such a spectacle.

I was put under the care of General Winder's Assistant Adjutant-general. This young man was courtly and most generous in bearing. I was seated in the cars alongside of an officer of the Confederate Army, who told me that his home was near Williamsburg; he was an intelligent and gentlemanly man, and talked without any bitterness. He said the first families of Virginia all mourned the loss of many relatives; that to the officers of the army it had been very fatal, and there had gradually grown up an intense hatred toward the North, which would render a return to the Union impossible; that when the war first commenced they despised and loathed the Yankees, but they had no such feeling to the men of New Jersey and Pennsylvania; that now they knew no difference; that the women and children were even more hostile to us than the men; that his boys of ten and twelve years of age could, with difficulty, be held at home; that they were daily practising with pistols and rifles, in order that they might be able to shoot the Yankees. He said if they should be conquered, not a single honorable person would remain in the South; that they would all prefer poverty and exile to submission to an enemy whom they hated and despised. I listened to him, and after a time turned the conversation to themes more grateful to both of us. He said their loss had been immense at Malvern Hill: it was a slaughter-pen; they never would have walked into it, if Lee had commanded.

We reached Petersburg, which is not more than twenty-five miles from Richmond, about seven o'clock, A. M. There was an immense throng of relatives and friends around the depôt, waiting for the arrival of the wounded, and there were many most tender and affecting scenes. I often stood transfixed, a spell-bound spectator of the joy and grief, tears, and eloquent demonstrations of affection — their dead were alive again, and their lost found.

I remarked that my evident sympathy did not, for a moment, thaw into gentleness toward a hated stranger; but when they looked at me, even in their tears, in a moment there came the scowl of anger over their faces. They were children in emotion, but mature in passion and pride.

Petersburg is one of the most beautiful cities of Virginia, situated at the head of Appomatix Bay, about twelve miles from James River. It is located on the hills surrounding this sheet of water; the streets are wider and cleaner than most Southern towns; many of the residences are elegant, and encompassed with objects of beauty and works of art. The inhabitants of the higher streets were evidently intensely aristocratic, and felt that no common blood flowed in their veins. Everything indicated that Petersburg had been very prosperous previous to the war. It is surrounded with one of the finest tobacco-growing regions in Virginia.

My friend, the adjutant, conducted me to Major Ker, who was Military Governor of Petersburg, and surrendered me into his hands. The major was very polite; he is a man of military bearing, having been for many years an army officer in the United States service. He directed me to return to the hotel, and that in the course of the day he would call for me, and place me on the train for City Point. I took occasion to walk through the streets; many of the houses were closed, and apparently abandoned; silence and gloom reigned everywhere; most of the ladies, indeed every one of respectability, were robed in mourning; almost every face wore the look of sorrow and despair; not a well, strong man, except the military, could be seen in the streets; all the others were blind, deaf, walking on crutches, armless, or shaking with palsy. Even in such stores as were open, not a man able to bear arms was found behind the counters: the persons engaged in business were old men, boys, and women. I was permitted, without molestation, to walk several hours around the city. I was fully aware that here, as in Richmond, a spy was ever in sight, and every word was noted, and every act watched. But, as they gave me unusual liberty, a sense of honor constrained me not to take advantage of it, and to ask no questions. I met at the hotel Major Wood, of a loyal Kentucky regiment; he had been taken prisoner, and confined in Richmond, and now paroled, was on his way to James River. He was a fine-looking man, affable and communicative to me, but could not be drawn into conversation by any of the Rebel officers or citizens.

About two o'clock, P. M., Major Ker came to the hotel, and requested me to walk down to the depôt. I went with him. While we were waiting here for a train coming from Richmond, the major asked me of my State. He then went on to say, " that Pennsylvania was the birth-place of his father; and that once the Southern people had a high regard for that State, but now felt as hostile, and even more so, to Pennsylvanians, than to genuine Yankees, for they had been disappointed in us. They had expected that we would have too much pride and principle to be dragged into this war by the selfish and scheming New Englanders. But now they had lost all confidence in us."

37

"Major," I replied, "you are an old army officer, and, therefore, I have no doubt seen service in the Northern States as well as the Southern, and you are familiar with the views and desires of the people of the free States, and must know this war was forced upon us. *We* had not been for years threatening hostilities and the *division* of the Union. *We* made the largest concession to the South. *We* yielded, in the spirit of compromise and for peace, everything you asked. *We* had no taste for war, the genius of our people did not run in that direction. The very thought of civil war was dismissed from our minds as a hideous dream, and no man amongst us dared to predict such a national calamity. But for years *you* had been preparing the public mind of the South for this very day by prophesying war; by urging your people to prepare for it. Even *your* schools were military academies; and *your* children were educated to look with the most ardent desire for the hour when they might draw their swords upon us, compel greater concessions, or secure the glory of illustrious deeds in arms. But such, you well know, major, was not the spirit of our people. *We* felt that in peace was our greatness, and that all the institutions we most dearly prized flourished under its shadow. *You* forced this war upon us, major, and having commenced it, you must take all the consequences."

"And we are ready to take them," said the major. "The people of the South will never demean themselves so far as to be associated with a people who have robbed us, wasted our country, burned our homes, stolen our negroes, and slain our sons.

Never! never! may I die first! If the South ever
submits to you, it will be as a desert. I have, for
my part, reached that stage now, that I desire to
take no prisoners. This war must be one of exter-
mination. I never read in the papers of prisoners
being taken without a sigh. I want to see no more
of you except in battle, or as dead men. This may
sound to you as savage and brutal; but we have borne
until endurance is no longer a virtue, indeed, it is now
a crime. You have robbed us of everything; we are
living in a poverty almost equal to that of the root-
digging Indians. Every day our dead are brought
to us. You are shutting us out from the whole
world; publishing all manner of infamous slanders
in regard to us; branding us as traitors, and con-
fiscating our homes. Our wrongs are as great as
were ever endured even by the martyrs. Our patience
is exhausted, and the strongest desire we have now
is for revenge, and we will have it."

During this conversation, there had gathered
around us a large number of gentlemen and officers
of the Confederate army. The words of the major
stimulated several of them to frenzy, and they turned
and glared upon me with the fiercest anger.

"Yes," said one, who, I afterward learned, was
a grandson of the great Samuel Davies, and himself
a lawyer of the highest respectability, and an elder
in the Presbyterian church of which the Rev. Dr.
Plumer was formerly pastor — "yes," said he, "I
fully endorse, and with all my heart, all that the
major has said. I am too old to be drafted, but I
am going into the army this fall, and will have the
gratification of killing one Yankee before I die. I

am for taking no prisoners; we have been too gentle and merciful."

At this moment loud and vehement were the words of the bitterest scorn and rage which were poured out from the lips of the men of even grey hairs. With one voice they exclaimed : "No, we are done with war upon humane and civilized principles; we are for the knife and the death." Their words increased the excitement, until many were livid with rage, and others tossed to and fro with a frenzy beyond control. I placed my back against the wall, and calmly surveyed the spectacle. A noble, humane-looking North Carolina colonel edged his way through the crowd, and placed himself alongside for my protection. Major Ker was soon ashamed of the storm he had created; lifting his voice above the din he made himself heard, reminding the crowd that Dr. Marks was a prisoner, and much that had been said was ungenerous and unbecoming.

"But, doctor," said he, turning and looking me in the face, "go home and preach peace, and you will be a great deal better employed than marching and fighting with those cursed legions who have invaded us."

All eyes turned on me, expecting my answer. "Major," I said, "all that you and your friends have uttered here has greatly surprised me; listening, as I have done, the question has arisen in my mind, 'Are they Christians?' Have they rejected all the teachings of the great Master, who has taught us to love our enemies, to forgive, as we hope to be forgiven, and to return good for evil? I

most solemnly assure you that I never heard such
sentiments in the North. We think you have done
wrong, and we take up arms to defend the Constitution and laws of the land; but toward you, per-
sonally, we have no feeling of bitterness. In all the
public meetings I have attended North, and in all
assemblages in the army, I have never heard one of
our men speak as you have done to-day. And as
for preaching '*peace*,' what shall I say? Shall I
say you have repented of your errors, and are disposed to lay down your arms? Shall I say that all
you ask is your independence? I have heard it intimated that you want much more than this. What
shall I say as coming from you?"

"Say," one replied, "that our negroes must be
restored to us, or paid for; that all debts incurred
during this war shall be paid by the United States;
that half the territories are to be ours; that the
Border States, Missouri, Kentucky, and Maryland,
are to be left free to choose the Confederacy or the
old Union, as the majority shall determine."

"Very well, gentlemen," I replied, "let me assure
you, peace on those terms is an impossibility. Had
you taken Baltimore and Washington City, Philadelphia and New York, such demands might be
reasonable; but every one of these concessions forced
from us would be the cause of another war. No,
you ask everything and concede nothing. We must
pay all your debts, hunt your negroes, give up to
the jail and the gallows the loyal men of the Border
States, give you the Mississippi, and allow you to imprison or drive into exile the inhabitants of Western
Virginia. *Peace* on such terms would cover us with

37 *

perpetual shame.   No, gentlemen, peace is of great
value to us, but it would be the greatest curse if
purchased on your terms; for we would stand before
the world degraded, and transmit to our children
the heritage of shame.   Be assured that if I should
go North, and be so foolish as to be the advocate
of peace on the basis you ask, I should not be bowie-
knifed, ridden on a rail, nor hung to a lamp-post.
They would not even honor me with a riot; but I
should be pitied as a man whom the miseries of
Libby Prison had bereft of reason, and whose friends
would consign to a lunatic asylum."

The whistle of the train from Richmond called
away, in the midst of the conversation, those who
were looking for wounded sons and brothers.   Only
two persons, one an officer from North Carolina,
and the other a citizen, lingered to express their
sorrow that such a scene of vindictiveness should
disgrace them, and to assure me that all did not
partake of the malignant animosity that had been
expressed.

The train containing the Federal wounded did
not arrive until after two P. M.   In this were eight
hundred men, on their way to James River for our
transports.   The rail track to City Point runs along
the banks of the Appomatix, through fruitful fields,
and a land then smiling and green.   As we approached James River, we came to many encampments of Confederate brigades.   The most of these
troops had recently arrived from the South and West,
and had not been engaged in the recent battles.   In
order that they might see us and enjoy the spectacle,
the train halted every mile; and thousands of long-

haired, dark-featured men gathered around us. Innumerable were their questions, and firm their conviction that the war was over; they were most
anxious to wring from our officers the confession of
defeat, and that we participated in their expectation
of peace.

When we reached the shore, the entire scene was
quiet and beautiful. The rays of the setting sun were
falling gently, after a day of tropical heat, on the hills
west of James River. The placid stream, the sleeping
islands, the dark wooded shore, the radiant glow of
the heavens reflected in the waters, the serene repose
of all nature, brought the highest enjoyment to
those who for weeks had gasped in prisons, and
drank in the air of pestilence and death.

Many of those tottering, haggard men, when they
were lifted from the cars, and saw in the river our
noble steamers, and flying aloft the Stars and Stripes,
shed tears of gratitude; others fell on their knees,
and thanked God for their deliverance; others said
to one another, "I have never felt the old flag so
dear to us as now, and we were never so willing to
die for our country as now." "We know now the
spirit of the men we have to deal with." In a few
moments those able to walk staggered and limped
to the space in front of the *Vanderbilt*. Those
who were more ill were borne on stretchers. There
were arranged on the shore several Confederate
officers, and two or three of our Government, in
whose presence the name of each man was written,
and he subjected to such examination as was deemed
essential for the satisfaction of the Richmond representatives.. Of these last we had no reason to com-

plain; they were considerate and humane. But the
conduct of Dr. Watson, the surgeon in charge of
the *Vanderbilt*, was in the highest degree ungentle-
manly and rude. In order to display "his entire
impartiality," he seized every possible opportunity
to snub, abuse, and insult our men. Never, in the
course of my experience in my own country and in
foreign lands, have I seen an officer of any government behave in a manner so dastardly and brutal.
The whiskey must have been unusually bad to have
developed so many loathsome traits. After the
work of the parolement was finished, though there
were many men on the boat dying, and others so
exhausted that the least noise brought to them
torture, yet Dr. Watson took the Confederate officers
up to his state-room, and for hours, even until long
after midnight, there were perpetrated the most indecent and barbaric orgies; shoutings, stampings,
yells, songs, and toasts, gave variety to the exercises,
and cemented the bonds of friendship.

I was grateful to the officer who assured me that
Dr. Watson was not an American, and I should
have been more grateful if he could have convinced
me he did not belong to the human race. On the
following morning, Sabbath, the 20th of July, we
dropped down to Harrison's Landing; and in the
course of a few hours I was in the midst of the men
from whom I had been separated through many
eventful days. We had so much to say, so many
inquiries to make, that it seemed we had been parted
for years.

I soon reported myself to General Kearney, and
was received with the most flattering expressions of

regard. He made me detail in full all I had seen and heard in Richmond, all my experiences in the hospitals of the field and in the lines of the Rebel army. He expressed the deepest sympathy for our poor wounded soldiers, and asked by name for many officers; his whole manner was that of a man of heart.

From this time I had no personal intercourse with General Kearney, until the fatal day of Chantilly. While the army was yet at Centreville, I entered his room to obtain permission to visit the wounded at Fairfax Station. This, without a moment's hesitation, he granted, and urged me to remain with him for a few moments; during the course of our conversation he spoke of the causes which led to the disastrous defeat of the previous Saturday, and then of the spirit which animated the South. For the first time in our intercourse he spoke on the subject of religion. He regretted that it had been so little his study, but said his knowledge of the world and experience taught him that the only hope of the future was in the gospel of our Lord, and that everything else would signally fail in producing peace on earth and good-will amongst men. He said the scenes in which we were living more deeply impressed him with the value of the teachings of the Bible.

We parted, and in the sanguinary struggle of the evening General Kearney fell, and with him a thousand hopes for the country and the army. He was a man of far more talent than many have been willing to concede to him. While ardent and impulsive, he was capable of the most wily caution;

while often stern and withering in rebuke, he was generous and forgiving, and though ambitious, he was above all low, mean jealousies. No officer in the army was more laborious and sleepless; his keen eye was everywhere; and with an energy that never faltered, he corrected every abuse, and fully investigated everything that pertained to the discipline and well-being of his division. If he had lived, his brilliant and chivalrous qualities would have won for him a very high place in the admiration and gratitude of his country.

In a few days afterwards the army was recalled from the Peninsula and sent to reinforce General Pope on the Rappahannock, and with this move ended a campaign which has scarcely a parallel in human history, if we consider the splendor and magnitude of its commencement, the sufferings and heroic endurance of its progress, and the disasters which darkened its close. Many of the causes which led to a termination so unpropitious are palpable, but others are yet to be revealed from the secret history of councils of war and political conclaves. Every year will pour increasing light on the darkness of *that* past, but, alas! will not shed a ray of comfort on the homes which are made desolate, nor bring back one of our dead from unknown graves.

The subsequent history of the Army of the Potomac properly ranges itself under the heroes of those ever-memorable campaigns which followed.

APPENDIX.

AFTER relating the scene in the jail at Yorktown, and the language of one of the slaves to my estimable young friend, G. B. Patch, of Washington city, in a short time I was gratified to receive from him a song, arranged in form and shaped into poetical symmetry; and I am glad to subjoin it here:

I.

Come, children — bless de Lord for heaven,
  De negro's happy home,
For there no storm, no angry cloud,
  No dark night eber come;
There ebery tree and ebery bush,
  Grows eber fresh and green,
And there no chilly, biting frost
  Upon de grass is seen.

CHORUS.

Come children ob de morning ob de Lord —
I long to go to heaven in de morning,
I hope to go to heaven in de morning,
   O, de morning ob de Lord!

II.

Come, children — bless de Lord for heaven,
  For there de birds sing gay;
And there de sweetly laughing flowers
  Do neber fade away;
There all de long and changing year
  Is but de month ob June,
And there de voices and de harps
  Be neber out of tune.

CHORUS. — Come children ob de morning, etc.

(443)

III.

Come, children — tell me, if you can,
  How goes poor negro there?
Oh! I will tell you : — he must go
  By faith and humble prayer:
Prayer's de *key* ob de door ob heaven,
  And this will let him in ;
But there's a *bar* will shut him out,
  De mighty bar ob sin.

CHORUS. — Come children ob de morning, etc

IV.

Come, poor sinners — look to Jesus,
  For he will take de *key*,
And break de bars and ope de doors,
  And lead in you and me.
Bless de Lord for Jesus, Jesus,
  Who died for you and me,
We shall meet Him, if we serve Him,
  At de morning jubilee.

CHORUS. — Come children ob de morning, etc.

THE END.

www.ingramcontent.com/pod-product-compliance
Lightning Source LLC
Chambersburg PA
CBHW022022110726
47901CB00006B/1628